THE LOST ART OF HEART NAVIGATION

"Heart-centered living has been failing in the Western-influenced world with dire consequences for us and the earth. Nixa takes us on a journey that becomes a self-help manual for reviving our human nature through the deliberative and intuitive nurturing of our heart minds. In the process, we learn to rebalance our minds and center our spirits in life more broadly, opening ourselves to our unique gifts. It's a book for anyone ready to move forward toward self and community transformation."

Darcia Narvaez, Ph.D., professor of psychology at the University of Notre Dame and author of *Neurobiology and the Development of Human Morality*

"With metaphor and poetic prose Nixa describes practical exercises, to which everyone can relate, for implementing the ancient wisdom of complementarity both within ourselves and in the world around us. Enjoy the read, follow the guidelines, and feel the joy of legacy you can start 'leaving in your wake.'"

Four Arrows (Don Trent Jacobs, Ed.D., Ph.D.), American Indian activist and author of *Primal Awareness, Teaching Truly,* and *Point of Departure*

"Nixa's lovely book offers both an inspirational and grounded approach that requires embracing the 'four shamanic steps of hearing, honoring, acting, and protecting as core requirements' on the navigational path of the heart."

Linda Star Wolf, Ph.D., director of Venus Rising Association for Transformation and author of *Shamanic Breathwork* and *Visionary Shamanism*

"Jeff Nixa has created a valuable spiritual field manual for discovering and attending to our inner growth work. His ability to combine the practices of core shamanism with leading-edge spiritual psychology comes from his many years of serving from the heart. If you follow Jeff's practices and programs you will experience greater ease and freedom in your life as a result of expanded consciousness and the awakening of your dormant gifts, strengths, and talents. Every page of this essential book is filled with the love he exudes in all of his work."

MICHAEL STONE, HOST OF KMVR'S *CONVERSATIONS* AND THE SHIFT NETWORK'S *SHAMANISM GLOBAL SUMMIT*

"*The Lost Art of Heart Navigation* acts as an insightful guide for the journey home to one's authentic self. It explores how the path of the shaman reconnects each of us with our soul, personal empowerment, and sacred creativity. This book is heartfelt, innovative, and greatly needed at this time."

ANNA CARIAD-BARRETT, D.MIN., AUTHOR OF *SHAMANIC WISDOM FOR PREGNANCY AND PARENTHOOD* AND COAUTHOR OF *SACRED MEDICINE OF BEE, BUTTERFLY, EARTHWORM, AND SPIDER*

"The brain is loaded with neurotransmitters but so is the heart. In this remarkable book, Jeff D. Nixa helps his readers follow the path of the heart, a route well known to tribal shamans but one all but ignored in the modern world. Drawing upon ancient wisdom as well as the work of contemporary Jungian psychotherapists, Nixa provides exercises, rituals, and tools that are informative, visionary, and—most important—transformational."

STANLEY KRIPPNER, PH.D., COAUTHOR OF *THE VOICE OF ROLLING THUNDER*

"Relying on the wisdom of helper spirits, Jeff Nixa has designed *The Lost Art of Heart Navigation* to serve as a guide for those of us seeking purpose and meaning in our lives. With valuable tools such as breathing meditations, guided imagery, and outdoor moving meditation Jeff leads us through the challenges of modern life and into our own heart path. Join me on the adventure of saying yes to our heart's invitations!"

TERRI HEBERT, ED.D., ASSISTANT PROFESSOR OF SCIENCE EDUCATION AT INDIANA UNIVERSITY

THE LOST ART OF HEART NAVIGATION

A Modern Shaman's Field Manual

Jeff D. Nixa, J.D., M.Div.

Bear & Company
Rochester, Vermont • Toronto, Canada

Bear & Company
One Park Street
Rochester, Vermont 05767
www.BearandCompanyBooks.com

Bear & Company is a division of Inner Traditions International

Originally published in 2016 by Bison Press under the title *A Modern Shaman's Field Manual: How to Awaken Your Power and Heal the Earth*

Library of Congress Cataloging-in-Publication Data

Names: Nixa, Jeff D., author.
Title: The lost art of heart navigation : a modern shaman's field manual / Jeff D. Nixa, J.D., M.Div.
Other titles: Modern's shaman's field manual
Description: Rochester, Vermont : Bear & Company, 2017. | Originally published under title: A modern's shaman's field manual : how to awaken your power and heal the earth. Middletown, DE : Bison Press, 2016. | Includes index.
Identifiers: LCCN 2017007912 (print) | LCCN 2017036739 (e-book) | ISBN 9781591432852 (pbk.) | ISBN 9781591432869 (e-book)
Subjects: LCSH: Shamanism. | Spiritual healing.
Classification: LCC BF1611 (e-book) | LCC BF1611 .N59 2017 (print) | DDC 201/.44—dc23
LC record available at https://lccn.loc.gov/2017007912

Printed and bound in the United States by P. A. Hutchison Company

10 9 8 7 6 5 4 3 2 1

Text design and layout by Priscilla Baker
This book was typeset in Garamond Premier Pro with Grotesque and Gill Sans used as display typefaces

Cover art by Elspeth McLean (www.elspethmclean.com)

To send correspondence to the author of this book, mail a first-class letter to the author c/o Inner Traditions • Bear & Company, One Park Street, Rochester, VT 05767, and we will forward the communication, or contact the author directly at **www.GreatPlainsGuide.net**.

Contents

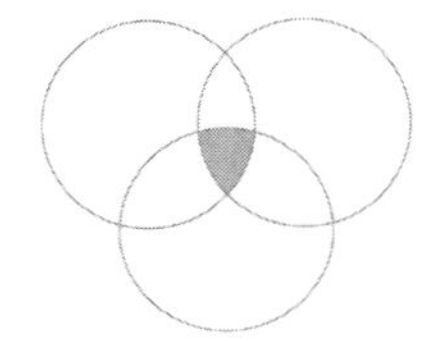

PART III
Shapeshifting

PART IV
The Shamanic Journey and Return

Foreword

This book that you hold in your hands is a tremendous resource, packed with lineage wisdom from shamanism, Jungian psychology, and multiple strands of influence. It is aimed at providing you, the reader or student of shamanism, with a solid base of information, principles, and powerful practices that will transform your life if you take advantage of them. The real creative genius of this book is the way it weaves so many useful sources and resources into a practical manual that is highly accessible and user friendly for the beginner and useful for the professional practitioner as well. I wish I'd had such a manual for my own clients and apprentices early on. It takes a lot of creative thinking and intuition to write a book like this.

Jeff Nixa has honored me in this book, as his first teacher on the shamanic heart path, and in doing so has honored my own traditions and lineages, the Quechua Taita Iachak and the Cherokee path of my own teachers, but also other teachers and traditions Jeff has become exposed to and experientially worked with. These include the modern Mexican Toltec system and the Lakota Red Road wisdom, as well as mentoring in soul retrieval and leadership with renowned shamanic practitioner Sandra Ingerman. Jeff's own interest in a contemplative life, and in wild nature, finds expression outside shamanism in his Zen meditation and his love of the life and work of the Trappist monk

Thomas Merton. Jeff has conducted many contemplative retreats, and Gethsemani Abbey and the fruit of all of these influences are woven into this book as well.

When I had the privilege of meeting Jeff, he came to Crows Nest Center for Shamanic Studies in the southwest Michigan woodlands near Dowagiac. We had what I call a fire talk, which is a heart-to-heart talk around or near a sacred fire. We connected with the sacred fire, and then moved to my little guest cabin in the Crows Nest forest. After we were comfortably seated on the cabin's porch, Jeff said he wasn't sure why he had come to the center. But he knew something in him was curious about it and what we did here. So I asked him to tell me about his life, and I asked the two very powerful and strategic core questions that helped us cut to the root.

The first question was: What kind of life do you really want? Once Jeff had laid this out and made it relatively clear, I then asked: What seems to be in the way of this? Jeff replied to these questions by telling me he had been something of a career gypsy: he had been a lawyer, a hospital chaplain working with the sick and dying, and a massage therapist. But he had always felt restless, a feeling of not quite being on the beam of his precise calling. I could sense, from what he said, that he wanted to do something spiritual and connected with healing, a component of which would be contemplative and yet also involve nature. I didn't have to be a rocket scientist to feel the path Jeff was unconsciously groping toward might indeed be that of a shamanic life and a shamanic way of practice. More deeply, I gleaned from Jeff's story that he was restlessly searching for a path that would be a homecoming to his true self and a solidly felt sense that he was doing and living what he was here for.

I could also sense Jeff's gifts, intelligence, and great potential. I felt he was a little too centered in the head, however, and that his powerful intellect, shaped as it had been by his training as an attorney and chaplain, had led him to make life decisions based in security rather than in inspiration and inner guidance.

The shamanic heart psychology teaches us that the intellect has no idea what we are here for or what we really want. It is the heart that guides us in these matters. I could see that what would help Jeff would be a shifting of the crown from his head to the heart, with his mind as its servant. I thus invited Jeff to a vision quest. As I was talking about this, a doe and her baby fawn walked by the cabin porch. This seemed synchronistic not only for the obvious coupling of the doe and fawn, which the doe was mentoring, but also because the symbol of the deer is associated with shamanism and the heart (hart).

Thus it was that Jeff made a big "act of power" by deciding to go on the vision quest with us on South Manitou Island and enter into an apprenticeship at the center.

After the vision quest, Jeff employed his creative ability as a storyteller to air a story on a local NPR radio station in which he talked about his quest and how he had shared it with his family around the dinner table in a language that was clear enough for them to get the crux of the vision. I took note of the power of his storytelling gifts, his talent for forming user-friendly analogies, and I immediately saw beyond Jeff's abilities as a healer to his potential for teaching and leadership at this early stage of our relationship.

Over the next six years Jeff surrendered to initiation and study. He went through two certification programs, one in shamanic counseling and one in Sacred Breathwork—a very powerful form of holotropic healing in a shamanic community and ritual context. Jeff learned many things during his time at Crows Nest, including much about sacred ceremonies, shamanic journeying, shamanic dreamwork, due ritual process and leadership, shamanic counseling skills involving the heart, otherwise known as the navigational guidance system (NGS) of the heart, how to listen for what is felt but not said, and so on. He learned the Four Acts of Power for concretely embodying your archetype and its vision in the world. He studied diligently, and I could see him applying it all to himself and then to his client work. He also developed and successfully grew his shamanic counseling practice.

I felt honored to witness him progressively shift the center of his living and creativity from his head to his heart. As he did so it was clear that he was coming home to his true self and thriving because he was following his navigational guidance system and continually living the Four Acts of Power, of which this book is proof.

Jeff continually applied what he learned to himself, courageously doing his own initiatory wounded healer work and moving into an advanced stage of apprenticeship centering on leadership skills. Jeff became a respected Crows Nest elder, known as a wise, solid, and generously accessible presence with a big heart, and everyone in the community loved and trusted him. He came to facilitate our powerful Sacred Breathwork ceremonies and journeyed with me to the Peruvian Amazon to study plant medicines and enrich his knowledge through learning about Amazonian shamanism.

I am delighted to recommend to you this book and Jeff Nixa as a shamanic healer and teacher. I know that whoever comes to Jeff for guidance, soul healing, or a workshop or retreat is in the steadiest of hands, for Jeff has a heart full of love, empathy, and compassion and a clear mind filled with wisdom. The reader will find that this book is chock-full of stories, examples, analogies, autobiographical vignettes, and step-by-step instructions. It is a multilevel tapestry that reflects the creative synthesis of a variety of important shamanic topics organized around the central theme of the Heart Path and how living from it brings forth your true self, with vision, love, and service.

Jeff has been among the very best of my apprentices worldwide, and I know he is a real gift to the world as a shamanic healer and teacher in his own right. I know you will be blessed to receive his teachings.

C. MICHAEL SMITH, PH.D.

C. MICHAEL (MIKKAL) SMITH is a practicing psychologist trained in medical anthropology and Jungian psychology. Through his teaching membership, the Cercle de Sagesse, he has worked for many years with more than one hundred forty shamans from eighty-five indigenous cultures. He is the author of the acclaimed books *Jung and Shamanism in Dialogue* and *Psychotherapy and the Sacred*, for which he won a NAAP Gradiva Award in 1996.

He is also the director of the Crows Nest Centers for Shamanic Studies, which are teaching-learning communities operating in several countries. They originated in southwest Michigan before spreading to France, Belgium, Switzerland, and South Africa. The Crows Nest mission is to mentor and train individuals called to a shamanic life. Its overarching goal is to offer initiatory and powerful healing rites of passage and to offer shamanic counseling and leadership skills. In so doing, it imparts the basic principles of an Earth-honoring shamanic Path of the Heart and helps each individual develop their true self and creative potential and put it to service in the world. The very center of this work is to see that each apprentice is thoroughly grounded in the shamanic heart psychology and an Earth-honoring spiritual practice. Crows Nest International fosters the vessels of learning-healing communities, which provide the necessary support, challenge, and containment for individuals to rapidly transform. http://crowsnestshamanism.com/blog.

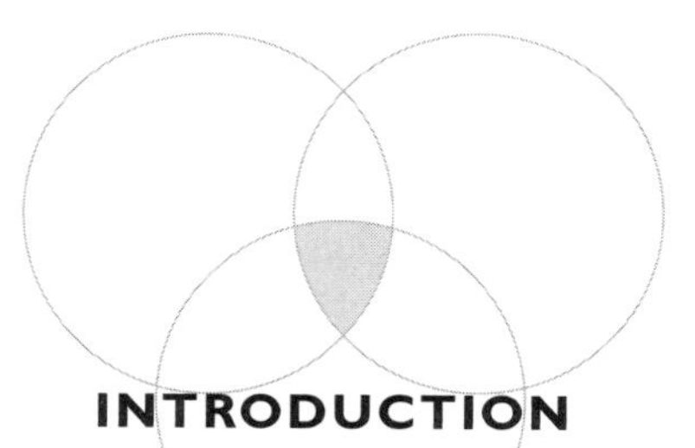

INTRODUCTION

Calling Down the Song for Your Life

I wasn't looking for a shaman. I didn't know anything about shamanism or the growing interest in indigenous healing worldwide. I am not a Native American, and my great-grandmother was not a Cherokee princess. My Christian upbringing, schooling, and graduate theological training did not address shamanism. In thirty years of work in the best medical centers in the world, I never heard the word *shaman* mentioned once.

Then one day in May of 2009 as a client was getting off my massage table, I asked if she had any plans for the weekend.

"I'm going to go see a shaman," she said, "up near Dowagiac."

"A shaman?" I asked her. "Like a medicine man?"

"He's a psychologist," she replied, "and a shamanic healer."

I got his name, Mikkal, and called him up. "I'm not exactly sure why I'm calling you," I said, "but I'm curious about your work." He welcomed me to his home for a visit.

I drove up the gravel road to Mikkal's wooded property and parked next to a rustic structure I assumed was his house. A small fire was burning in a well-used fire pit carved in the earth, surrounded by a careful pattern of stones. He greeted me on the porch, and we walked down through the woods to a little cabin facing a magnificent old tree. As the sun dropped through the trees, we sat on the porch and talked in a relaxed fashion.

Mikkal listened intently to my story of lifelong spiritual searching and my struggle to balance work, family, community involvements, and fitness routines with the needs of my aging mother. I was surprised how quickly I felt comfortable with the man, and as it grew dark I shared that throughout my life I often felt I was not living the life I was supposed to be living, as if there was something different waiting for me. But what? After law and then hospital chaplaincy, I was on my third professional career and tired of big changes.

During a pause in our conversation I looked out to see a stately doe step out of the forest directly in front of us, followed a few moments later by a gangly little fawn. Mikkal acted as if this was the most ordinary occurrence. "You might want to consider doing a vision quest," he said, gazing at the deer.

By the time we finished talking, I had agreed to participate in a traditional wilderness vision quest Mikkal was leading in northern Michigan. During that week in August, after two days and nights of fasting from food and water on a remote island beach, a vision came to me that changed my life. Subsequently, Mikkal accepted me into his shamanic apprenticeship program that fall, and I began learning the program for personal healing and life change that he called the Path of the Heart.

The focus of his teaching that fall was shamanic counseling skills. With my background in pastoral counseling, combined with my love of the outdoors, my concerns about climate change, and my personal search for meaning, I instantly recognized the treasure I had found in this healing methodology, which addressed all three of my biggest concerns at once:

1. A methodology for finding my purpose and way in life, *my* way "home"

2. A deep, intuitive, strength-based model for helping others, based in soul and our spiritual connection with nature
3. An Earth-honoring worldview that directly relates human health and happiness to the health of and balance of the living Earth

This book describes the core principles and practices of the *Path of the Heart.* Rooted in the Earth-honoring spiritual ways of our indigenous ancestors, the Heart Path blends ancient shamanism and modern depth psychology to help you uncover your core vision or purpose, conquer the fear barriers that stand in the way of that vision, and become a shamanic shapeshifter of your life. In these pages you will learn to access your spiritual core directly, clear out old emotional wounding patterns, retrieve vital energy, and become an artist of the soul. You will learn the shaman's art of connecting directly with spirit to navigate by the great "Heart of Everything That Is." You will learn of the powerful teachers I have studied with, including Mikkal, Sandra Ingerman, faculty of the Foundation for Shamanic Studies, spiritual elders of the Oglala Lakota people, plant-spirit medicine of the Amazon jungle, and, of course, my own helper spirits.

These pages are packed with introductory tools, which include penetrating core questions, shamanic journeys, recapitulation practices, dreamwork, outdoor ceremonies, artistic expression, and mindfulness practices—all supported by engaging client case studies and stories from my own journey. By the time you have reached the end of this book, you will have learned the following:

- What shamanism is and how it relates to modern religion, psychology, and Native American cultures
- How to connect with the spirits of animals, plants, and trees for personal healing, guidance, and support
- How to make a shamanic journey into the spirit world, find a power animal or helper spirit, and journey for guidance on particular life problems

- How to seek a shamanic vision for your life
- How to use the navigational system of your heart to turn that vision into reality
- How to distinguish the guidance of your heart from passing moods and fleeting emotions
- How to overcome the barriers that block the life you really want to be living
- How to bring your life's unique gift and power into the real world

Of all these objectives, the main thing is to find out what you are here for. When you get clear on this, you will understand what your medicine is for the world. You will know your unique path, your way of being, your "angel mission" on Earth. You will be able to call down the song for your life that is yours and no one else's. This is the most important thing, and this entire book is devoted to helping you figure out how to do this and make it so.

There couldn't be a better time to be learning these practices. Our people and our planet are in big trouble. We are so distracted with busyness and urgent but unimportant demands on our attention that we cannot stop and listen to the guidings from our soul, causing us to suffer from soul loss and "hurry sickness." Earth is sick too, suffering the consequences of our consumer lifestyle, which is poisoning and depleting our natural resources. We turn to our doctors for relief but discover modern medicine to be incomplete in both its perception of illness and the tools required for healing. We discover that our consumer culture does not have a core economic or political system that values a sustainable balance with nature. Even our churches can seem oddly detached from the ecospiritual crisis around us, focused as they are on issues like sexuality, scripture proofing, and personal sin and salvation to the exclusion of the global environment we depend on for life itself.

Our modern way of being in the world is unsustainable. Our thinking and living will have to be closer to that of indigenous people, understanding that we don't just have an economic, military, or political role in world but also an ecological role in the whole web of life.

This book contains the medicine that is missing from our lives and social institutions. Rooted in the forgotten Earth-honoring spiritual ways of our own ancestors, you will find here a personal healing path with teeth; a spirituality that is ecological and concerned with all your vital parts: body, soul, nature, and the greater spirit world.

Compared to conventional medicine and psychotherapy, the shamanic approach to happiness and health is fast, inexpensive, and free of pharmaceutical side effects. It penetrates quickly to the core of the pertinent presenting issue or issues, and then puts the primary means of healing directly into your own hands rather than creating dependency upon a doctor, therapist, pastor, or spiritual guru. The Path of the Heart is an "open-source" wisdom path, uncompromised by personal, financial, or institutional interests. For the price of this book, you will get priceless, time-tested wisdom and information gathered from the best modern teachers of these ancient traditions around the world.

My entire life has led to the writing of this book and I teach what I know: how to break the paralysis of uncertainty and stagnation, retrieve your soul, get clear on your life purpose, and then make the real changes necessary to live that life. I have been on a restless search for meaning since college and endured three long and expensive vocational changes before discovering the Heart Path. When I finally learned the methods described in this book, and identified my Core Self (in about thirty minutes!), I instantly saw my problem. I had been trying to find my way in life with my primary navigational system disengaged. There was nothing wrong with me at all!

That navigational system is my heart, and I continue to use all the practices in this book to maintain my vision and power in daily life. This helps me personally, but it also benefits my marriage, my ability to parent well, my friendships and clients, and my contributions to the community. I have gone from a young man unhappily studying for a law career he did not want to waking up each morning fully alive, going outside and standing in the sun to call down the song for my life that day. I am living a joyful and deeply meaningful life, able to cross dark valleys of old anxiety and depression on the real wings of inner purpose and power. Misfortune, criticism, illness, loss, and injury still occur in my life, of course. But they are like strong gusts of wind that no longer stop me in my tracks or poison me with negativity and despair.

A Modern Shaman's Field Manual stands apart from other books on shamanism in its breadth of resources, down-to-earth voice, practical utility, and tools for addressing the most common barriers blocking positive life change and happiness. The structure of the book follows the motif of the hero's journey, taking you through the four archetypal stages of leaving home (chapters 1–4), descent (chapters 5–7), shapeshifting (chapters 8–10), and shamanic journey and return (chapters 11–13).

These chapters will first familiarize you with the shamanic worldview and practices of our indigenous ancestors, using relatively simple heart-opening exercises. Then we delve more deeply to explore the "spiritual cartography" of the human heart and the modern psychological workings of the mind. Using the motif of the great hoop of life, we will move onward and upward in a spiral of learnings and exercises to engage directly with the spirit world, using classic tools like dreamwork and shamanic journeying. With each chapter, you will learn to deepen, heighten, and strengthen your new shamanic practice.

This book anticipates the inner resistance you will encounter when attempting to make heart-centered life changes. Where many other books emphasize only traditional shamanism (like Celtic traditions, Native American rituals, healing ceremonies, or shamanic journeying), this book also provides insights from modern depth psychology, like the Jungian interpretation of dreams and how to disarm the self-sabotaging ego psyche.* Few books address the importance of doing one's inner

---

*The terms *ego* and *ego psyche* referred to in this book are not used in their popular sense of egotism or self-absorption but rather in their specialized psychological sense, referring to the self-conscious "I" or the social "me" that sees itself as distinct from other persons. We will explain this in more detail in chapter 3.

work on the healing path, and those that do either fail to explain what that inner work is or to provide tools to explore and transform one's own shadow psyche.

The humble spirit of this book comes from my own life journey: a man with thirty years' experience in law, ministry, health care, and counseling who has helped thousands of individuals find their way through major life change, traumatic loss, illness, and fear. The book is written to help you solve real barriers, analogous to military field manuals that are written to help soldiers in the field. It will point out common pitfalls along the way, booby traps of self-sabotage, doubt, and criticism. But most of all, it will awaken your wild and free heart.

The shamanic Heart Path activates your wildness, your power, your inner "indigenous self." This is a part of you that you may know nothing about, raised as most of us are in a society that has completely forgotten or suppressed it. Shamanism is rooted in your wild outdoor self and heart, not your domesticated indoor self and mind. The indoor self is comfortable, habitual, and lazy in its conditioned thinking, like a fat house cat served a dish of canned food at every meal. But the soul is wild, with all the natural instincts and powers that wild animals have. It is strong, intelligent, quick, and powerful, with a unique set of survival skills and defenses at its disposal. All day long you listen to the self-sabotaging voice of the fat cat in your head, the impotent self that stands in your pajamas and complains, "I can't lose five pounds." This book is written to awaken the *other* part of you, the inner jaguar that crouches in the jungle unconcerned with weight or diets, with both gleaming yellow eyes fixed on its prey, ready to leap with the power and grace of nature, instinct, and the full force of life.

As the author of this field manual, I don't want you just to learn something about shamanism. I want you to *do* something with your life. I want you to use the tools in this book to get up and take action toward creating the vibrant life your heart is programmed to seek out. This book is not written as a scholarly work on shamanism, psychology, comparative religion, or theology. Nor is it an anthropology of Indian cultures. It is a practical manual for changing your life that uses our forgotten shamanic heritage as a supportive toolbox for perception and navigation.

My strength is as a generalist, a synthesizer able to present complex material in a readable way through story, example, imagery, and metaphor. This is the book I needed when I struggled to decide on a major in college, felt misplaced in graduate school, lost a job, and chose a life partner. It's the book I needed when I was feeling stuck, puzzled by a big fork in the road, forced to make a difficult choice, or finding myself depressed and lost, far away from home.

For the modern reader adept at racing through information from the Internet, television, newspapers, and social media, it's important to understand this book is about making a soul journey. It is not a quick informational pit stop on the racetrack of your life. To help you downshift into a deeper mode of experiencing, each chapter contains exercises to slow your mental racing and begin to detect the dynamic felt-sense guidance of your heart. This is *the* essential skill for walking the Heart Path. The exercises in the two appendices allow you to go even deeper into crucial areas like deactivating trauma-based emotional patterns and understanding the precise contours of your authentic self and visionary heart.

On behalf of your wild heart and our wounded planet, thank you for picking up this book. Something in your heart—not just your intellect—is drawing you closer to read it. That same quiet but persistent voice in you is inviting you to begin a hero's journey to a more joyful, rewarding, and purpose-filled life today.

Come join me now as we begin to walk an amazing adventure together!

PART I

◎ ◎ ◎

Leaving Home

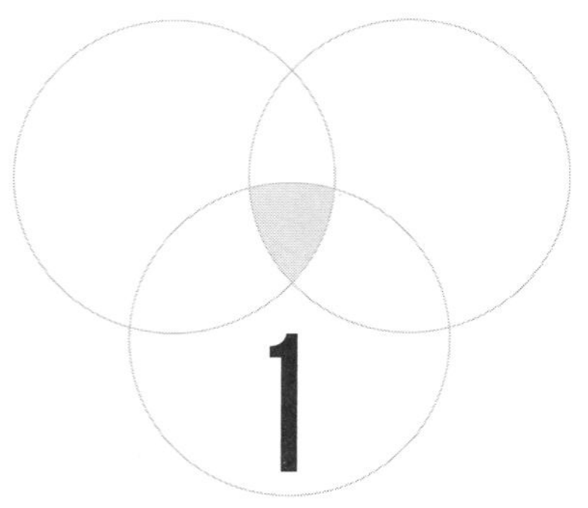

1

Searching for Heart in a World of Reason

Ask yourself one question. It is the question that only a very old man asks: Does this path have a heart? One path makes for a joyful journey. The other path will make you curse your life.

Carlos Castaneda, The Teachings of Don Juan

Thirty-three years ago I was sitting in a first-year law school class in Portland, Oregon, with an uneasy feeling in my gut. It was a vague but insistent sense that I didn't belong there, that I didn't want to become a lawyer after all. But instantly that feeling was shoved aside by a scolding voice in my head. *Are you* crazy? *You quit a good job, paid for entrance exams, and moved across the country for nothing? What will people think?* So I suppressed the feelings and completed my first year of study. That whole time I was haunted by anxiety, muscle tension, and stomach problems. At the end of the academic year, I left school and moved to New York City to explore what really interested me: more soulful creative work like writing, art, and photography.

In New York I waited tables during the day and drove a taxi at night so I could chase my dream, and for a while I felt happy, alive, and even heroic. My anxiety and physical problems disappeared. But city life was harsh and lonely without a support group, and I still lacked clarity on my personal gifts and life purpose. My energy fell off and the doubts returned. That fall I withdrew to my hometown of Rochester, Minnesota, and spent a long, awful winter working nights as a janitor and security guard, waking up every morning in my childhood bed, feeling like a complete failure. I was too embarrassed to talk with anyone about the depression and panic attacks that had returned, and I took my stomach pains to the Mayo Clinic actually hoping for a diagnosis of "ulcer" to explain these symptoms and obtain relief for them.

But after a series of negative GI tests, my physician took off her glasses and asked, "Jeff, is there anything unusual going on in your life right now?" I about hit the ceiling in a panic of confusion and shame. I lied, said no, and walked out. For the rest of the winter and spring, I distracted myself with classes in studio art, history, and philosophy at the local community college. I enjoyed these, yet failed to understand what that enjoyment was telling me. By summer I had decided to return to law school in the fall, opting for a secure life over an inspired one.

When I returned to law school, the physical and emotional problems resumed. I again distracted myself with busyness, and by sheer effort, I began to succeed. I was accepted on the law review editorial staff for my writing skills. I won my class mock trial competition for my rhetorical skills. At age twenty-three I began arguing criminal cases in front of real juries for the Portland district attorney's office, and by graduation I was interviewing with Oregon Supreme Court justices for clerkships.

I was on the road to success as a lawyer, and I was good at it. My reasons for seeking the law degree were still as well reasoned as ever: it was a logical application for my undergraduate degree in political science, I would be acquiring powerful tools to help others, and a career in law would provide an established social role, a steady job, and financial security. Yet I was mentally exhausted, emotionally fragile, and spiritually empty. I hardly recognized myself anymore. I had gone from being a happy, free-spirited, contemplative soul in college to a fake persona in an expensive suit trying to fit into the hard-driving legal culture and the urban singles' nightlife of Portland. My heart continued to whisper, *not this.*

I remember studying one rainy day in my tiny apartment, a converted garage behind a wealthy home with an apple orchard in the hills of southwest Portland. Surrounded by my papers and stack of law books, I noticed the Mexican gardener had arrived to prune the landlord's apple trees. Even perched on his ladder in the cold drizzle I could see the quiet joy and care in his purposeful movements. I deeply wanted *that:* not his job per se, but his simple way of being and working, physically connected with nature. Yet I was too mired in the momentum of my career path to recognize this longing or understand its meaning for my life.

In the midst of this confusion I wandered into a Catholic church one Sunday for mass. I had been raised in the church but had long since stopped attending. There I met a beautiful, self-assured young woman named Regina who led the worship music and introduced me to the fields of lay ministry, contemplative spirituality, and social justice. She invited me to play guitar in the little folk group that accompanied Sunday mass. In her low-paying but meaningful job at the parish, I recognized a person doing work that flowed authentically from her heart, who was rich with friends, vitality, and purpose.* My heart was leaping around in my chest. *Like that! Like that!* It seemed to be saying. *Like what?* I wondered. *Doing church work? Seriously?*

Years later I would understand that it wasn't Regina's church *role* that my heart was resonating with. It was my witnessing a life fully aligned with her authentic self, her core gifts and vision. As we will see in the chapters ahead, the goal is to find your own authentic spiritual core,

*Regina and I were married two years later and celebrated our twenty-ninth anniversary in 2017.

essence, or archetype of soul (e.g., "a servant to the poor"), not a mere job or social role ("outreach minister at St. Joseph Church"). The latter can easily change with time, age, or misfortune; the former will never change.

After graduation and more months of study I sat for the Oregon state bar exam, a two-day ordeal that consisted of analyzing dense legal cases in the arenas of civil and criminal law. I failed the exam by two points out of several hundred. Panicked, I buckled down harder by paying for a preparatory course and spending three more months sequestered in my apartment studying. When I finally received the second form letter from the Oregon State Board of Bar Examiners, this one beginning with "Congratulations, Mr. Nixa," I had an unexpected reaction: *I can leave now.*

So in 1986 I walked away from the legal profession. I had no job prospects or alternative career plans and faced seven years of deferred school loans coming due. But I began volunteering at Regina's parish, reading contemporary theology and spiritual authors like the monk and activist Thomas Merton, and eventually retooled my life into a rewarding twenty-year career in spiritual care and counseling.

Still, that process took years and was akin to groping blindly in the dark to determine what worked and what didn't. Although I was clearer on what I did *not* want for my life (a law career), it still wasn't very helpful in finding the thing I *did* want. The ministry field for me was essentially "way better than law." But I still lacked a specific, forward-directed aspiration or vision for my life. I was not trying to be picky! I puzzled at friends and colleagues who seemed content with the very same roles and careers I was unsatisfied with, who even had the same complaints about them. What the hell was wrong with me? Why did that quiet but insistent voice in my heart keep saying *not this, not this?*

It wasn't until I met with Mikkal in that little cabin so many years later that I began to acquire what I had been missing: a set of practices that would help me detect and track the specific forward-directed invitations of my soul; instructions for the navigational guidance system installed in every human vehicle.

Looking back, I had another question: How had I gotten so far off the beam in the first place? I'd had a good childhood, received a fine education, and had been given a solid religious upbringing. By the time I finished my first year of law school, I had the skills necessary to research the most arcane points of legislative history, wetlands regulation, or international treaties. Yet I didn't know how to research—or trust—my own gifts and spiritual heart and had completely disregarded the communications of my body, which were warning me I was off the path. Wasn't this the job of a good education, a caring family, and a religious community? To help me know myself?

What had happened?

What had happened was that half of the information I needed for fully conscious living was off-line and inaccessible to me—as it was to my teachers, parents, and church leaders. And that missing information was all related to the heart. It turns out I'm not the only one suffering this condition, known among shamanic practitioners as soul loss. Our entire culture is suffering soul loss, evidenced by our disregard for our bodies, our inability to hold still, and our abuse of the living Earth.

Although my particular story involves the struggle to discern a career path, this book is for anyone realizing that their outer life is not in alignment with their inner self and natural way of being. It is for anyone who feels out of joint with their job, friendships, partner, house, church affiliation, spiritual practices, neighborhood, social group, even the annual family vacation or their fitness activities. (Do you really enjoy going to Disney? Or straining on a fitness club treadmill for hours a week? What ways of relaxing, or being active, would be more natural and enjoyable for you?)

TWO PATHS

Mind and Heart

In our lives there are two great sources of information available to us for perceiving and navigating the world: the rational, analytical way of the mind and the soulful, felt sense of the heart. The mind is the king of conscious reality and specializes in the logical, verbal, archetypal masculine realm of visible information, matter, analysis, clock time, science, technology, reasoned principles, ideology, judgments, and knowledge. It parses things into their individual components, emphasizing separateness and differences. But the heart is the queen of unconscious reality and specializes in the intuitive, nonverbal, archetypal feminine realm of spirit, nature, darkness, mystery, dreams, and poetry. It emphasizes the relationships among things and our connectedness to all life. The mind *thinks,* but it cannot perceive mystery or unconscious reality. The heart *feels,* but it cannot speak in words or be dispassionate and logical.

Of these two available ways of perceiving our environment, the conscious mind completely dominates our modern approach to healing, life navigation, and decision making. The king, the loud, chatty, thinking conscious self—the voice in our head—always wants the microphone of control in our decision-making process and is quick to dismiss the quieter whispers of heart and intuition that come from the deep kingdom of the queen. But we learn, slowly, that the loudest voice in our head is not always the wisest voice in our life.

The problem is not that our rational minds or our achievements in modern science, technology, and civilization are lacking in value. The problem is that we don't equally value and use the heart. So when our rational approaches fail, or even cause us harm, instead of consulting the heart with its entirely different realm of experience and information, we go *back* to the failed approach and repeat the same mistakes from the same playbook of reason. We seek a "bigger hammer": more data, more research, more words, a stronger medication, a different technology, another scripture verse.

All of this falls into the archetypal masculine realm of *rational* intellect, science, and ideology. At no point do we stop and ask the huge missing questions that dwell in the archetypal feminine realm of the body, soul, spirit, and Earth itself, questions such as: Who am I? What am I doing here on this Earth, really? What is my place in the world beyond my job, possessions, favorite sports team, and social network?

We don't ask those questions because we don't have a social, economic, political, or religious system that honors the heart, the wisdom of the body, or balance with nature. I am referring to the implicit values and belief system(s) underlying American business, consumer culture, and mainstream religion. Contrast this with the startling actions of Ecuador (2008) and Bolivia (2010), which rewrote their constitutions to give nature—trees, rivers, animals—legal rights and protections similar to human beings and corporations. These include the right to life and to exist; the right to continue vital cycles and processes free from human alteration; the right to pure water and clean air; the right to balance; the right not to be polluted; and the right to not have cellular structures modified or genetically altered. Controversially, these laws will also enshrine the right of nature "to not be affected by mega-infrastructure and development projects that affect the balance of ecosystems and the local inhabitant communities."[1]

Synchronistically for me, the week I finished my second draft of this book, Pope Francis released his encyclical, *Laudato Si',* on the relationship between climate change, consumerism, and social injustice. This was a rare, welcome, and blunt demand for care of the whole planet and everything on it, not just for our particular human aspirations, institutions (the church!), human security, and profit. Later Pope Francis stood before the U.S. Congress and gave a pointed challenge to the leaders of the most powerful nation in the world to better address the causes of climate change, the unjust distribution of wealth, the protection of life in all stages and forms, and other issues, including the unjust treatment of indigenous people.

As I listened to the pope's speech, I was struck by the warmth of heart that shone through his slow and heavily accented English. Despite his plunge into the most politicized of social issues (and his own rational training as a chemist and theologian), Francis led with his heart, not with ideology or scripture. By speaking from the heart, he was able to connect with the hearts of his listeners. The following day, I noted a conspicuous absence of negative political reactions to Francis's speech.

We have reached a turning point in our progress as a nation and as a civilization. At this critical time in the life of our planet, our primary need is not for more data, doctors, or different technologies for industrial growth. Instead, we need different *people*—more heart-open people living from their spiritual center. We need people with broader states of consciousness than any superficial label of "Democrat" or "Republican," "American" or "Chinese," "Christian" or "Muslim" can offer us. We need people with "a psyche the size of the Earth," as psychologist James Hillman says. We need a spirituality and spiritual practices that are ecological, not just anthropological, and a religious mythology concerned not just with human sin and salvation but with the whole planet and everything on it.

We will find this mythology right where it was abandoned or suppressed centuries ago: in the beliefs and practices of our own indigenous ancestors. Their innate Earth-honoring consciousness kept them anchored in the heart and intimately connected with the natural world around them. Their shaman healers saw human illness and unhappiness as indications of soul loss first, not a lack of technology, research, or medication. This ancient wisdom is still practiced today and making a big comeback in popular interest, spiritual practice, and academic study.

THE HEART PATH

The shamanic approach I will describe here is not a religion but a set of general tools from Earth-honoring cultures for living a life in balance with soul, nature, and the world of spirit. The core methodology is called the Path of the Heart, a four-stage process of psychological individuation and spiritual maturation. Derived from the work of C. Michael Smith, it involves an archetypal initiation, a classic hero's journey deep into one's soul to identify and confront the issues that are causing the trouble and then eliminating or transforming them into a new vision and power for living. The goal of shamanic healing is to help individuals become more vital people, living lives of purpose, joy, and service to others. This includes walking on Earth more gently as a healer, rather than as a parasite consuming its resources and returning nothing of value to the planet.

This is not a book of religious beliefs, popular psychology, or new age thinking. The wisdom contained herein is very "old age," derived as it is from the experiences of our indigenous ancestors who used it to navigate, heal, and stay alive for tens of thousands of years without our modern technology, weapons, agriculture, or medicine.

Anyone can learn the techniques contained in this book. You don't need to be a spiritual medium, a mystic, or even a person of faith. Like a person who wants to learn how to swim, however, you *will* need to get wet. More than just reading a book about swimming technique (the history and traditions of shamanism), you will need to step off the shore and take a plunge into the wet and deep realm of the spirit world. You may have never done this before. But the spirit world has been here all along—inside us, all around us, influencing us. We've just been socialized to ignore it, fear it, or deny it even exists.

THE CRUX OF IT ALL
Getting Clear on Your Center

The realm of shamanic practice is vast, ancient, and deep. Reading this book will not make you a shaman. Shamanism is a difficult life path and shamans "in the wild" often spend their lives from childhood on apprenticing and working with ancestor and animal spirits and plant medicine. Modern teachers like Sandra Ingerman have devoted entire books to single aspects of shamanic healing such as shamanic journeying and soul retrieval. But what we can do in this book is help you to get clear on your Core Self, your soul or spiritual center. These are all names for the heart.

And that will change everything.

When you get clear on your center, you will have great power in the world. You will have a clear vision for your life and know where you are going. You can say yes and no with ease. You can laugh when others criticize you because you see their own fear and lack of direction. You will be the captain of your ship, born to handle the wind and waves. You can steer to ports of your choice, navigating by the compass of your heart toward the destiny of your life. Opportunity will open before you, and trouble and pain will be like mere gusts of wind. Your relationships will be positive and supportive, or you will end them. You will be surrounded by vibrant people because the influence of a vital person vitalizes others. You will walk the Earth as a light, a healer, and as a true sorcerer living from your source.

If you are not clear on your center, you will suffer. Without a vision and navigational system, you will be adrift in the sea of powerful and self-interested voices inside you and all around you. You will doubt your actions and be stung by criticism. Without power inside, endless family demands and work dramas will push you off course like big waves hitting a small boat. You will labor on someone else's ship, working for their dreams and their profit. You will keep yourself small and unnoticed to minimize risk and pain, preferring stagnant harbors to the open sea. You will fill your days with busyness, work, watching TV, cleaning and shopping, eating and complaining with friends—but never setting forth. And you will feel alone. The Great Spirit will not be able to reach you because you have not found yourself.

In my own life, thanks to gifted teachers and the practices I share in this book, I am now clear on my center. I know exactly why I am on this planet, what my purpose is, and when I am "on the beam" or "off the beam" of my life. With this knowledge, I periodically sit back and actually sketch out the kind of life I want to have in the months and years ahead, including activities, workshops, travel, and personal and family time. Knowing my purpose, I can easily say yes or no to relationships, new opportunities, potential distractions, family issues, and friendships. I know who I am, and I am no longer confused about this. It doesn't really matter to me now what others think as I go about living my authentic life, a life now aligned with my heart and not the other way around. I have detached from my old life-support system based on social approval and have plugged it into a new support system based on the vibrant, guiding intelligence within me and around me.

For example, to get this book written, I had to turn down many new potential clients and social engagements and change my daily chore and fitness routines. But I did so without hesitation, guilt, or regret because I knew that getting the book written was the prime directive. I explained my changes to others as needed, but whether they understood this or approved of my priorities was of little importance to me. This kind of deep conviction, clarity, and inner power has been a huge and positive change for a man who was raised "Minnesota nice" and was unable to express my real feelings or deal with conflict earlier in my life.

HEART COMMUNICATION 101

In order to get clear on your spiritual center, you need to be able to perceive the subtle communications from your heart on a moment-by-moment basis. In their simplest form, these communications can feel like the three colors of a traffic light: a green (yes/move forward) signal; a red (no/stop this course) signal; and a yellow (caution/slow down/wait) signal. Like a traffic light, these three basic tones change constantly. Each signal can be physically felt in the body and is experienced as

- A pleasant attraction or invitation (green light/yes)
- An unpleasant sense of repulsion or a feeling of disinterest (red light/no)
- An unclear hesitancy (yellow light/not yet)

To better illustrate these basic heart communications, here is an exercise to help you experience them as they shift back and forth, as the light changes. You will be *sensing* these different felt tones, not thinking about them conceptually, through shifts in feeling, bodily sensation, imagery, emotion, and intuition.

EXERCISE

☼ Experiencing the Heart's Navigational Guidance System

1. Sit comfortably on a chair with both feet on the ground. Take three deep breaths, exhaling slowly through your mouth. Close your eyes.
2. Imagine a real person you love to be with. Picture that person in front of you. Imagine their clothing, posture, facial expression, eyes, and mannerisms.
3. Holding that person's image in front of you, draw your attention to your chest and belly area. Notice what you are experiencing there physically. Scan your body for subtle sensations and pay attention to *where* in your body you are feeling them. Take your time. Notice your breathing and inner feelings.
4. Take three deep breaths and clear the image of that person.
5. Now picture a real person you can hardly stand to be with, a person who may have hurt you or caused pain. Picture that person right in front of you. As before, clearly note their clothing, posture, facial expression, eyes, and mannerisms. Now do the same body scan of yourself and notice what you are experiencing physically, in your body, especially in the chest and gut area. Take your time. Notice your breathing, and the area around your heart. Note anything different from what you sensed with the first person.
6. Take three deep breaths and clear your imagination and bodily felt-sense completely of this person.
7. Now for a second time, imagine the person you love to be with in front of you. Smile. See him or her smile. Again, do a body scan of your physical, felt response to the presence of this person in front of you. Notice the differences and where you are feeling these differences in your body.
8. Clear your imagination, and repeat with the unpleasant person.
9. Return a final time to the person you love to be with. Enjoy that felt sense.
10. Open your eyes. Take a few minutes to write down what shifts you felt in your body between each person and where you felt those shifts in your body.

The shifting physical sensations you experienced in the exercise above are the dynamic *feeling tones* of your heart. Feeling tones are the nonverbal language of the heart—and of spirit itself—experienced through your physical body. When honored (carefully explored and skillfully interpreted), they can help you navigate complex life situations as reliably as a compass or GPS unit. Should you take this job? Marry that person? Move to a different state? Your heart knows the answer, and its navigational guidance system is locked on to your unique destiny and no one else's. When ignored (as I ignored my own persistent body signals in law school), unfortunate things will happen and will continue to happen, just as when you ignore the colors of a traffic light.

We will be fine-tuning your heart navigation skill throughout this book; it is the most important skill of all. And we will learn the big difference between the reliable invitations of your heart and the unreliable nature of passing moods, emotions, impulses, or libido. But first we will explore the hero's journey motif as a road map for the spiritual transformation work ahead and look more closely at the heart itself. We will define what the heart is, look at the four stages of the hero's journey, and explain the innovative dual-source approach of the Heart Path that draws from both shamanism and modern psychology. Then we will peek into the three realms of the shaman's spirit world or cosmos and learn the benefits of walking the Heart Path in real life.

Ready to learn more about your heart and your own hero's journey? Read on!

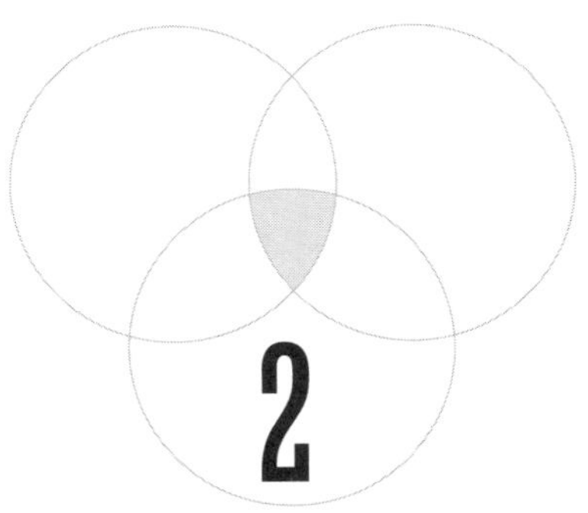

2

The Heart Path as a Hero's Journey

I had ambitions to set out and find, like an odyssey, going home somewhere. I set out to find this home I'd left a while back and couldn't remember exactly where it was, but I was on my way there and encountering what I encountered on the way was how I envisioned it all. I was born very far from where I'm supposed to be, and so I'm on my way home.

Bob Dylan, *No Direction Home*

FINDING YOUR WAY HOME

Years ago I had an experience that foreshadowed my call to shamanism and illustrates what walking the Heart Path feels like. I was standing in an Indiana state park campground filling a water jug. As I stood to carry the water back to my waiting family, I heard a faint sound in the air. *Boom-boom, boom-boom, boom-boom*. It sounded like the beat of a Native American powwow drum.

I looked around. *What was that,* I thought? I saw tents and campers, children on bicycles, and people walking their dogs. But no Native American drummers. I began to carry the water jug back to our campsite.

I heard it again. *Boom-boom, boom-boom, boom-boom.* The dull thumping was far off, more like a low pulse from Earth than an audible sound. I cocked my head to lock in on the direction. Again, only silence. Was I actually hearing this? I set down the jug and listened with full attention. I heard children shouting, dogs barking, music from a radio. No one else seemed to notice the sound. I reached down for the jug but heard the drum beat again. It was real and drifting out of the woods on my right. I left the water jug and began walking toward the drumbeat.

I had to find it.

I started up a gravel path that led through the campground toward the sound, but the path soon ended at the edge of a woods. A narrow dirt trail continued into the forest, however, so I took that. Once I was inside, the forest trees muffled all of the campground sounds, and I stood long minutes in silence, straining to hear, turning slowly in a circle, my animal senses on full alert.

Nothing.

Then the drum pulse returned. It was sharper now and directly ahead of me. I followed the dirt path until it veered away from the sound, and then I left the path and continued forward, plunging on through deep brush. A chipmunk dashed out of my way. I was getting closer to the drumming but farther from camp. I ducked low under a toppled tree, and then picked my way through a low boggy area. I had no idea where I was now. *You could get lost out here. This is crazy,* I told myself. Raspberry thorns scraped my arms and spider webs swept into my face, but I stumbled ahead like a thirsty person honing in on the sound of water.

Eventually I emerged from the woods into a large clearing. People sat in a circle around a large Indian powwow drum lying on its side, drumming. Ha! There *was* a drum in the park! Each person was striking the drum together with long beater sticks and singing together in a low chant, "*Hey ya ha. Hey ha ya aa. Hey ha ya. Hey ya ha eh ya.*" I walked over and the group welcomed me and invited me to stay and watch. As they drummed, each beat seemed to pulse from deep in Earth and move outward like a great sonar wave into the trees and up into the sky. I looked around at this area I had never known before, even though I had been to the park dozens of times, hiking, camping, and exploring the established trails.

At some point I remembered that my family was waiting for me back at the campsite. I left the drummers and returned through the woods with a big smile on my face. My crazy march through the woods had paid off, and I had discovered a new group of like-minded friends and a lovely part of the park I could return to.

A DIFFICULT BUT ESSENTIAL JOURNEY

Learning to sense and track with the heart is a process exactly like what happened to me in that story: hearing or smelling something enticing on the breeze that you cannot see but you know is there and luring you toward it. The invitations come from spirit, through your heart, and are calibrated to bring you home to yourself and your full aliveness on Earth. They are from the same source as the guidance that leads a V formation of Canada geese to Mexico and back, or draws a salmon to return from the depths of the Pacific upriver to a remote creek that was its home.

Following the Heart Path is not complicated. A child can do it. But the resistance from inside your mind and from the world around you creates a lot of static in the signal and can be very difficult to navigate through. These challenges arise at every stage. The first is being able to simply hear the calling of your heart among all the other noise in your life and trust that its longings are important. Then you must "put down your jug," listen carefully, and discern a course of action. After that, you need to actually *do* something, to move and follow the invitations of your heart. ("Being *on* the Heart Path is not *walking* the Heart Path," a teacher told me.) This will often seem foolish to your rational mind and to other people, so you must continually protect your progress against sabotage from within and without.

These four steps of *hearing, honoring, acting,* and *protecting* are the core requirements of walking the Heart Path.

When you do follow the heart, you will light up with energy you had long forgotten. Unexpected helpers will come into your life, including people of similar interests and passions. Opportunities will open before you that you could not have anticipated or caused to happen all by yourself. You will begin to experience the effortlessness of flow-state living, as if you had acquired wings of lightness and mobility. As long as you are "on the beam" of living your life's purpose you will have great power, a quiet but purposeful determination that comes from the great powwow drum beating in your heart.

This chapter will explain the Path of the Heart in more detail, define what the heart is, and describe the benefits of living the Heart Path day to day.

A PATH-BASED WISDOM TRADITION WITH ANCIENT AND MODERN ROOTS

The Heart Path blends traditional shamanism with insights and practices from modern depth psychology. This hybrid psychoshamanism draws from ancient traditions such as the Mexican Toltec, Andean Iachak, and North American Cherokee traditions, as well as contemporary Jungian and transpersonal psychology.* In short, shamanism provides the Earth-honoring spiritual core of the work; depth psychology provides the self-awareness necessary for mature consciousness.

The spiritual path or journey motif is found in many shamanic traditions and goes by many names: the path of the warrior, hero, healer, or sage, for example. From ancient oral traditions to modern writers like Carlos Castaneda, the emphasis is on knowing one's authentic soul, dropping masks of self-illusion, conquering fear, and walking a good path as a strong voice of truth and healing in the world. The core process involves

*The term *psychoshamanism* was coined by Alejandro Jodorowsky, a Chilean filmmaker, writer, poet, and spiritual teacher.

getting clear on a vision for your life, then embarking on an inward hero's journey toward that vision, confronting your inner hesitations and the self-deceptions that keep you from realizing that vision in the world.

The journey involved is not about traveling somewhere in the physical world. Rather, it is an inner process, a spiritual *initiation* or deep transformation that is necessary to undergo if we are to become psychologically individuated, spiritually mature human beings. Though each person is different, the journey process has similar phases for everyone. This is seen time and again throughout human history and mythology and involves several predictable and sequential phases. The classic work on this is Joseph Campbell's *The Hero with a Thousand Faces* (New York: Pantheon Books, 1949, and later editions).

1. In phase one a mythological or historical hero (e.g., Prometheus, Moses, Jesus, Joan of Arc, Luke Skywalker) experiences the call to an unexpected new life or adventure, leaves the security of home (literally or psychologically), and ventures forth from the familiar world of day-to-day routine and relationships into a darker unknown or unconscious region. In his book *Soulcraft: Crossing into the Mysteries of Nature and Psyche,* Bill Plotkin describes this phase as surrendering "the summer house of your first personality and early adult worldview . . . the house you have been carefully building, furnishing and accessorizing since puberty."[1] The big surrender, says Plotkin, "is the idea that someone else (or some institution) is going to protect you, save you, or show you the way."
2. In phase two the hero descends into this unconscious region and encounters resistant forces, temptations, dragons, or demons there, namely *fear:* fear of change, fear of societal reactions, fear of psychological or physical harm. But our hero can also encounter temptations of wealth, pleasure, or status that would distract the hero from his or her life purpose.
3. Phase three is the battle or crisis the hero must endure with these forces, during which the hero suffers the little death of the

individual self or ego. Eventually, the hero prevails in a decisive victory over the resistant forces and acquires a new self-understanding and personal power that integrates his or her divine self (Buddha nature, Christ consciousness, inner healer, or shaman). Thus the name I have chosen for this phase is shapeshifting.

4. In the final phase four, the hero returns to the everyday world with this new self-understanding and uses the personal power to address some unmet need in society. In other words, the ultimate purpose of the hero's journey of initiation is not for the individual but for the community. Harley SwiftDeer Reagan, founder of the Deer Tribe Metis Medicine Society, taught that life has two primary acts or movements: the survival dance and the sacred dance. Our first task in life is mastering the survival dance, creating physical, emotional, and social security for ourselves. Once these individual needs are addressed, however, it is necessary to shift our focus outward to identify and begin our sacred dance, the unique work we were born to do in the world.

Variations on the hero's journey abound. Clarissa Pinkola Estes's bestseller *Women Who Run with the Wolves* collects intercultural world myths and stories illustrating the particular initiatory tasks women must attend to for psychological individuation and spiritual transformation. A feminist critique of Campbell's work is that he assumes every person must literally leave home and battle for self-achievement in a masculine corporate, academic, or political culture. But the authentic hero's journey is not outward into the world but downward into the soul, requiring a psychological descent into one's unconscious to acknowledge and confront one's own barriers to full living. The demons for women may indeed be different than for men, but demons abound nonetheless. In her own counterpoint book, *The Heroine's Journey: Woman's Quest for Wholeness,* Maureen Murdock outlines the particular wounding of women who have rejected their feminine self (by associating it with the unwanted dependency and controlling behavior of their "witch" mothers) and overly

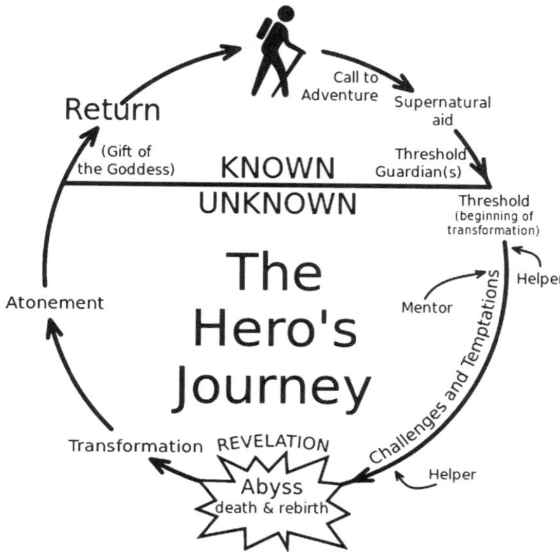

Fig. 2.1 The hero's journey.

identified with their masculine energies, only to find themselves fighting exhausting battles in institutional settings for an illusory boon of success.[2] The real journey for a woman, says Murdock, is to descend to her "dark feminine" goddess self, become intimate with her body, emotions, sexuality, values, and mind. Only then can she properly integrate and balance both masculine and feminine energies to create lasting gifts for the world.

Figure 2.1 is a visual depiction of the hero's journey, showing the threshold (depicted by the horizontal line) between the known conscious realm and the unknown unconscious realm the hero must penetrate and explore.

DEFINING THE HEART

The heart is a key concept in shamanism, a specialized term that refers to one's deep source of aliveness, spiritual center, soul, or core. The word *core* itself comes from the French word *coeur,* meaning "heart." It is understood to mean our individual, localized expression of the Great Spirit, God, or Universal Consciousness. It is our individual wave moving upon the greater sea of spirit.

Indigenous people didn't explain what the heart was because they didn't have to; their cultures and beliefs were so immersed in heart-based living it was taken for granted, just as Americans don't have to explain individualism or promote rationalism: it's what we do. But we moderns do need a broader definition of heart and a set of tools to help us get clear on our Core Self.

Our Western conceptions of the heart are simplistic and incomplete. They reflect our overly rational assumption that the mind is fully logical and concerned only with reliable facts and information, whereas the heart is irrational and corrupted by unreliable emotions, poetic nonsense, or libidinal desires. But for indigenous societies, the heart was the locus of intelligence, of knowing and inner guidance, a dynamic multiplex of human consciousness. The simple navigational guidance system (NGS) exercise in chapter 1 illustrated how the heart can communicate directly in real time via physical sensations, and feelings of attraction or repulsion.

We have forgotten how to access the heart's abilities, and like a person suffering amnesia, we do not even perceive what we have lost. To get a sense of that, here is a brief look at the complex, multilevel spiritual cosmos that shamanic cultures access and interact with through the heart. The heart is the perceptual consciousness that lies at the intersection of all realms of perceiving and knowing.

THE THREE REALMS OF THE HEART

Shamanic cultures worldwide have uncannily similar views of the physical and spiritual realms of consciousness. These realms include

- A higher *upper world* realm of shared universal consciousness, that of the higher self or transcendent aspect of the Creator active in us. This is "the Great Spirit that dwells within the heart of each creature, even the tiniest ant" (Black Elk).
- A *middle world* realm of physical, here-and-now waking consciousness that includes awareness of our bodies and the material world around us, as well as our self-concept, ego personality, and social role identity.

- A *lower world* realm of individual subconscious, the more hidden, earthy instincts and appetites, fears and aggressions, attractions and repulsions, including sexuality and hunger. This way of knowing has its own intelligence and intuition, likes and dislikes. (The NGS exercise in chapter 1 gave you an experience of this intelligence in action.)

In many ancient traditions, these three realms are symbolized by a sacred tree with upper branches (the higher realm), a trunk (the middle realm), and roots (the lower realm). This tree-of-life motif is found around the world in cultures that had no prior contact with each other, such as the ancient Hebrew and Norse tribes.

Some cultures have more levels and sublevels, for instance, Dante's nine circles of hell in the *Inferno* or the seven chakra levels of Hindu belief. At the deepest level there is only one cosmic consciousness, beautifully portrayed in the Buddhist metaphor of the jewel net of Indra, which hangs over the palace of the Vedic god and represents the interconnectedness of the entire universe. The net stretches out infinitely in all directions and in each open eye of the net a single glittering ruby hangs suspended. Reflected in each facet of every polished jewel is the image of every other jewel in the net.

This three-worlds metaphor is a simple but effective sketch of the so-called spirit world that shamanic healers enter during shamanic journeys. It gives shamans a conceptual map or cartography of the soul to work with when journeying: "up" into the upper-world consciousness, "down" into the lower-world unconscious, and laterally out into the visible living world of created life and relations. For example, seeking to connect with the spirit of a deceased person could be an upper-world journey; discerning whether to take a new job could involve a middle-world journey; finding a solution to chronic anxiety or depression could transpire in the lower world.

Implicit in this three-worlds cosmology is the understanding that we need to be fluent in and engaged with all three realms for a strong, whole, and balanced life. Like a tree, we cannot grow and rise high without deep and nourishing roots. Unless we "branch out" from the solitary

Fig. 2.2. Yggdrasil or the sacred tree of Norse mythology (1847 depiction).

trunk of self, regardless of strong roots, we will not be of fruitful service to others. The roots are hidden from the aboveground perspective of our ordinary, middle-world consciousness. But this does not mean they are unimportant or unrelated to the condition of our trunk and branches.

A shaman's preparatory rituals and drumming are simply tools to help the shaman attain a trance state and drop down into and remain in the consciousness of his or her own heart, which by its nature is in dynamic relationship with the larger, surrounding spirit world. This is the core principle of shamanism: when you connect deeply with your heart, you are connecting with a portal to the Heart of Everything That Is.

Figure 2.3 is another representation of the interconnected realms of the shamanic spirit world, all intersecting with and in the heart.

The point here is that when shamanic healers talk about the heart, they are referring to a multidimensional realm of intelligence and experience far beyond our limited Western understanding of human consciousness, science, or psychology. They do not mean the cardiac muscle, an emotional or poetic impulse, an energy center or chakra, or the practice of electrophysiological heart entrainment as in HeartMath. They mean the sacred, conscious, guiding center in each one of us. There is much to be said here regarding the current insights of neuroscience, Bohm theory, and quantum mind consciousness. For now, just know that the Heart

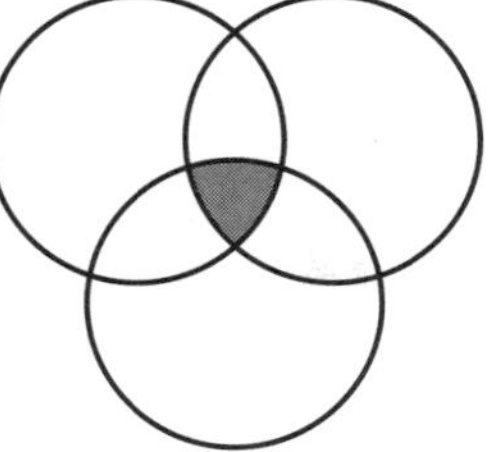

Fig. 2.3. The three realms of the heart.

Path takes you to the doorstep of a far more vast understanding of the physical world and nonphysical consciousness than we are accustomed to.

Most important, it is through the heart that the Creator Spirit *actively sends invitations into our lives,* beckoning us forward to our life purpose. The heart tracks us and signals us to let us know when we are on or off course for this purpose. As any sea navigator lost in fog knows, if you can locate just two or three objects and their compass bearings, then you can triangulate your own location precisely on a map—even on a vast ocean, in the wilderness, or in complete darkness.

This can save your life.

WALKING THE HEART PATH

To walk the Heart Path means saying yes to the heart's invitations and responding to them accordingly, just as a ship captain responds to a ship's compass, a navigational buoy, or a lighthouse. Trusting that the information from these signals is accurate and unchanging, a captain can navigate his ship for hundreds of miles without being able to actually see anything beyond the next buoy or lighthouse beam. Yet one buoy at a time, the individual course corrections aggregate into an entire journey, and the ship can emerge safely out of darkness or fog at its destination.*

*The ancient Polynesians were legendary transoceanic navigators, able to make their way thousands of miles to the tiny Hawaiian Islands without compass or maps, by following star patterns and detecting island proximity through changes in sea color, wave size, wave speed, wave patterns, and bird and fish behavior. Their seafaring knowledge was passed on from navigator to apprentice by oral tradition, often in the form of song. Modern navy officers are still taught to use the sextant, which can locate a ship or island on the vast ocean within a single mile's point of accuracy using only the sun and stars.

Conversely, ignoring the invitations of the heart will result in negative consequences. The "Issuer of Invitations" will be forced to send those out in more urgent and unavoidable forms: physical illness, pain, emotional issues, and spiritual malaise. Rather than a spiritual emergence, the individual will find herself in a spiritual *emergency*—upset and wondering why God has forsaken her. Yet God is no further away than before; it is one's own neglect that has forced the Issuer of Invitations to become the Issuer of Symptoms.

In my years as a hospital chaplain visiting thousands of individuals in various states of illness or injury, I often found myself thinking about auto repair. That is, like a car owner, you can be attentive and proactive about your body's health by checking the oil and coolant, rotating the tires, and getting spark plugs and wiring replaced at proper intervals. Or you can ignore these key functions and keep driving until one day the engine "suddenly" overheats, the car refuses to start, or you blow a bad tire in some remote area. Much of the human physical suffering I witnessed (for example the amputation of the toes, feet, and legs of medically noncompliant diabetes patients) seemed avoidable and unnecessary.

I recall a hospital patient I met years ago as a chaplain, a hard-charging corporate executive whose nonstop work and travel had led to stress, poor self-care, and obesity and had landed him in the intensive care unit with a serious heart attack. When I walked into his room, I found him alone, sitting up in bed on full oxygen and IV drips, with a heart monitor bleeping away over his head. And he was working on *two* open laptop computers sitting on his overbed table. "What am I supposed to do?" he said. "Cut back on my work?" His spiritual (and physical) heart seemed to be shouting the answer with an unqualified, *hell yes!* But he was unwilling to listen to it.

True accidents and random illness are not as frequent as we imagine.

BENEFITS OF THE HEART PATH

My experience of walking the Heart Path has felt both magical and natural at the same time. Being off the path (my time in law school) was like struggling to drive through sluggish downtown traffic and hitting one red light after another, stressed and worried that nothing seemed to be going right. Being on the path is like realizing all those traffic lights are synchronized: as long as you maintain the correct direction and speed, the lights "magically" turn green as you near them, allowing you to glide through the entire city without a single stop. All you have to do is find the right speed and stay in the flow!

That's what walking the Heart Path feels like. The green lights are opportunities and openings in your life; the yellow and red lights are indications you are getting off the beam or needing to turn onto a side street with a whole new direction and its own set of sequenced lights. You start to trust and follow the leadings of the green lights and drop your prior destination agenda.

In walking the Heart Path, I've experienced the following personal and societal benefits:

1. A program for life transformation and change, complete with full navigational guidance, energy, and free support from an unlimited source.
2. More effective help with illness, anxiety, and depression. The methods of shamanism are fast, deep, purposeful, low cost, and free of harmful side effects.
3. A deeper relationship with nature linked to a nuanced awareness of the body and its own natural cycles and sensations.
4. A set of priorities and ecoethics for our time far deeper than our obsession with information, technology, and the narrow goals of industrial growth.
5. A spirituality that is ecological, not just anthropological, and concerned with the soul of all created things, not just humans and human institutions.
6. Restored interest and respect for the wisdom of indigenous societies.
7. A happier life: greater authenticity, purpose, personal power, and resilience.

8. A return of mystery and wildness to our rationalistic society that has sucked the mystery out of everything, including our religious practices.
9. A natural desire to serve others out of personal joy and abundance, rather than moral duty, social obligation, or fear of hell.

In this chapter we explained the Path of the Heart as a hero's journey comprised of four stages, an archetypal map for spiritual transformation. We learned of the three-tiered shamanic universe and defined the heart as being far more complex than conventional understanding assumes it to be. It is our sacred core of aliveness, and it stands at the crossroads of spirit, matter, and instinct, able to access and communicate with all three realms. We described the heart's capacity to invite us forward to our life's purpose and help us navigate along the way, and we articulated the practical benefits of walking the Heart Path in our lives.

In the next chapter we will explore the world of shamanism and learn how modern shamanic practice relates to religious faith, psychology, and Native American and other indigenous traditions. We will learn what exactly a shaman does, explain the shamanic practice of altering consciousness for shamanic journeying, and learn several exercises to open your imagination in preparation for doing your own shamanic journeying later in this book. We will also look at the three main categories of shamanic practices: heart-opening tools, mind-management tools, and mindfulness tools. These tools include traditional shamanic practices like acquiring a power animal, soul retrieval, and vision quest, as well as modern practices like core questions work, Jungian dreamwork, body-focusing exercises, and outdoor moving meditations.

Ready for the nonordinary journey ahead? The Heart Path awaits us. Let's go!

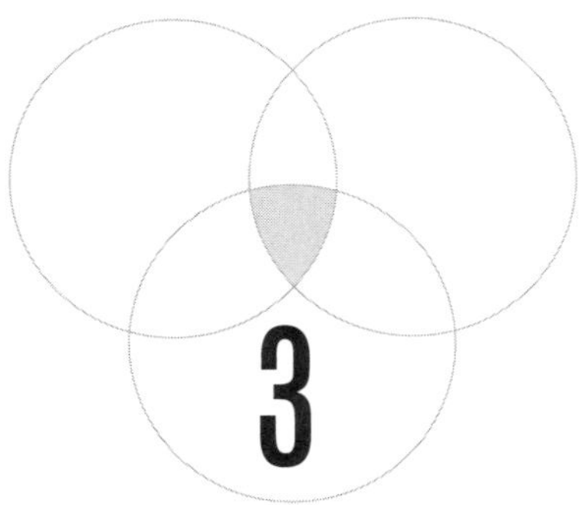

3

The Shaman as Guide to the Spirit World

Shamanism is for skeptics. It is for those who walk their own path. There are no intermediaries. You don't accept these things because I say so. What's important is finding what works. The way is open, and the first step through it only requires, as it would for a true scientist, honest curiosity, an open mind, and some courage.

Michael Harner, "Science, Spirits, and Core Shamanism," in *Shamanism*

WHAT SHAMANISM IS

Shamanism is a modern name for the oldest spiritual healing traditions on the planet. These Earth-honoring practices were all concerned with the health and restoration of the soul, and predate the major contemporary world religions of Buddhism, Christianity, Hinduism, Islam, and Judaism. The word *shaman* is borrowed from the Tungusic-speaking people of Siberia and can be translated as "one who knows" or "one who sees." Although the abilities of the shaman can be extraordinary, he or she is an ordinary person recognized for his or her abilities—in spirit journeys and ceremonies—to connect with the spirit world. A shaman is like a reference librarian or database administrator, except that the shamanic database includes all of the shaman's ancestors back through history, every creature in the Amazon rain forest and the Chihuahuan desert, the energy of the farthest star, and the collective consciousness of the entire web of life.

The first academic studies of shamanism are attributed to Mircea Eliade (1907–1986), a history of religions scholar at the University of Chicago. The first teacher of shamanic practices to general audiences in the West was Michael Harner (1929–), an anthropologist who studied in the Amazon and taught a core shamanism of spiritual beliefs and practices that he found to be similar across cultures. Some scholars have insisted there is no such core set of shared principles and that it is more accurate to speak of "shamanisms" than of a single shamanism shared by all traditions. Others have used terms like *shamanhood* or *shamanship* to emphasize that shamanism is not a religion of sacred dogma but is linked to everyday life in a practical way.

Today shamanism is a rapidly growing area of study in anthropology, sociology, medicine, and psychology as well as in spirituality circles. Forty thousand international visitors per year fly into Iquitos, Peru, the main entry point for those seeking shamanic healers in the Amazon rain forest. The United Nations designated 1993 the International Year of the World's Indigenous Peoples to recognize the 370 million native people living in five thousand traditional cultures worldwide.

The vision quest ceremony, shamanic journeying, and soul retrieval are examples of traditional shamanic practices used to gain clarity on one's life purpose, eliminate patterns of fear and wounding, restore vital energy, and move forward in life with great intention and creativity. As mentioned previously, in my shamanic practice I borrow from the Toltecs of Mexico, the Quechua of the Ecuadoran Andes, and tribes of the American Great Plains. Regardless of the particular culture, all shamanic traditions hold that healing, vital health, and personal power require good relationships with one's own soul, the world of nature, and the spirit world.

WHAT A SHAMAN DOES

A shaman is a healer. People come to a shamanic practitioner because something is wrong physically, emotionally, or spiritually. The shaman provides help by altering his or her ordinary state of consciousness, entering the spirit world, and actively *doing* things there: seeking information and guidance for others, removing spiritual intrusions, and finding and returning lost soul parts. For example, in classic shamanic psychopomp (Greek for "conductor of souls") work, the shaman helps assist lost or wandering souls of the deceased over the threshold of death. True to this image of shaman as a master conductor, two of my shamanic teachers in Peru would refer to each other respectfully as Maestro Raul and Maestro Mikkal.

To alter his or her consciousness, the shaman typically uses percussion—hand drums or rattles—dance, breathwork, chanting, and/or music and, in some cultures, entheogen plant medicines such as ayahuasca or peyote. The shamanic journey is used to help with needs ranging from difficult life decisions that an individual may be facing to serious emotional and spiritual suffering such as PTSD resulting from war, trauma, or sexual abuse.

The process of the shamanic journey is very purposeful and workmanlike, not a passive or mood-altered state of relaxation or dreaminess. Rather, a shaman on a journey is "at the office," and the practice requires mastery and great focus. During my early shamanic training, when I met with my teacher for supervisory sessions, he would often ask, "Have you been journeying?" If I had not been, then I was not really "doing the work."

The notion of altering consciousness can raise eyebrows in Western society, but be clear on this: we alter our consciousness *all the time.* Have you ever had a cup of coffee? Eaten chocolate? Lit up a cigarette, or sipped a glass of wine? Have you ever played a video game, danced at a club, screamed at a ball game, or sung in a choir? Church worship alters consciousness with music, ecstatic sermons, incense, candles, booming organs, ringing bells, and stained-glass windows—all methods of shifting awareness to a more excited or deeper way of experiencing reality.*

With this in mind, we will next look at the different shamanic practices and tools available to set us on our Heart Path and to keep us moving along it.

THE SHAMANIC TOOLBOX

An Overview

The practices used on the Heart Path can be grouped into three broad categories or strategies for healing: heart-opening tools, mind-management tools, and mindfulness tools. These tools are selected by the shamanic practitioner or journeying individual based on what the individual needs in any given situation. These three categories of practice lead to the same place of heart-open living and navigation, but each uses a different focus and strategy.

Here's a summary of the various practices I have used on my own journeys and in the shamanic counseling and healing work I do with others. (We will explore many of them more fully in other sections of this book.)

Heart-Opening Tools

Heart-opening tools comprise the first strategic route of shamanic practice. These are methodologies used to help identify and honor the heart's deepest longings. They include:

- Answering Core Questions: carefully crafted questions that get to the heart of who you are (examples will be found in chapter 5 and appendix 1)
- Creating a mandala vision: a method of eliciting a vision for the kind of life the heart really longs to be living (see exercise in chapter 5)

*At two opposite extremes, Adolph Hitler and Martin Luther King Jr. were both very "shamanic" in their public speaking, able to move people to ecstasy and action with their passion, intonations, and gestures. The poet Allen Ginsberg referred to the early performances of singer-songwriter Bob Dylan as shamanistic.

- Listening to feeling tones: exercises to detect and track the navigational guidance system (NGS) of the heart
- Dreamwork: engaging with dreams to draw out the wisdom and directives of the heart
- Power animal retrieval: a classic shamanic journey to acquire a primary spirit helper or animal guide
- Dismemberment journeys: a foundational shamanic journey to experience oneself as a pure and conscious soul self without a body
- Shamanic journeys: used with endless variations to gain needed information from the spirit world and can include journeys to consult with particular helper spirits such as an inner shaman, Mother Earth, or an ancestor
- Journeys to connect with the spirit of another living thing for guidance: this spirit could be of a plant, animal, or stone, consulted for information and support
- Wilderness vision quest: a traditional Amerindian rite of passage involving several days of fasting and prayer alone in the wilderness to obtain spiritual knowledge, clarity, and life direction. Done in the context of advanced preparation and the close support of a teacher and spiritual community
- Journaling vision quest: an intensive journaling process to clarify a vision for your life by looking at three key arenas of life and your uniqueness, particular loves, and calling
- Sacred Breathwork: connected breathing, ritual process, and powerful music help you enter nonordinary states of consciousness, engage with spirit, and creatively express visions through breath, artwork, dance, poetry, and chanting
- Ecstatic movement and dance: traditional and contemporary methods that employ powerful percussive rhythms and music to help you release mental barriers and open the heart
- Plant medicine: ingesting natural entheogens derived from such plants as the ayahuasca vine (Amazon jungle), San Pedro cactus (Andes mountains), and the peyote cactus (Mexico and southwest

Texas) to break through mental barriers and induce nonordinary states for deep healing journeys

Mind-Management Tools

These mind-management tools—the second strategic route of shamanic work—address the thinking component of our problems, helping to release and transform negative or trauma-based belief patterns into positive energies in service of the heart. We use these tools to identify and break the trance of our habitual negative thought patterns and to identify and restore areas of soul loss.

- The Four Agreements: these are four rules for living developed by Don Miguel Ruiz, which he explains in his bestselling book of the same name; Ruiz uses Mexican Toltec shamanism to help readers see the "parasite" in our mind comprised of the inner judge, the victim, and our negative belief system (explained in chapter 7).
- Smoky Mirror: a Toltec exercise to observe the inner judge at work in our life and transform the energy of this parasite into usable power for a satisfying life (see chapter 7).
- Recapitulation: a practice for systematically rooting out old trauma-based belief patterns (see chapter 7 for a journaling version of this traditional practice).
- Clearing of the heart: a practice from Andean shamanism for healing a trauma-based pattern using the bodily felt sense; the practice Journaling from the Heart (see appendix 1) is inspired by this.
- Shamanic journeys: the classic methodology for seeking information and guidance in the spirit world. This practice crosses the boundaries between heart-opening and mind-management tools.

Mindfulness Tools

Mindfulness tools, the third strategic route of the transformational work that I do, are practices that pull your mind, heart, and body together, helping to decrease distractedness and the compulsion to dwell on past hurts or future worries. Although not all are traditionally shamanic, these tools are essential for keeping our focus and power in the present moment as we navigate the challenges of modern life.

- Ritual beginnings for ceremony: burning sage, calling in the directions, drumming or rattling
- Simple breathing meditations
- Body-focusing exercises
- Guided imagery
- Outdoor moving meditation (Fox Walking, for example, which we describe in appendix 2)

Traditional shamanism provides three powerful additional tools that do not easily fall into any single category above:

1. Soul extraction: the shaman identifies and removes unhelpful spiritual intrusions from a person's life.
2. Soul retrieval: the shaman journeys to locate and retrieve a person's soul essence, which may have been lost after a traumatic event.
3. Psychopomp: the shaman journeys to help dying or deceased persons transition from bodily to spiritual life as an end-of-life doula.

Now that you have a basic understanding of shamanism and the tools available in the shamanic toolbox, let's take some easy first steps to get you started on your exploration of the shamanic realms and give you some direct exposure to this world. Below are several warm-up exercises to loosen your imagination and allow your creative heart to move freely, without your analytical mind getting in the way.

EXERCISE

❋ Opening the Imagination

Allow yourself to quickly imagine and feel each of the situations below, however it comes to you. Don't overthink the images or feelings that your imagination comes up with. Just read the paragraph, close your eyes, and see, feel, or hear the experience unfold.

1. Imagine you are sitting in your living room. The doorbell rings. You get up and open the door. You see a golden retriever standing there. Pat him on the head. He wags his tail. Close the door.
2. The doorbell rings. You open the door. It's the same retriever with a red ball in his mouth. He drops it at your feet. Pick up the ball and throw it into the yard. Watch the dog run after the ball and bring it back to you, wagging his tail. You pick up the ball. It now has dog slobber on it. Throw it high into the air and at its highest point you say "Bird!" and the ball turns into a white dove and flies away. Notice the expression on the dog's face. Close the door.
3. The doorbell rings. You open the door. Santa Claus is standing there. *Ho, ho, ho!* You say hello and decide to put Santa in your pocket. Make Santa very small so that he fits in your hand. You bend down, he climbs into your hand, and you slip him into your pocket. Close the door.
4. Imagine you are standing on the south rim of the Grand Canyon, enjoying the beautiful view. Your arms and hands begin to feel funny. They are turning into wings, great, long feathered wings. Your feet turn into raptor's talons that grasp the railing you are now perched on. Your eyes become as powerful as telescopes, and you can see a rabbit half a mile away under a bush on the canyon floor. Look around you, then lean forward and drop into the canyon. As you fall, spread your great wings out wide. They catch the air and you carve a turn upward in the wind, and you are now soaring on the warm air currents rising up from the canyon floor. Make a few powerful strokes with your wings. Circle the rabbit. Feel the wind rippling through your wing feathers. Your vision is incredible. Go back to your living room now.
5. The doorbell rings. You open the door. A small child is standing there. The child is you, when you were little. Spend some time looking at your small self: notice what you are wearing, from your head down to your shoes. Your small self is wearing a little backpack and perhaps holding your favorite toy. Remember the details. Notice how the child is feeling and note his or

her expression. Say hello to the child, and give the child a big hug. Now the child reaches into the backpack and pulls out a small gift box. It was wrapped awkwardly with love by this little you. The box is *for* you. There is something inside for your healing, your happiness today. Open the box.

What is inside the box? Be patient. It may take some time for the contents of the box to come into focus.

With these exercises, the particular imagery you generate is not that important. Not everyone is a visual journeyer. The point is to create situations with your imagination, fully sense those situations, and use your intention to navigate and interact with those situations at will. Some people will experience these mini-journeys and actual shamanic journeys visually, others will hear them audibly, still others will sense them intuitively. Over time you will learn which manner of experiencing these journeys is most natural for you. Note that you close the door after each situation above. This is important because the shamanic journey is purposeful work: when the job is done, you close the portal to the spirit world and return to ordinary consciousness.

EXAMPLE OF A SHAMANIC JOURNEY

The following is a good example of the practical help that shamanic journeying provides me in daily life. Last year I was invited to speak at a local university where I would be the guest lecturer for a one-hour class, a very short time to introduce shamanism! There was so much information I wanted to share that after several hours of attempting to create an outline on index cards I stopped, frustrated. I was trying to cram too much information into the allotted time yet still was unable to arrive at the core teaching I wanted to convey.

I decided to do a shamanic journey to ask my spirit guides for help.

I burned some sage and drummed for a few minutes to open my senses and shift attention from my thinking mind to my creative heart. I turned to each of the four directions and called to mind the powers, images, animals, and spiritual teaching of each. Then I picked up a rattle, closed my eyes, and began to rattle at the steady rate I use while journeying.

I quickly entered an altered state of consciousness and journeyed to my familiar departure station, a solitary campfire out on the prairie of the Great Plains. Once there I summoned my spirit guides, which this time, in addition to the usual characters, included the Trappist monk and writer Thomas Merton and the novelist Cormac McCarthy. (In my previous journeys, Merton and McCarthy had been skilled helpers in matters of writing and creativity.) I explained to the assembled guides that I needed help organizing my talk.

Instantly the scene in my imagination shifted to a classroom I recognized as the university I would be visiting. I was standing in front of the class with the stack of index cards I had prepared. As I began to read through them, my buffalo power animal barged into the room, knocked the student chair desks out of their orderly rows, and arranged them into a large circle. In the center of the circle was a small campfire. At that point, Thomas Merton walked up to me, grabbed most of the cards, and threw them into the fire.

I was shocked. The remaining cards flew out of my hands, circled around the fire, and settled on the floor in a pattern I recognized as the stone layout for a Cherokee medicine wheel: four large stones at the four compass points, with three smaller stones between each of those. *Ah, a medicine wheel,* I thought, *which contains the core of all the teachings. I've taught the medicine wheel principles many times in outdoor settings.*

I realized I had my answer: I would organize my talk around the four main compass points that I wanted to convey, with three subpoints for each. That was plenty of content for a short talk. I had a few cards left in my hand when Cormac McCarthy walked up and growled, "Keep it simple, for God's sake!" and the remaining cards flew into the fire. I had to laugh because I always overtalk my presentations and run out of time.

I thanked my guides, each of whom bowed to me except for McCarthy, who just rolled his eyes in mock impatience. I opened my eyes, turned back to my desk, and easily rewrote my talk.

The class was a big success: I created a ceremonial fire on the classroom floor using chunks of split wood and small candles elevated in the center. With the classroom lights dimmed, I slowly walked around the fire as I talked, to emphasize each main point. The students were captivated.

This example is characteristic of my journeys in several ways. The helpers I summon are often familiar but the help they bring is always unexpected. The information that comes is usually symbolic or telepathic. I don't "talk" with my spirit guides and power animals verbally. And although I begin the journeys by making up the initial scene in my imagination, another creative hand enters the picture and things come back to me that I don't make up. These things are always helpful and usually quite striking. Finally, there is often an element of lightheartedness, even in the most serious of journey circumstances. In this journey McCarthy's gruff yet fatherly impatience is an example of that. The journey experience typically feels like I'm reconnecting with old friends to help me address serious matters needing resolution.

In the pages to come you will learn how to go on your own shamanic journeys and will read examples of how the journey is used to acquire specific information and guidance for yourself and on behalf of other people (an advanced practice).

WHAT IS SHAMANISM?

First, let's look at what shamanism is and what it is not.

Not a Religion

Shamanism is not a religion, and the shaman is not the pastor or spiritual leader of the tribe in any modern sense. "Shamanism is a path of knowledge, not faith," writes Michael Harner, scholar and founder of the Foundation for Shamanic Studies. "To acquire that knowledge . . . it is necessary to step through the shaman's doorway and acquire empirical evidence."[1] Joseph Campbell clearly distinguishes the role of the shaman from that of the priest in world religions: "A priest is ordained as a functionary of a social sort, to carry on a social ritual of a deity who existed before him. [But] a shaman's authority comes out of a psychological experience of ecstasy, not a social ordination. He becomes the interpreter of things not seen for others. He interprets the heritage of mythological life."[2]

Although the particular practices of shamanic healing have been aligned with specific cultures over time, the shamanic spirit world is as inclusive as Christ consciousness or Buddha nature. One can practice shamanism without being an American Indian just as one can practice yoga without being Hindu or sit in meditation without being a Buddhist.

This nonreligious character of shamanism can be confusing to people raised to divide the world into believers and nonbelievers, into people of faith (*their* faith) and people with no faith. They find it hard to imagine a path of authentic spiritual experience that does not involve a sacred book, a dedicated building to worship in, or ordained clergy. Yet the practice of shamanism does not need to conflict with one's individual beliefs. It is not based on belief in a sacred book or religious hero but in direct experience of the sacred. Shamanic practices can help anyone and even build bridges back to a spiritual practice for those disillusioned with organized religion.

Not about Playing Indian

Shamanism is not about dressing up in Indian regalia, mimicking sacred ceremony, getting an Indian name, or obtaining pseudo-Indian artifacts (eagle feathers, peace pipes, deerskin medicine bags). In the United States, the current fascination with all things Native American frustrates many Indians who see this as a second wave of exploitation and cultural appropriation by the descendants of the very Europeans who destroyed Indian societies in the first place. Some Indians find the situation ironic: first, the Europeans perceived the Indians as uncivilized; now their descendants want to copy Indian culture and learn their most sacred beliefs.*

*The opinions of Indian people differ on this, of course, depending on the individual and his or her group's historical experience. For example, I met several Lakota people on the Pine Ridge Reservation in South Dakota who were devout Christians and seemed to have little interest in the spiritual practices of their traditional healers.

The goal of shamanic healing is to open people's hearts and do what we can to heal and learn from Earth. The Path of the Heart is rooted in Earth-honoring ways common to all indigenous peoples, including the ancestors of white Europeans. Every human being has a relationship with nature and the spirit world. And every human being has the responsibility to honor and protect Earth.

Not Psychotherapy

Although the Heart Path includes insights and tools borrowed from Jungian and transpersonal psychology, my one-on-one shamanic counseling sessions are not psychotherapy. Conventional psychotherapy is rooted in Western culture and rationalistic assumptions about the mind, illness, and healing. Shamanism is rooted in ancient Earth-honoring societies in which the whole created world, not just the human one, is considered sacred and of equal importance. The psychological and shamanic approaches can work together; this book integrates aspects of both. But the shamanic approach is not primarily interested in explaining why an individual is unhappy (examining past trauma or diagnosing family dysfunction). The emphasis is on restoring the spiritual heart and bringing the person more fully alive in the world. In psychotherapy, the doctor is the therapist. In shamanism, the doctor is the Great Spirit.

To illustrate the difference between conventional psychotherapy and shamanism, picture a frightened person surrounded by wolves in a forest. In psychotherapy, you might study the wolves (problems, past traumas, emotional wounding patterns), speculate about how they got there, and look deeply into your childhood and family history over weeks and months of therapy so that you can make each wolf go away and be happy again.

In shamanic healing, you pick up a branch, light a torch (the power of the heart), consult the compass in your pocket (the navigational guidance of the heart), and begin walking straight ahead *through* the circle of wolves. The wolves may snarl and follow you a ways, but you are moving toward a luminous vision for your life. Many of the wolves you encounter are lazy and don't like light or confrontation and so they slink away. As you move forward and discover you aren't "eaten," you become stronger and can better contend with any remaining wolves from a position of power and confidence. It's an entirely different approach, and it works.

I often use a similar approach during shamanic couples' counseling. The emphasis is not on developing a mutual understanding about the past hurts and current emotional needs of the partners. The emphasis is on helping each individual come more fully alive in the world. I help each person become the other's "shaman" so that he or she can help the other explore a vision for his or her life. This works because it turns out that a more fully alive, purpose-driven partner is a lot easier to live with than an angry, depressed, or stagnant one.

Here is an exercise in calling together your own circle of support prior to your journey.

EXERCISE

Calling in Your Helper Spirits

1. Find a quiet place at home or outdoors. Turn off all distractions. Put the cat out. Create a special, protected space that is just for you at this time.
2. Light a small candle to represent your heart and the spirit all around you. Burn a little white sage or incense if you wish. Breathing deeply, take a moment to shift your attention to your body and breath.
3. Use a rattle or hand drum to begin a simple, rapid, monotonous beat without flourishes. For a rattle you can use an empty water bottle with popcorn kernels or dry beans in it; even a Tic Tac breath mint dispenser will work as a shaker. Find a percussion rate that feels natural for you. Continue drumming or shaking through the whole exercise.
4. Sit or lie down with eyes closed. You are going to use your imagination to envision and feel some things. There is no place for the critical voice in your head to say "this is silly" or "I'm doing it wrong." You are going to *make this all up,* initially. But as you'll see, you won't be making it all up.

5. Now picture the key people who have helped you during your life: grandparents, family members, teachers, coaches, friends, lovers, neighbors. Include those who have died. Visualize each one of them coming to you now. Be open to someone you had forgotten about also appearing to join you.
6. Now include all the animals you have loved. Call out to them and see them coming to you. Be open to a surprise animal visitor or two.
7. Look at each face around the circle. Give thanks for all of these helper spirits in your life. Now ask if anyone of them has a message or gift for you and wait. Be patient. Keep drumming or rattling. Don't *think,* just be alert with your brain in neutral, holding your attention on the scene in your imagination. See what happens.
8. Return your attention to the room and open your eyes.

Shifting consciousness for shamanic journeying is a learnable skill. Some people are able to do this easily, while for others, their first experience is often "nothing happened" or "I think I saw a few things." Don't worry. There is no one who can't journey, though there are many who need to do it several times to get the hang of it. Children can shift consciousness easily; it's the adults who typically must overcome a certain level of intellectual resistance.

AM I MAKING ALL THIS UP?

Whether you had a vivid full-color experience above with your spirit helpers gathered around you or nothing much seemed to happen, the question arises, "Isn't my mind making this up?" I asked my teacher this early in my training, and his immediate response was, "Yes, you're making it up. But you're not making it *all* up." In shamanic journeying, we use our conscious, intentional mind to create an imaginal bridge to the unconscious, a shaman's portal to our psyche and the spirit world. And when you create a bridge, *things come back to you across that bridge.* In the words of Lakota elder Fools Crow, the healer strives to be a clean hollow bone or tube, empty of ego and personal desires, so that Wakan Tanka (Great Mystery) and the spirit helpers can come through for healing.[3]

There is solid science behind shamanism.[4] We have neurobiological pathways in our brains that correspond to habitual thought patterns. The practice of shamanic journeying opens up new perceptual pathways in the physical brain and in greater nonphysical consciousness. Like any untraveled path through a wild area, the first time you walk it is difficult, but the more you walk it, the more established the path becomes.

In this chapter we defined shamanism and learned how modern shamanic practice relates to religious faith, Indian traditions, and psychology. We looked inside the shaman's toolbox to see the whole array of available practices for healing and journeying. We began to learn the skill of shifting consciousness for shamanic journeying.

To find support and encouragement for our walk along this path together, we are now going to visit the world of your indigenous ancestors. We will meet the people whose relationship with nature was so intimate they referred to it as their mother or mama. We will see the animals, plants, and trees around them as they did: as kin, spiritual beings, and teachers. We will learn how to communicate directly with the spirit of a plant, tree, or animal. And we will begin to see paradise as our ancestors did: the simple way of being in the providential care of the living Earth all around them—not just in some faraway heaven or a rarified spiritual state.

These people have disappeared from view, and many of their cultures are gone. But they are not unavailable to us. The spirits of our ancestors—of *your own* ancestors—are real and are with us here; they will be your helpers and guides.

It's now time to meet these ancestors, so we can call out to them for help on our journey.

Ssshhh! Quiet your mind and open your heart. If you close your eyes, you may be able to smell the wood smoke, see the glow of their council fires, and hear the whispering voices of wisdom gathered around you now.

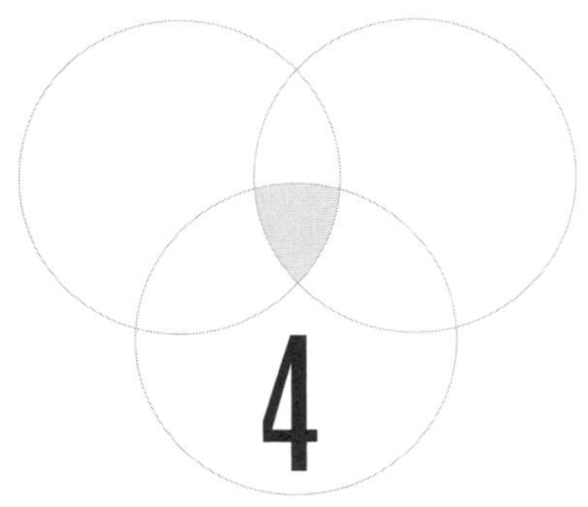

4

Gathering around the Sacred Fire

The world is holy. We are holy. All life is holy. Daily prayers are delivered on the lips of breaking waves, the whisperings of grasses, the shimmering of leaves.

TERRY TEMPEST WILLIAMS

YOUR ANCESTORS

Intimacy with the Heart of Nature

In 1932 in New Mexico, the Swiss psychiatrist Carl Jung met with Ochwiay Biano, a Taos Pueblo Indian, an experience that Jung recounted in his book *Memories, Dreams, Reflections.* Jung wanted the Indians to teach him their spiritual ceremonies, which they would not do. But the chief did share his observations of white people with Jung.

"See how cruel the whites look," the chief said to Jung. "Their lips are thin, their noses sharp, their faces furrowed and distorted by folds. Their eyes have a staring expression; they are always seeking something.

What are they seeking? The whites always want something. They are always uneasy and restless. We do not know what they want. We do not understand them. We think that they are all mad."

Jung was surprised, and asked the chief why he thought the whites were mad. He replied, "They say the white people think with their heads."

"Why of course," said Jung. "What do you think with?"

"We think here," replied the chief, pointing to his heart.

In this chapter we are going to journey back into the physical and spiritual world of our ancestors. This is a preparatory step that mirrors the shaman's practice of invoking the spirits of his or her ancestors before undertaking journeys into the spirit world. This calling in of one's ancestors is no mere ceremonial custom; it is a practical matter that allows the shaman to be strong during the shamanic journey. This is especially important when a shaman is performing advanced work like soul retrieval or spirit depossession, during which the shaman may encounter uncooperative or harmful spirits.

It is important to understand that when I refer to ancestors, I mean *your* indigenous ancestors, not just those of, say, American Indians, African tribes, or Australian aborigines. The word *indigenous* is from the Latin *indu* or *endo* (from within) and *gignere* (to beget). We all come from indigenous people somewhere. Many Caucasian Americans think of themselves as originating from modern European states like Ireland, Italy, or Belgium, but their heritage extends much further back—tens of thousands of years before those nations existed. Caucasian ancestors may be found in a Celtic or Germanic tribe, the Sami of Scandinavia, the Mari of Russia, or the Goral people of Poland and Slovakia, for instance. The Judeo-Christian religious tradition itself arose out of tribal, nomadic cultures. The early books of the Old Testament originated in the oral stories of the twelve Hebrew-speaking tribes of Israel, in the land of Canaan in ancient Palestine.*

***Caucasian* is an imprecise eighteenth-century term for people from the Caucasus region of Armenia, Azerbaijan, and Georgia. I am focusing on Caucasian or white Americans here (my own group) and the Judeo-Christian identity because I believe many of this

Let's go visit the world of your ancestors now, no matter where they are from!

INTIMACY WITH WILDNESS

For over fifty thousand years human beings lived and moved in small bands of fewer than sixty people each. Life was immediate, purposeful, and very physical. Adults, infants, elders, and teens were constantly on the move in search of food, water, better hunting grounds, or safer areas to raise their families. This transient life was difficult but close-knit, vital, and enjoyable. Early societies enjoyed far more leisure time than modern capitalist and agrarian societies. They worked an estimated two and a half days per week, approximately five to six hours a day.[1]

Our ancestors had no significant personal possessions other than what they could carry with them. They owned no real estate, had no social classes, nor had any sense of rich or poor. There were no kings or peasants, employers or employees, haves and have-nots. Violence and crime within the clan was unheard of because this would have endangered the survival and smooth functioning of the entire community.

The attention of our ancestors was constantly engaged with the nature around them. During my own wilderness trips I have been struck by the immediacy of outdoor survival and the present moment, all day long. *Don't trip on that root. Are those storm clouds? I need to find water. Look, an eagle!* It's hard to be dwelling on past regrets when you are paddling down river rapids and a large submerged rock is coming right at you. You forget about future worries when you walk face-first into a spider web hanging across the trail. A single misstep on a slippery rock can end a trip in a moment. To live in the wild is to be a student in Earth School with its 24/7 emphasis on mindfulness and coordination with nature.

By comparison, our modern disconnect from nature is almost

---

group have never considered their own roots in indigenous societies. A number of relatively low-cost DNA-testing services for determining one's ancestral origins now exist, such as Ancestry.com and National Geographic's Geno 2.0.

complete today. Our primary contact with large wild animals is more apt to result from a car collision than witnessing them in their natural settings. Yet instead of feeling remorse for building a highway across the animals' habitat and sorrow for the death, many people are apt to react with distaste and repulsion: *Why doesn't the highway department pick that thing up? It's disgusting to look at!*

One of the great losses that has come with urban living is the constant reminder of our own animal nature, an awareness that is inescapable in a natural setting. On a wilderness trip when I watch my own urine draining back into the earth or squat in the woods to defecate, my kinship with animals is undeniable. In the wilderness, the impact of my life on the natural world is obvious and immediate: I know where my poop goes. Do you know where your poop goes? Do you know where anything that you flush down the toilet, pour into the sink, or drop into your garbage can really goes? In modern living it can appear as if our lives have no impact on the environment whatsoever, as if our waste just disappears. This individual lack of awareness becomes a much bigger problem when it aggregates into the collective lack of awareness, as in the case of climate change. If we do not see where our own waste goes, how much easier to not see the impact of invisible greenhouse gases from our industrial, power-generating, and agricultural sources?

THANKING THE ANIMALS

Our ancestors learned in the "classroom" of interdependent life all around them and took their nourishment directly from the same source. The natural world was a caring and connected world, despite the obvious risks of daily survival: it provided food and shelter, healing plants, and clothing. A Plains Indian would see how the shallow depression left by a buffalo wallow filled with rain in the spring, creating a little ecosystem that allowed seeds to sprout in a dry climate and thus keep the prairie ecosystem alive. "People think we learned plant medicine by praying or experiments on plants," a Lakota elder once told me. "But we just watched the animals. We saw which plants an animal would go to when it was sick or for healing a wound." Our ancestors' dependence on nature for survival was stark and undeniable.

Our ancestors ate what they hunted, fished out of the waters, pulled roots from the ground, and took fruit off the trees. "It was life eating life," as Joseph Campbell says, "and they knew it."[2] Because of their direct dependence on nature for survival, our ancestors didn't thank an unseen God in heaven for their food; they thanked the animal or plant itself for its life. "You, buffalo, thank you. You, brother salmon, thank you. You, sister corn, thank you. Thank you for your sacrifice for the life of my people. We have a special dance to honor your death for my life. We dance it before the hunt. We dance it after the harvest. We promise to take only what we need, and you promise to come back next year."

To paraphrase Joseph Campbell, their mythos and rituals helped our ancestors relate their actions of killing and taking from nature to the greater cosmos and spirit world. It kept them whole, relieved of guilt from what they knew they were doing: killing fellow creatures to stay alive. Contrast this belief system with the modern meat industry, which kills our animals for us, some ten billion per year in the United States, and sells us neatly packaged meat, completely detached from the source. Emissions of the greenhouse gas methane from the same livestock industry are a greater contributor to climate change than CO_2 from the entire U.S. transportation industry.[3]

Children instinctively sense the connectedness of our human lives to the natural world, but this awareness gets pushed aside early on by social values and religious constructs, like the belief in a soul for humans alone. As a child, I would get in playground debates with classmates related to the question "Do dogs have souls?" This was an important subject. But unless the animal in question was a family pet or otherwise cute and cuddly, things generally turned out badly for the animal.

When we stop seeing other creatures as a *thou* and begin treating them as an *it*—as an object—then the killing can begin. When I was a boy I had a friend named Tim, whose father was a big hunter and handgun collector. Tim and I were constantly outdoors and explored every vacant lot, forest, and field within five miles of our homes. We often discovered birds, animals, and insects, but Tim's first reaction to them was usually as a predator, not as a fellow creature.

"Look, a deer!" I'd say to Tim.

"Yes, that's about three hundred fifty yards away," he'd say coldly. "I could drop that easily with my dad's .30-06." This way of seeing creatures only as prey is deeply wired into our modern psyche, especially in men. I was gazing at a pristine river in northern Michigan recently when another man walked up to me.

"Beautiful river," I said.

"Yeah," he replied. "Can you fish here?"

THE GREAT HOOP

Our ancestors experienced the world as a great circle or hoop of life. It was a revolving wheel of springtime birth, summer growth and expansion, autumn harvest and aging, and winter dying and stillness. Then it was springtime rising and rebirthing all over again. The medicine wheel of some Plains Indian traditions beautifully represents the dynamic processes of the cosmos. Each of the four cardinal directions are represented by four stones around a sacred fire, and each one is packed with multiple layers of meaning that are endlessly adaptable for teaching, prayer, and ceremony. The direction of east, for example, can represent the power of the rising sun, springtime, new life, infancy, vision, hope, the Fire People or white people, and the eagle's powerful vision.

The hoop embodied the dynamic womb of Mother Earth, the fertile source of all life on Earth as depicted in figure 4.1.

Unlike our modern world, in these nature-embedded cultures women had special social and spiritual power. All life seemed to come from the female; women could create new life and provide new members to sustain the tribe. They had mysterious bodies influenced by the moon and the tides and by the cycles and seasons of nature around

Fig. 4.1 Life on Earth within the hoop or womb of Mother Earth

them. They were sent apart during menstruation not because they were unclean but because they were so power filled at that time.

Some societies like the Lakota were matriarchal and/or matrilineal in social structure. And God was female, obviously: an Earth goddess. In the high Andes of South America, the Quechua-speaking people still call on the divine by her familiar name Pachamama, "World Mother."

THE SPIRITUAL NATURE OF ALL CREATED THINGS

In South America, this spiritual cosmology of our ancestors still exists today. The intimate relationship of humans with the Pachamama extends to each of her children—the animals, plants, rivers, and stones—and that relationship is characterized by the three core elements of kinship, spirit, and teaching wisdom.

- Kinship: Given that humans, animals, and plants all have the same Pachamama, they are related to each other, like brothers and sisters. Some indigenous people believe that the outer appearance of natural forms (an animal or a tree, for instance) only masks the human being within. So they look around them and see tree people, stone people, star people, and so on. Humans are not considered more God-favored than animal and plant forms, just different in outward appearance and talents.

- Spiritual beings: Every living thing is a sentient being with a soul or inner spirit. Even stones are conscious and considered the wisest of all things because they are the oldest. Our ancestors related to other life-forms as friends, not as objects: as a *thou* rather than an *it*. When shamans call on the spirits of plant and animal life, they are not invoking *a* bear for help; they are invoking Bear Spirit.
- Teaching wisdom: We learn things from our nonhuman kin that we would not learn anywhere else. From a river flowing around boulders, we learn how to deal with obstacles. From a coyote, we learn how to be resourceful and clever. From a snake, we learn how to shed our external appearance and grow. From a caterpillar, we learn how to undergo self-transformation.

Communicating with the spirit of a plant, tree, or animal sounds like a strange idea until you have been helped by one. And herein lies a deep truth in shamanism: opening your heart to another creature opens your heart to its Creator. When you greet another thing as Brother Oak rather than "that tree," you are creating a bridge to love. And when you create a bridge to love, things come back to you across the bridge. So our ancestors didn't "talk" to trees and plants, they connected with the *spirit* of the tree or plant that animates and guides it through its life cycle.

This is the basis of shamanic healing. Everything has a spirit; every cell in your body has a spirit; your fear has a spirit. So when you open your heart to another creature, you plug your individual awareness directly into the shared intelligence, spirit, or consciousness of that creature, into *wahmunka oganunka inchante,* the Lakota name for the sacred Black Hills of South Dakota, meaning "the heart of everything that is."

We will use this same conceptual basis later in chapter 10 to communicate directly with the spirits of your fears and to learn directly from them as teachers.

EXERCISE

☼ Shamanic Journey into a Plant or Animal

This is a foundational shamanic practice to help you connect directly with the living spirit of another life-form. You will need your journal and a pen or colored pencils.

1. **Go to a natural outdoor setting.** Find some place where you won't be disturbed by noise, pets, or other people. Take a few minutes to center yourself and connect deeply with your breath. You can do this by sitting down and drawing your attention to your breathing for several minutes. As you notice your mind wandering, just bring it gently back to your breath, focusing on the exhale each time it comes around.
2. **Walk around the area.** Walk at a very slow, strolling-the-park pace. With the same bodily felt sense you used in our earlier exercises, look around as you walk. Use your intuition to be alert for some natural thing that you feel drawn to, such as a tree, a flower, a line of ants. The felt sense will be a subtle feeling of curiosity, interest, or concern for the other being. Sit down in front of it.
3. **Establish a connection.** Greet the tree, plant, or creature that catches your attention just as you would a new acquaintance: "Hello, maple tree." "Greetings, turtle. How is the pond today?" Send your communications from your heart.
4. **State your purpose or question.** "I am here to connect with your spirit and see if you have anything to teach me." If you have a question, write it down in your journal and share it from your heart. Be specific in stating your need. For example, "I am not sure how to proceed with this new relationship. I am afraid of being hurt. Should I move forward?" Vague questions will elicit vague responses.
5. **Listen and wait for a response.** Now shift your perspective and imagine you are experiencing the world from the other's (tree, plant, or animal's) perspective. Your new friend can communicate with you the same way you can understand a whimpering dog, a purring cat, or the look in the eyes of a horse. Attend with your shared intuitive, nonverbal,

creaturely senses rather than your human intellect. If need be, send your question again, from your heart. Be patient. Any delay or muddledness in response will likely come from your side of the relationship, from the skeptical or impatient voice of your human intellect.

6. **Write down the response you get.** The response may come back to you as a feeling, image, metaphor, or a flash of knowing. You may get a brief glimpse or a deep understanding. There is often an element of the unexpected when you connect with the spirit world, like surprising tenderness or sharpness—even humor: *Jeff, you're so intense. Relax. Lighten up!*
7. **Thank your friend for its communication.** You may leave it a small gift: tobacco, a rolled-up paper with a poem or drawing on it, water for its roots. Take some time to journal or draw your encounter so that you will remember it.

I first tried this exercise in September 2009 during preparation for my wilderness vision quest. I was open to the idea but doubtful I could communicate with a tree or plant. I walked out into a little meadow and sat down by a common Queen Anne's lace wildflower, *Daucus carota*. That late in the season, the elegant, leggy plant was drying out; its stem was brown and the green leaves were curling up. It was clear the plant's glory days were over, and it was dying. I felt a sadness for the plant and, after introducing myself to it, asked it how it was doing.

The response I received, like an internal awareness or sudden insight, was unexpected: *This is what we do! We shoot up in the spring, show off all summer, and we die in the fall. We drop back to Earth, like we're supposed to.* I noticed dead stems of the previous year's flowers and grasses matted down at the feet of the Queen Anne's lace, half decomposed, already returning their biomass to the earth.

Then another thought came, *Why the sad face? We're supposed to die in the fall.* It felt like a gentle reprimand to my human assumptions about what constitutes a good life. Then the flower drew my attention upward to the tree line fifty yards away. Towering above all the other plants and trees was a tall, majestic oak that appeared to be more than a century old. *Now him, he lives a long time,* said the Queen Anne's lace. *That's his thing. But I wouldn't want to have to deal with the winters like he does.*

Amazing! This wilting wildflower was content, not envious. That simple exchange left a deep impression and taught me about the assent and joy of created things to be living their appointed role with full esteem in the great web of life.

In this, I am reminded of a favorite reflection by the Trappist monk and writer Thomas Merton:

> A tree gives glory to God by being a tree. For in being what God means it to be it is obeying Him. It "consents," so to speak, to His creative love. It is expressing an idea which is in God and which is not distinct from the essence of God, and therefore a tree imitates God by being a tree.
>
> The more a tree is like itself, the more it is like Him. If it tried to be like something else which it was never intended to be, it would be less like God and therefore it would give Him less glory . . .
>
> [T]his particular tree will give glory to God by spreading out its roots in the earth and raising its branches into the air and the light in a way that no other tree before or after it ever did or will do.[4]

Since 2009 I have had many shamanic interactions with fellow creatures, which include a horse, a tree in the Amazon jungle, a group of white swans on Lake Michigan, a monarch butterfly, the Saint Joseph River, a Canada goose, a desert lizard, a tall thistle plant on the Great Plains, and a swarm of gnats on a lakeshore. Each has provided me with real information and wisdom about their life or mine that I could not have made up or gotten anywhere else.

CASE STUDY

Randy's Tree Medicine

The following is an example of a deep physical healing resulting from an encounter with a tree spirit. This occurred at a workshop I was leading. Randy arrived in physical distress from a nagging lung infection, which made breathing difficult. This prevented him from joining in our sweat lodge ceremony and our Sacred Breathwork session. He even had to stand back from the short outdoor group blessing we did with burning sage. But things changed as soon as he began his medicine walk into the woods.

Here is the letter he sent me afterward:

> The first words I heard while walking on the path were "cultivate intimacy." I was drawn to a large tree on the side of the trail that came out of the ground in two trunks. I introduced myself to the Spirit of the Tree and told it how beautiful it was. I was noticing all of the life that was around, upon, and within the great tree and I thanked it for providing so much life to other creatures in the forest.
>
> After I established a connection with the tree I informed it of my intentions, my personal prayer, and I wrote them in my journal. I told the tree spirit that I wanted to "bring my medicine to the community in a natural, authentic, and indigenous way." After that I stepped up onto what felt like the two feet of a great parent. I wrapped my arms around the tree and began to hug it as I felt it was hugging me.
>
> All of a sudden I felt like the tree was leading me through a breathwork session. The tree became my ally, and my teacher in this work. I began to spontaneously breathe like a person does in holotropic breathwork. This did not feel contrived nor was it planned, it just happened in an organic and natural manner. In a very short time, only after ten or twenty breaths, I began to cry because it felt safe for me to breathe! So I continued, but then I began to get light-headed and frightened. I then heard or felt the tree communicate with me to not fear the light-headedness either. All I know is that the great tree spirit was my ally, and she led me through a spontaneous breathwork! I then got off of the tree and sat down because I felt it was speaking to me and I wanted to write what I was about to hear. These are the unedited words as I wrote them:

"Trust the Breath Become Intimate with the Breath Be the Breath Release through the Breath Make the Breath your Ally Guardian Lover Confidant Source of LIFE Sustaining Giving Cleansing Power. Come and Breathe with Me and my Relatives. We are here to share our medicine and you are here to share yours. You breathe us as we breathe you. Let us rejoice in LIFE together."

The teaching that came to me was that we humans have to "cultivate intimacy" with the spirits of the natural world. It takes effort, like it takes for human beings to have healthy relationships with one another. Consistency and intentionality = DAILY!

THIS IS PARADISE

We have seen how our ancestors honored the entire ecosystem, from the smallest creature to the metaprocesses of the seasons, weather, tides, and migrations. They saw new life rising from death and recognized the intelligence behind it all. They saw a conscious planet capable of responding to opportunity, adapting to injury, and rebalancing its systems just like the individual creatures within the system, from the blue whale to the tiniest ant. To live as human creatures in balance with all the other creatures in this greater web of life was to dwell in the real Garden of Eden. For our ancestors, paradise meant balance in this life, not some afterlife with streets of gold.

Our ancestors and their shamanic healers remind us what our modern civilization has forgotten: that *this* land is the holy land, right under our feet here in South Bend, Indiana, Portland, Oregon, or New York City. The holy rivers of Earth are not just the Ganges, the Nile, and the Amazon—but the Missouri, the Ohio, and the Saint Joseph. "Moses had been standing on holy ground his whole life," writes Bill Plotkin, "but he didn't know this until he heard God's voice for the first time. Afterwards, Moses was a transformed man, forever conscious of the Great Mystery in everything."[5]

The river flowing past your local mall or factory is a sacred river.

"But that river is polluted," you may say. No, the river is *not* polluted. Rather, the river carries our pollution. The river *itself* is sacred. That river flows from the love of the Pachamama for the benefit of humans and all our animal and plant kin. The fact that we may be utterly unconscious of this does not render it a commodity for our exploitation or pollution.

Having paused in this chapter to call in the spirits of your ancestors, experience the living Earth through their eyes, and connect with a helper spirit in nature, we are now ready to return to the Heart Path. In the next chapter, you are going to get clear on your life's spiritual cargo, the unique potential that you're carrying with you during this life. We will use a powerful core questions exercise to get to the essence of your heart, and then select a physical talisman to represent that essence. From the viewpoint of that essence in you, you will then cast your vision outward and ahead to imagine a life that would most fully serve and express your hidden cargo into the light of day, a life that is aligned with your heart. We will use some creative artwork to make that vision more clear, and read several case studies from my shamanic counseling clients, showing how they used this same process to release their inner visionary.

This is an enjoyable section of the Heart Path.

Let's go see where it leads us.

PART II

The Descent

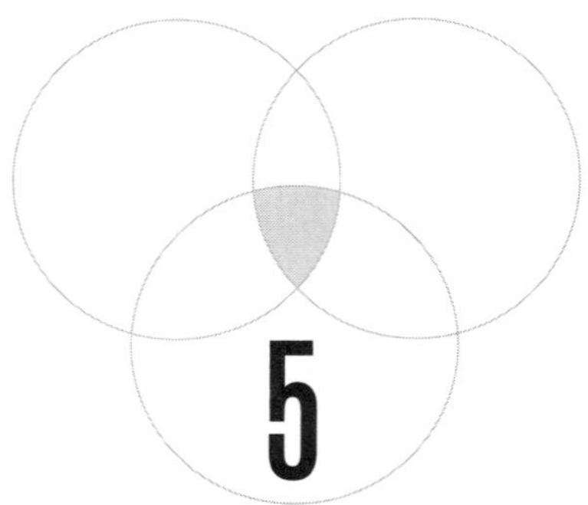

5

Getting Clear on Your Cargo

For me to be a saint means to be myself. Therefore the problem of sanctity and salvation is in fact the problem of finding out who I am and discovering my true self.

THOMAS MERTON,
NEW SEEDS OF CONTEMPLATION

CAREFUL PREPARATIONS FOR THE JOURNEY

When I take people out on wilderness programs, we do not simply unload our gear from the car, shoulder our backpacks, and start walking up the trail. We first sit down and review our maps, the weather forecast, our supplies, and the safety procedures that we should adhere to. We get clear on our destination and compass heading before we take our first step or dip a paddle into the water. So if anyone gets lost or injured, everyone knows exactly what to do.

The Heart Path requires similar preparations, and the first step is to get clear on your spiritual center or heart. This is your core nature, your unique soul-self. It is the cargo you are carrying in the hold of the beautiful ship that is your life. Only when you know your cargo can you know your destination and route to get there. Only then you can begin actively living *your* life and nobody else's.

When I talk with clients about the importance of following one's heart, some look worried. "But isn't that selfish?" they say. The answer is no, for following one's authentic, spiritual heart does not mean setting off on a self-absorbed path of emotional, financial, or sexual impulses that can result in harm to self and others. It does not mean "doing whatever I want," as in, "I am married but followed my heart and had an affair." Living the life your heart deeply desires—responding to the *call*—is the opposite of narcissistic self-absorption because the heart is an instinctively relational creature naturally drawing you into concern for other people. The Lakota form of prayer includes the words *mitokouye oyasin,* meaning "all my relatives," so that whatever is sought in prayer is sought not only for oneself but for all one's relatives. And for the Lakota, relatives include all of the animals, plants, and created things on Earth.

In heart-centered living you give freely out of the new abundance you are experiencing rather than because of social duty or a fear of divine punishment. Valuing your own core opens the awareness that others have a unique path as well; you stop expecting other people to think, feel, and live as you do.

If you are actively living a life that is following your heart, you are closely aligned with your Core Self. But what is your Core Self, exactly? It is your particular chemistry of natural interests, energies, drives, and spiritual sensitivities. It is that part of you that comes alive when you are doing certain things and that finds other things boring. It is your sense of some things being innately beautiful and other things intrinsically ugly. It is the part of you that senses holiness in certain people, places, or situations and feels that other things are intrinsically empty, false, or wrong to do. It is your unique, deeply imprinted spiritual DNA that shows up in everything you do.

The following exercise will help you perceive a basic outline of your Core Self and the soul cargo you are carrying.*

EXERCISE

☼ Ten Core Questions

This exercise is best done with a partner, or the voice-recorder function of your smartphone, to record your answers. This allows you to speak naturally and quickly without self-editing. We want to hear from your spontaneous heart here, not the carefully packaged ego self. Your partner's job is to ask the following ten questions and write down your answers verbatim without interpreting, commenting, or summarizing. She will provide a holding environment for your heart by listening without interrupting as you respond. This is very important.

Each question has a follow-up, asking you to name the crux of your prior answer. The crux just means the essence or the heart of something: "the crux of the matter," its core feeling or meaning. A crux is a deeper felt-sense kind of knowing than our intellectual understanding. It involves getting under the surface of the words or experience to feel the *sensation* of the thing, thus it can be hard to describe at first. So be patient, wait for the deep response, and get the right words. Here's an example of this process:

Q: Give me an example of a deeply satisfying time from your life?

A: (My exact words.) Well . . . writing this book was deeply satisfying. Difficult, a lot of time and work. And rewriting! And research. But when it was finished, I was very proud. Satisfied.

Q: What is the *crux* of this deep satisfaction for you?

A: (Long pause, thinking.) Um . . . *completion*. Yes. And *creativity*. Like giving birth to something. A baby, almost.

The entire dynamic arrangement of this book and your soul self-awareness pivots on this exercise. So first, take a moment to center yourself. Draw your

*Core-question inventory adapted from C. Michael Smith and his work with Kye Nelson.

attention to your breathing and its natural flow in and out of your body. Slow down. Then draw your attention farther down into your body, particularly the area around your heart and gut area. This is the felt-sense zone we want your responses to come from, not from your head and its thoughts. Indeed, the first response you have to each question will typically come from your intellect because the verbal function is more accessible (and more superficial) than the felt sense of the body and heart. But we want the slower, deeper response. Allow at least thirty seconds for that felt-sense response to rise up into your awareness.*

Here are the ten questions for you to answer. Key words in each question are in italic.

1. Give me an example in your life when you felt *naturally yourself* with no hindrance. Allow at least thirty seconds for your heart to respond and then record all your words. When you have done that, respond to the follow-up question, in a few words, or a short phrase: What is the *crux* of this naturalness for you?
2. Describe an instance of a *radiant* moment or *luminous* time in your life. As before, record every word and then ask, with a few words or a phrase: What is the *crux* of this radiant luminosity?
3. Tell me about a deeply *satisfying* time, as recent as possible. Record every word and then ask: What is the *crux* of this deep satisfaction for you?
4. Bring to mind some good thing in your life you are deeply *thankful* for because it so enriches your life and brings you peace, happiness, or inspiration. Then ask: What is the crux of your thankfulness for it?
5. If you could freely express your *wild* self, how exactly would you do so? What is the crux of that wildness in you?
6. What are three situations or activities during which you felt *physically vital,* resilient, or capable of surprising work or stamina? What is the crux of this physical vitality for you, in each example?

*This technique is based on two practices, Focusing and Thinking at the Edge, developed by philosopher and psychotherapist Eugene T. Gendlin. See his groundbreaking book *Focusing* (Maharashtra, India: Everest House, 1978).

7. What do you instinctually feel to be *beautiful?* In people? In places? In things? What is the crux of that beauty in each instance?
8. Recall a time in your life when you instinctually knew something was *right* to do even though others disagreed. Write that down. Where in your body did you feel that rightness? What is the crux of this rightness for you and in you?
9. Think of an activity that you easily become passionately *absorbed* in, such that the hours just fly by as if you were lost in time? What is the crux of that "absorbingness" for you?
10. Looking around your everyday life, the big and little things, give three examples of where you have experienced a sense of the sacred? (The sacred can be defined many ways. For example, feeling a presence of the holy, being emotionally moved by incredible beauty, a sense of awe or reverence in the presence of something, feeling deeply connected with your surroundings, or a sense of great mystery.) What is the crux of the sacred in each of your examples?

If you are alone and using a recording device, replay your answers above and transcribe the entire thing.

Next, underline all the key words in your answers that seem to have a significant heft or energy to them, that feel more heavy or dense than others. For example, if you wrote "the time I ran into my old girlfriend from high school and I felt oddly connected to her," you might underline the phrase *oddly connected* as feeling particularly significant, dense, or energetic.

Also go back and scan the full text of your initial responses, underlining any additional key words or short phrases that seem significant.

List each of those key words and phrases separately on a fresh piece of paper. This detaches these key feelings, memories, and ideas from the original questions so you can consider them on their own as freestanding attributes.

Now, look at this whole new list of key words and phrases together, as if you are looking at the full cast of a play onstage: separate individuals all contributing to a coordinated whole.

Get a felt sense of that whole collection of key words in your body, the feel of the whole thing as a unity, the *aura* of that whole assembly of key words.

Now write a fresh paragraph or two on this question: What do you know in your heart to be true about you? Be as elegant and precise as you can, using the key words you have selected as elemental parts of your statement.

This is your *Core Self*.

Get a felt sense of your Core Self now. What image or symbol would capture this essence of your most natural self? In looking for that image, we are seeking an elemental metaphor or archetype for your soul, not some social role or occupation (mother, nurse, teacher, engineer). We are seeking metaphors like the following: I am like a *bridge* between people . . . I am a *lighthouse* in the darkness . . . I am an *artist* of words . . . I am a *bringer of peace* . . . I am a shining *ruby* . . . I am a *healer* of broken hearts . . . I am a *lover* of Earth . . . I am a strong *leader* of people . . . I am a *dancer* between worlds.

When you are clear on that elemental metaphor for your soul, find a physical symbol or talisman to represent this Core Self. This is important to bring into full conscious awareness that which was previously held in the unconscious mind.

Congratulations! You have created a simple but accurate sketch of your Core Self. This is your most authentic self, the part of you we want to hear from when you are responding to the next exercise. You could do this exercise multiple times and get different responses over time, but all would be in alignment as complementary aspects or views of your Core Self.

If you had difficulty understanding or responding to one or more of the Ten Core Questions, don't worry. For many people their own heart is a complete stranger to them or has been missing so long they don't remember it. This is particularly true for people from addictive or abusive families. To help you get to know your heart in more detail, I have included a journaling exercise in appendix 1 called Thirty-Three Questions. This exercise is a longer version of Ten Core Questions above and will help you get to know your heart better by noticing the places in your life where your heart opens and closes, where it comes alive and where it closes down and backs away. *It is important to stop and do that exercise now if you need further clarification on your heart.* All of our work from this point on assumes you have reasonable clarity on your heart and Core Self, and we will be relying heavily upon your sense of that.

SEEKING A VISION

A View from Your Higher Self

Now that you have a clearer sense of your spiritual core, we want to ask *that* part of you to teach us something. Surprisingly, few of us have been encouraged to think about ourselves in this way. We don't realize that we have a spiritual consciousness or intelligence distinct from the ever-chattering (and often negative) voice in our heads. Even people of religious faith who believe in the soul may have little or no experience getting to know their own soul directly. We are more likely to be asked if we "know the Lord" than if we know our own heart! Yet the two are intimately connected.

Not being clear on one's Core Self is a spiritual problem, because if we do not know our deepest self then whatever we are calling "Lord" or "God" is likely to include a psychological projection of our unconscious desires and fears onto the Divine nature. To combat this tendency, Christianity (and all the other modern "world" religions) have a long tradition of mysticism and direct, experiential connection with the Divine, reaching back to Jesus and the disciples and found in the gnostic gospels, the desert fathers, monasticism, the writings of the Christian mystics, and centering prayer. Yet outside Roman Catholic, Anglican, and Orthodox Christianity, few Christians seem to know of this tradition and its associated spiritual practices. In Judaism, the mystical tradition is known as Merkabah and Kabbalah; in Islam, the mystical tradition is known as Sufisim. Zen Buddhism, Hindu yoga practice, and Taoism can be considered direct expressions of mystical traditions from the East.

The big question that needs to be asked of our Core Self is: What does it really want? What is it inviting me toward in my life? What is my purpose or angel mission in the community and in the world? This question is so important that indigenous societies had entire rite-of-passage ceremonies, with up to a year's preparation and support, to help individuals get clear on their vision. The Lakota *hambleycheya* or vision quest is an example in which young men went out into the wilderness alone for four days and nights of fasting and prayer, calling out for a vision for their lives. The vision they received was then brought back to their family, clan, and future partner, so that all would know the man's place among his people.

This is not the way we choose a path in modern life. Instead of starting with the heart, we start with the mind and attempt to reason our way into a career with logical questions such as: Where are the best jobs? The most secure? Which pays the most? As I write this book, the top fields that young students are being encouraged to pursue are engineering, mathematics, computer science, software development, management analysis, medical science, and technical writing. These are all fields dominated by the archetypal masculine energies of intellect, logic, science, and technology, which are so adept at parsing things (and people) into their separate, isolated component parts.

No one is encouraging our most talented young hearts and minds to become artists, musicians, spiritual healers, nature advocates, organic farmers, or stewards of animals and Earth. As Romanian writer Andrei Codrescu says, "America is a land of engineers, not poets." We are creating an entire generation of technicians, ill-equipped to show us how and why to live soulfully in the first place.

No one is asking our youth the one question I most needed in high school and college: Who are you? What does your deep heart actually like? What does it want to be doing? These questions are much more reliable in navigating a purposeful life than job trends in the ever-changing Bureau of Labor Statistics report.

So let's ask this great unasked question of your own life now, perhaps for the first time. We will do it with the following exercise.

EXERCISE

Creating a Mandala of Your Life Vision

1. Get a large piece of paper the size of a newspaper, or a flip-chart easel pad.
2. Find an array of bold-colored pencils, crayons, markers, or paint and brushes.
3. Draw a very large circle that reaches to the borders of the paper. This will be the perimeter of your mandala art. We are seeking a big vision here, not a small and shy one.

We are now going to ask a very important question of your heart, so important that we will first take a moment to refocus your attention there. The previous exercise left you in the right heart-open state to do this, so review the crux summary of your Core Self above. Then, from that heart place and deeper level of consciousness, consider the following question: What kind of life do you long to be living, really?

When you're ready, use the coloring supplies to draw or paint the life your heart really wants inside the mandala circle of your paper. Take as much time as you need—the more detail the better. The mandala will be a very important landmark on your Heart Path.

A few guidelines as you do this:

- First, you are capturing a personal vision here, not creating great art. Do not allow the negative voice of the inner judge in your head to stop you by insisting that you can't draw. Would you say that to a child who proudly brought home a drawing from school? The spirit behind the drawing is the main thing.
- Second, do not allow that negative voice in your head to insist you be realistic and cut down the scope of your vision. Imagine you will have all the time, money, and support you need, so don't get bogged down in how this would ever come about. We're not implementing your vision here or creating a family budget. We're just trying to flesh it out.
- Third, we want to hear from your authentic, natural self, not your inner good boy or good girl concerned with what others might think of your

vision. We really don't care what anyone else thinks about your personal vision. It's *your* vision, not your mother's or your partner's.

- Finally, this vision needs to be about *you* and *your* way of being in the world, not about your family or work plans. For example, "I just want my children to be happy" is not a vision for *you* (it's a vision for your children). "We will increase our gross revenue by 7 percent next year" is not a vision for you. We want *your* personal vision at the center of the mandala and no one else's. Other people can read this book and create their own mandala!

The following are photos of three mandalas I painted on newsprint some years ago immediately after my own Sacred Breathwork sessions. (The breathwork sessions are a very different kind of exercise; they're not about "the kind of life your heart wants to be living." But they illustrate the spontaneous feel of each of the visions generated. Each mandala—approximately thirty by thirty inches—was painted quickly to capture the vision I experienced in each case.)

This first painting captured a vision of myself standing high on a mountain in the ancient Inca palace ruins at Macchu Picchu in Peru. (I had recently returned from there.) In the vision, I found myself being transformed into a great bird, surrounded by attendants in their

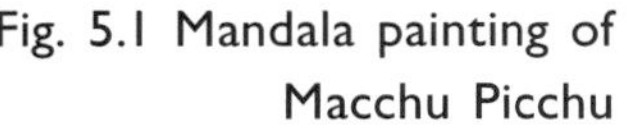
Fig. 5.1 Mandala painting of Macchu Picchu

Fig. 5.2 Mandala painting of mystery ship

traditional dress. The feeling was one of growing power in my personal life and as a healer; this feeling was aligned with the support and well-being of my family members who also appeared in the vision.

The second painting in figure 5.2 is of a beautiful mystery ship crossing a vast ocean. I was below deck in the ship's hold, surrounded by crates of supplies. When I opened them, I discovered great quantities of my favorite foods and beverages and plentiful supplies, even a case of fine scotch whiskey for special occasions! The feeling was "you have all the provisions you need to make this long journey."

The third painting (figure 5.3) had three different themes going at once: being surrounded by my key power animals and spirit guides (upper left); my oldest daughter graduating and moving away toward her new life in a big city (upper right); and my own departure station for my shamanic journeys, a simple setting by a campfire on the Great Plains (bottom).

Again, these illustrations are from my shamanic journeys, a different practice than the more literal focus intended for your mandala art here. The point is that I'm encouraging you to capture quickly whatever images and feelings come to you, without using words—which pulls your consciousness right back into the head and out of the heart.

Fig. 5.3 Mandala painting of spirit guides and departure station

CASE STUDY

Jessica Just Wants to Play Her Music

One of my fire-talk clients, Jessica, used this exercise to get clear on her life vision in the midst of a stagnant professional life. She was a student working as a therapy assistant in a facility for children with autism. The work was important; she liked children and had thought that someday she would use her artistic abilities to be an art therapist. But the work proved to be emotionally and physically hard. Some of the larger teen residents would get violent when upset and hit Jessica. The staff was unwelcoming to her, and the facility was poorly managed. She was just working a job and felt trapped because, as a student, she believed she had no other options for a professional position with the flexible hours her schedule required. Worse, she was beginning to realize that the actual life of an art therapist with that population was not what she had imagined. She was nearly finished with her degree, yet facing the wrong profession. She felt so lonely that she had developed a pattern of getting into unwise relationships with men, all of which had ended badly.

When Jessica completed her mandala exercise, she looked up and with unusual resolve said, "You know, I just want to play *music*." It turns out Jessica was a guitar player, composer, and singer who had dabbled in music over the years, but her mother had considered it too impractical for her to pursue professionally. Yet it was clear from her response to the Ten Core Questions and mandala art that what really brought her alive was writing and performing her music.

I told Jessica to honor this desire by considering a few small but real steps toward taking her music vision seriously.

The following week Jessica arrived smiling. "The strangest thing happened," she said. "A guy told me about an open microphone night at a coffeehouse, and I decided to go play there. The people were really great, they applauded and wanted to buy my music CDs." As she was selling the CDs after her performance, another musician approached her. He said he was looking for a singer for his new band and asked if she would be interested. Jessica was already on her way. All she had to do was show some real interest in the longings of her heart, and the Great Spirit that had issued the invitations to her heart in the first place was now helping her move forward by providing synchronistic opportunities. A month later Jessica quit her job at the autism facility and got a simple nanny job that paid well and allowed greater flexibility with less stress. Jessica is now playing, performing, and composing her music on a regular basis. (Her music CD is sitting here on my desk!)

She e-mailed me recently: "I noticed that when you follow your heart and your passion . . . the universe will come along and confirm what you are doing is right! I have had several people ask me to play different places, and even more musicians coming along to play with! To me, it is confirmation that if I believe in myself and believe in what I do, people will come along to join the process of growth and happiness!"

Clients who complete the Ten Core Questions and mandala-visioning activity above typically have one of three types of experience in the process:

- A good time visioning and coloring. Excellent! You now have a solid start toward a deep vision for your life that comes directly from your heart center.

- You had *some* ideas or images arise but also conflicting "logical" voice(s) in your head: "You can't take time to write a novel, what about the children?" "I can't afford to do this, we have too many bills." As a result, you are already feeling hesitant and unsure about proceeding. You may be saying to yourself, "I should probably stop this right here. This is nonsense."
- You had little or no vision whatsoever. Nada. Just a lonesome echo from an empty (or numb) place deep within you. Perhaps a scolding voice in your head responded that sounded like your mother or a pastor, "What do you mean, what do *you* want? Don't be selfish."

I have noticed that in some cases the question "What kind of life do you want?" seems to cut off all further thinking and the person enters a sort of emotional and visionary freeze and simply says, "I can't really do this." She just stops trying, like someone had suddenly pulled the plug on her brain. Sometimes this reaction is a symptom of trauma or abuse: the individual has been groomed or forced to never consider or protect his own needs and dreams, only those of others.

If you have similar thoughts here or no vision at all, don't worry. Don't allow *new* negative voices to begin their ritual flogging of this, your latest effort to be happy! For now, do the best you can—you can name *something* you would like to do—and know that I will provide tools in the chapters to come that are specially designed to break these barriers of hesitation, negativity, and blank hearts.

Recall that indigenous societies supported heart knowledge and navigation from birth onward and had powerful ceremonies like the vision quest to help the heart's vision become clear. We do not. If you had trouble with the Ten Questions or the mandala visioning exercises, there is nothing wrong with you. You just need to slow down and get more familiar with your basic core of aliveness. Take time now to turn to appendix 1 and complete the Thirty-Three Questions exercise before reading ahead. We are undertaking a deep transformative process here, not just drawing pictures in circles.

Even if you had a relatively easy time with this mandala-art exercise, stay alert. We are about to enter the dark forest of your most deeply resistant spirits and dragons. *And they know we're coming.*

In this chapter, we have completed two of the key, self-knowledge exercises needed for your journey and given you an additional resource in the appendix to hone your skill of listening to and clarifying the contours of your heart. You have been introduced to your Core Self, and from that deep place of authenticity, you have looked into your future and envisioned a more deeply satisfying life aligned to your Core Self.

In the next chapter we're going to step directly into the dim cave of your hesitations and fears and take a hard look at your personal "dragons." These are all the mental and emotional barriers that stand in the way of your living the beautiful vision you created in the mandala exercise above. We will first list these dragons—every hesitation about living out your vision. We will learn what fear-based living is and the big difference between being discerning about your life versus being paralyzed in your life. You will read a case study of a talented yet troubled young man who used the Heart Path to break free of his own fear-based living, and we will take a fresh look at Jesus as a shamanic-style healer. Finally, we will strike up a direct conversation with your fears to shift the balance of power to you and open a new doorway to change.

This next phase of the hero's journey can be one of the most difficult parts of the Heart Path because of the inner resistance that may arise. We will be exploring a part of you that does not want to be explored. Fortunately, many brave souls have gone before you, survived, and prevailed over their dragons with great success.

I did, and you will too.

Light up your torch, and let's step into the darkness of your fears together.

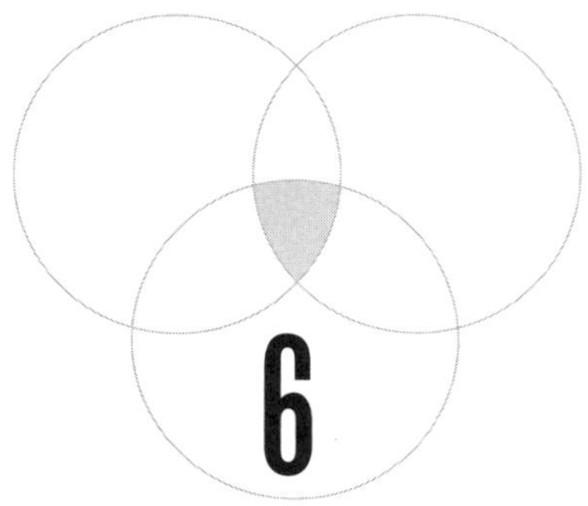

6

Facing Your Dragons

There is no coming to consciousness without pain. People will do anything, no matter how absurd, to avoid facing their own self.

C. G. Jung, *Contributions to Analytical Psychology*

FEAR AND THE SMALL SELF IN PARTNERSHIP

In the previous chapter we used your conscious mind to focus on your heart's core desires and created a positive mandala vision for your life. That was the easy part. Now we're going to descend into the dimmer regions of your unconscious psyche to see what is lurking there to keep you from moving toward your vision. As on sea journeys, it's the unseen barriers of underwater reefs and wrecks that present the most danger to ships, not the visible rocks and obstacles. But once detected, these unseen barriers can be raised to the surface and dealt with. This takes work.

I call these shadowy barriers dragons, a nod to these classic symbols of fear and psychological resistance in world mythology. Joseph

Campbell, the great scholar of comparative religions explains: "In European mythology dragons represent the binding of oneself to the ego. The dragon/ego guards the 'gold' and 'virgins' (the dragon) can't use, because he has no vitality of self, no experience of the gold or the virgins. We need to psychologically break open the cage of the dragon so we can experience a larger expression of our self. What your ego and environment wants from you is too small, it pins you down."[1]

EXERCISE

☼ Meeting Your Dragons

1. Go back and look at the mandala art you created in chapter 5. Holding the felt sense of your vision in your heart, now think of *all the reasons that you cannot or should not actually follow that vision*. Get very clear on the actual thoughts in your head, not just a vague sense that your vision won't work. For example, thoughts like, "This vision would be too expensive to follow." "It would take too long." "I'd have to go back to school." "John would be upset with me." "I might get hurt again." "The kids need me at home."
2. Now write down each of your own vision-stopping thoughts and feelings around the outside perimeter of your mandala circle on small pieces of paper. Do this quickly. We are not analyzing or problem solving here.

When you're finished you will have a whole list of words around the outside of your circle (see fig. 6.1).

Now sit back and look at what you've written as a whole. The beliefs and feelings you have written around your mandala are your personal dragons: your deep psychological demons of hesitation, self-doubt, and resistance. They are the particular beliefs you have created (or been taught) to prevent change in your life. Notice too that each belief contains some element of fear: avoiding certain behaviors, changes, people, or opportunities because there is some risk of being hurt or abandoned, or it will make you feel unsafe, vulnerable, alone, or financially at risk. For example, "I am too old." Or, "I don't have the talent."

A difficult area here involves self-defeating beliefs related to the death or absence of a loved one because these sorts of dragons appear to be caused

Fig. 6.1 Mandala painting with dragons

by someone else's situation or resistant behavior, for example: "I cannot be at peace because my beloved Mary is dead." "I cannot move for a new job until I get custody of my child." "I cannot be happy until my husband agrees to have another baby." These look like total dream stoppers because they seem to require another person to do something impossible (return from the dead, be cooperative after a divorce, want another child). But behind each self-stopping thought is a hidden wound or need that can be brought into the light and healed: the need to grieve, release, and find new love; the resentment and helplessness of a parent separated from her child; the need for an object of love and nurture. Each can be addressed in ways that do not require someone else to change or act first.

In my case I have long been burdened with a deep but dormant need for approval that does not manifest itself *until* I am about to put something I have created out into the world, like this book. Then the shaming voices of "What if people hate it?" and other dragons of that ilk come howling down upon me and I hesitate in my forward progress. It really is remarkable.

FEAR-BASED LIVING

The bottom line is this: at some point in your life you stopped responding to the positive longings *inside* the mandala vision and began to submit to the negative voices *outside* the circle. You changed from living a more open life of adventure and accepting risk to living a more closed life of caution and avoiding risk.

You are living a fear-based life.

A fear-based life does not mean you experience the emotion of fear or anxiety all the time. You may not even be consciously aware of any fear or anxiety. Rather, it means you have adopted a strategy of risk-and-loss avoidance that trumps your more spontaneous urges for new directions, relationships, creativity, and change. And you have come to believe this strategy is good, realistic, responsible, and/or living in reality, as in, "I'm not afraid to change. I'm just being realistic." This is the story you have been telling yourself for a long time. This sad story has grown into a whole belief system with tentacles that reach into every aspect of your life, sapping energy and hope. In religious terms, this negative self-sabotaging belief has become your god. You put your "faith" in it, trusting it, believing it to be true and unchangeable.

If you are not free to move toward the life your heart longs to be living, then you are not living your life. You are living someone else's idea of a proper life (that of your parent, teacher, or partner), and/or you have lost vital energy and personal power. Power loss points to soul loss.

At this point in our journey I have some good news, some bad news, and some more good news. The good news is that these dragons are not just your personal dragons, they are universal to all people. These are exactly the same challenges the heroes and heroines of world myth and religion have struggled with throughout human history. Jesus in the desert and Buddha meditating under the Bodhi tree were both faced with the same three temptations that stood in their way on the path to fulfillment: fear (of pain or dying), desire (for security, possessions, or power), and social duty (obligations to family and friends).

The bad news is these dragons can stop you in your tracks, and the most powerful ones are invisible and inside your own head (your belief system).

The good news is that the life force in you, the Great Spirit, is more powerful than the dragons and is tireless in its pursuit of your happiness. When you do face your dragons, they can even become helpful guides on your journey.

To illustrate, here is an example from my shamanic fire-talk counseling sessions of a talented man paralyzed by his unconscious-belief dragons.

CASE STUDY

Bringing Keith's Heart Back Online

Keith is a single man in his thirties, a software developer who first came to my massage therapy practice for chronic back tension. After several sessions it was clear to me that his physical symptoms were rooted in deeper issues of mind and heart because his muscle tension would return so quickly after a massage there was no way it could be caused by physical strain, injury, or posture alone.

We began meeting for shamanic counseling and exploring his heart for issues there. I soon saw the problem. Although Keith was highly intelligent, with a Mensa-level IQ, his heart was completely off-line; he could not feel or say what he wanted for his life, or even what he liked or disliked. In fact, he had mastered the art of rationalizing and neutralizing any positive feelings or desires he did have with his keen intellect, as the following exchange will illustrate:

Me: "How was your day today, Keith?"

Keith: "Well, I can't really answer that. It was neither good nor bad."

Me: "You said earlier you enjoyed working on the new software project at work?"

Keith: "Well, yes, but on the other hand I could argue that it was not real enjoyment but simply relief from the stress of the usual projects."

ME: "So when was the last time you remember being really happy, and enjoying yourself?"

KEITH: "Well, that would depend on how you define happy. One could argue that happiness is actually a relative state of mind . . ." (etc.)

Keith could literally go on like this for hours, session after session, with an emotionless tone in his voice, keeping the whole inquiry safely moored in the harbor of his mind and intellect. That's where his psyche felt safest. Only with much time and prodding did he step into the realm of the heart to feel some less manageable emotions and admit that he was unhappy at work and unhappy living with his mother and had no close friends in the area. Keith felt powerless to make any changes in his life. Though he could casually solve the most complex conceptual problems of database management at his job, he was unable to complete the simple action tasks of assembling a résumé, or calling the local university to explore a return to school. It was as if Keith were completely paralyzed in his personal life, stuck in a holding pattern of intellectual chess moves and countermoves—all leading nowhere.

When Keith and I did the dragon-listing exercise above, a whole *army* of self-stopping thoughts came to the surface. I learned that Keith had dropped out of college after his father died and he flunked a math class. This had set off a cascade of self-doubt that became deeply entrenched. "There's something wrong with my mind or I would not have flunked math in college." "If I went back to school I would probably fail again." "My mother is still grieving and needs me to stay in town." "My best friend in California is chronically ill and needs my financial support so I cannot quit my job now." "I don't have the kind of résumé I need for today's job market." Each belief related to an area of personal soul loss that Keith and I began to address in our fire talks.

Very slowly, one dragon at a time, Keith began to see how his unconscious beliefs were working against him. I told Keith these negative beliefs reminded me of a computer virus: they were faulty or malicious lines of software code that had infiltrated the operating system of his thinking. With this new perspective, Keith, a gifted software engineer, threw himself into identifying, extracting, and rewriting that code using a Toltec recapitulation exercise we will learn in the next chapter. Slowly but surely his self-sabotaging thoughts dissipated, and his vital energy returned. He completed a strong résumé and contacted a professional employment agency to find work that would be more rewarding for him. Once his résumé listing his talents actually began circulating, recruiters began contacting him almost daily including recruiters from the Bay Area where his best friend lived. Keith was facing his dragons, dragging them into the light of day, and prevailing over them—a true hero indeed.

JESUS AND OTHER SHAMANS

Shamanism teaches that healing has less to do with finding the right doctor, medication, or therapy than activating the inner healer, which releases the "medicine" of hope and power from the inside. The story of Jesus healing the chronically ill man (John 5:1–9) illustrates the shamanic approach rather well.

In the story, Jesus is in Jerusalem and comes upon a man lying near a pool of water known for its healing powers. The man has not walked for *thirty-eight years*. Jesus asks him, "Do you want to be made well?" This is a very strange question to ask a man who cannot move! A medical doctor would never ask such a question. But Jesus is not a medical man; he is a healer of souls.

The man answers, "Sir, I have no one to put me into the water . . . and while I am making my way, someone else steps down ahead of me."

Jesus doesn't respond to this complaint of powerlessness and victimization. He sees that the man's real illness is helplessness that has festered into hopelessness. Jesus disregards all the obvious contributing factors, like the man's physical condition, his lack of access to "treatment" (the pool), and his psychological depression. Jesus just says, "Stand up, take your mat, and walk."

At this, the man stands up and walks.

This is not a medical account of clinical cure from disease. It is a story by people of faith written for other people of faith, about healing helplessness with the power and authority of love. Like Jesus, shamanic practitioners see suffering and illness as spiritual issues first, the result of soul loss. Instead of beginning with a physical exam, lab tests, scans, and medications, the shamanic healer first looks for illness or paralysis in the heart.

The shaman addresses the spiritual dimension of physical illness.

This is not saying, "You don't need a medical doctor, just pray about this." Rather, the shaman focuses on conditions unseen by the medical eye. The shaman says, "There may be some deep soul issues here. Let's look into your heart and see what's there." Shamans do not believe in a spiritual or emotional "bypass," skipping over painful or fearful issues. They facilitate real open-heart surgery, supporting people as they engage with their deepest fears.

Many people are not interested in confronting their dragons and prefer the medical approach.*

In my own story of law school (in chapter 1), the physician at the Mayo Clinic brought me face to face with my own big dragon, the unconscious denial of my own feelings of failure and shame, my depression and anxiety. When I sought relief for my stomach problems, I was hoping the tests would find an ulcer or some other physical ailment I could treat with a pill to relieve my pain. But when the tests came back negative, the doctor looked me in the eye and said, "Jeff, is there anything unusual going on in your life lately?" She was right on the money,

*I'm reminded of a joke told by my chaplaincy-training supervisor years ago about surrendering control. A man is hiking the edge of a deep canyon and slips off the edge. As he is falling, his hand grasps a small branch sticking out from the canyon wall and arrests his fall. As the man hangs there above the void, he cries out, "Help! Is there anybody out there?" A voice answers him from the heavens: "Yes! I'm here!" The man asks, "Thank goodness! Who are you?" The voice answers, "It's God! I can help you!" The man says, "Great! What should I do?" God says, "The first thing is, you need to let go of the branch!" There's a long pause, then the man yells out, "Is there anybody else out there?"

so much so that my ego couldn't handle the truth that my life seemed to be collapsing in failure after leaving law school and ending up back in my hometown, in my childhood room. Sensing (unconsciously) that I had no social, spiritual, or emotional safety net to fall into, I replied by telling her that everything was fine. So the doctor had incomplete information, her final diagnosis was "not sick," and I failed to get any relief.

Carl Jung's words at the opening of this chapter could have been written for me; "There is no coming to consciousness without pain. People will do anything, no matter how absurd, to avoid facing their own self." My experience with the Mayo doctor turned out to be the low point, ground zero, in my own painful but life-changing social, vocational, and spiritual transformation in the months and years that would follow.

The following is an exercise that will enable you to identify and address your own dragons collectively, which is the necessary first step in overcoming them individually.

EXERCISE

❋ Talking to Your Dragons

For this exercise you will need to have at hand the small pieces of paper on which you wrote your respective dragons in the exercise Meeting Your Dragons earlier in the chapter.

1. **Collect about twenty small objects in a bowl.** Any natural objects will do: stones, seashells, walnuts, for example. These will act as placeholders for each of your dragons. Find a quiet place where you will not be disturbed and you can focus on the task at hand: no pets, kids, or TV. Silence all devices.
2. **If possible, sit on the ground or floor.** You should be physically close to Mother Earth, down from the high altitude of your normal mental thoughts and perspectives about things.
3. **Out in front of you, spread the pieces of paper that label all the dragons you have identified in the earlier exercise.**
4. **Select one stone or object for each dragon.** Lay it down on the

piece of paper that identifies it, while saying its name aloud: "Finances" (lay a stone down before you). "My son" (lay a stone down). "Migraines" (lay a stone down). "Too old" (lay a stone down). If you realize some of your dragons can be broken down into multiple or smaller parts, do so. For example, if one of your dragons is a more general issue like "Anxiety" you should break this down further into all its component parts such as "Anxiety about my upcoming knee surgery" and "Anxiety about paying for my knee surgery" and "Anxiety about pain from my knee surgery." (We are doing this *quickly* to prevent your intellect from getting overinvolved in the process and bogging things down with analyzing: "Well, actually, this stone might belong to my sister, because that time she betrayed me she really . . . " Keep your focus *here*.)

5. **Ask your heart if there is anything else in the way.** When you're finished laying down a stone for each dragon, ask if there are any additional barriers that need a stone. Often this step reveals another issue or two. After this, to make sure you have all the main issues accounted for, ask yourself, "If I didn't have these stones (issues) in my life anymore, if these problems were magically solved, would I then be truly happy and free to live the kind of life I want to be living?" If the answer from your heart is yes, then you are ready to move on to step 6. If not, put down another stone for whatever additional dragon has emerged that is holding you back.
6. **Address each stone one by one, from a place of detachment and compassion.** Some of these dragons are painful for you, so you don't have to be nice to them. But you do have to be as authentic and honest as possible. To assist you in this, imagine you are sitting on a park bench next to all of these dragons. Each is an old acquaintance that you will converse with by saying a few sincere words to each stone as you hold it in your hand. Here is an example: "Well, hello Guilt about My Divorce. Here you are, just as heavy and ashamed as ever. You have really weighed me down in my life and I am so sick of that! But I don't know how to get rid of you, so for now, I'm just saying hello." Set the "guilt" stone down, pick up the next stone, and repeat the process until you have addressed each stone, telling it whatever honest thing comes to you from your heart.

7. **Sit back and look at all those stones arranged before you.** Notice this: they are all resting on the ground, and you are sitting up and apart from them observing from a distance, from your *higher self*. You are like a spider looking down over her web. There may be some fearsome problems caught in your web, but notice three things:

   - These things may be stuck in your web, but it's *your web*. You are the spider.
   - These things are not *you*. Do not identify with *any* of that stuff in your web. These are just small parts of situations that exist in the greater web of your whole life.
   - As the weaver of your own web, you have choices. You are the shaman shapeshifter of your life! In this, you can do anything: You can add to the web. You can choose a few issues to address and others to ignore. You can *destroy the entire web* and create a new web somewhere else. You are the spider! You are not the problems in the web.

   You have great power. Let this sink in for a few minutes. The point is you are not a hapless figure caught in someone else's web. That's just a sad story you've been telling yourself for a very long time.

8. **Take a photo of your stone layout.** Use your smartphone's camera or some other device or camera. We will be returning to these stones later in the book and you need to preserve the layout for use at that time.

   You don't need to do anything more with these dragon stones right now. We're not making any changes or solving problems yet. It's too soon for that. For now, just remember:

   - The things stuck in your web are your dragons. But it's your web, not theirs.
   - The things stuck in your web are *not you*. They're just small parts of your whole life.
   - You are the spider shaman of your web. You are the shapeshifter of your life.

We have only begun this hero's journey of dragon slaying, but clients often report feeling a little better and less burdened at this point. This is because we are bringing you back to your place of true power and greater consciousness: your core spiderness or heart. This is where the Great Spirit itself is burning like a furnace in your life, awaiting your directions for change and transformation.

Let's summarize our progress on the Heart Path so far:

- We did a Ten Questions exercise to get clear on your Core Self, your heart.
- From that perspective we envisioned a more fulfilling life and then drew that vision in the mandala-art exercise.
- We then got clear on the barriers or dragons that keep you from following that vision.
- We addressed each one by name, opening a working relationship with each issue for the work ahead.
- We saw that these dragons are not you. They are distinct situations or beliefs stuck in the greater web of your life.

Good work for today! We have begun walking the shamanic Heart Path, a way of deep transformation. You are *moving.* Emotionally, you may still feel stuck and uncertain, but you will see that your emotions and perceptions are not always a reliable indicator of your actual situation, power, or capabilities. You are, in fact, beginning to use your power because any awareness of an unconscious fear or negative belief is itself progress. It is a spiritual intervention to break the trance of immobility. Unconscious fears and beliefs rely on darkness to remain powerful. Once you see them and their operation in your life, you've won half the battle.

You may have noticed that our shamanic path is not all about "Indians"—drumming, indigenous garb, incense, or dancing and chanting around a fire. It's about the soul and the real issues in your actual modern life. Also notice that you have now left your "home" of ordinary self-awareness and have begun to enter the dark forest of your psyche and the spirit world.

And you're fine!

In fact, you may be feeling a bit stronger as you explore the deep invitations of your heart. Enjoy the spring in your step, the reassuring heft of your pack, and the inherent wisdom of the power tools you are learning. You will get even stronger as you go, like a hiker on a month-long backpacking trip.

There are challenges ahead, but you will not be alone.

We will soon meet the helper spirits who have been with you all along. How far we go now, how successful your journey will be, is up to you. You will see that when you take a step forward toward real change in your life, the universe takes a step forward with you and provides additional new support and opportunity. But you have to take that first step, every time, not saying, as many stuck people do, "as soon as opportunity arrives, then I will make a change." You will make your changes not on blind faith but on your experience of what works; empirically, like a scientist.

We are now ready to return to the Heart Path.

In the next chapter we are going to explore the vast house of illumination, moving shadows, and mirrors that is your mind. We will first take a hard look at how your own mind—not other people or situations—creates most of your suffering. We will explore how this works: how negative emotional patterns can hijack your thinking, and how the mind can resist the very information it needs for healing and happiness. Then we will look at several of the powerful shamanic tools for taming the unruly mind that come from the ancient Toltec tradition, including the Four Agreements, Smoky Mirror, and Recapitulation work.

Heads up, and stay alert. This is no game. We will need your full attention to navigate this next portion of the journey.

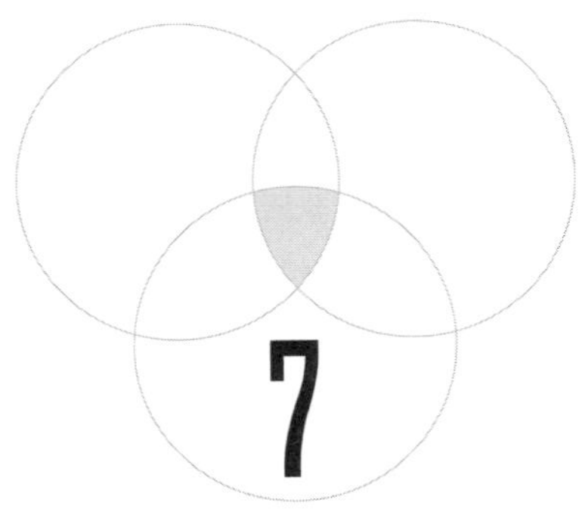

7

A Hard Look at Your Own Mind

Whatever an enemy might do to an enemy, the ill-directed mind can do to you even worse.
Whatever a mother, father or kinsman might do for you, the well-directed mind can do for you even better.

Gautama Buddha, *Cittavagga: The Mind*

THE ART AND SKILL OF MIND MANAGEMENT

In this chapter we're going to take a hard, unblinking look at the way our minds create our own suffering. This is a key learning on the Heart Path because when you begin to see what is really going on in your head most of the time you will gain the motivation and energy needed to change it. Shamanism provides time-tested tools for actively seeking out, stalking, and extracting the toxic thought systems of hesitation and fear that keep us weak and hold us back in life.

You will learn many of these in this and the following chapters.

I call this aspect of the journey mind management. This is the psychological part of our Heart Path, a unique set of insights and tools you will not find in other books on shamanism. Combined with more traditional shamanic practices, this teaching will provide you a much more effective approach to lasting happiness in the real world.

The human mind is brilliant at planning, adapting, and implementing change. But its inner workings, thoughts, and emotions go largely unseen and unsupervised and can get unruly at times. This is particularly true regarding our beliefs about ourselves, others, and the world around us. We create much of our unhappiness right between our ears, with negative thoughts triggered by old emotional patterns that are replayed over and over. This chapter and its exercises are about seeing, facing, and taming these more unruly and heart-suppressing aspects of your mind* and allowing the Heart its full voice in your life.

We are not seeking to suppress thinking or become illogical or irrational here. Rather we are seeking to enhance our intelligence with more careful and *mindful* thinking and a better balance between your mind and heart. Indeed, we will need the full power of your well-trained mind later in our journey, when we are implementing the steps for making your heart's vision a reality in the day-to-day world.

Beware: the *last* thing that our self-made ego personality wants to acknowledge are the ways we create our own unhappiness. So as you read on, be alert for signs that your own mind is resisting further movement. That resistance can manifest as boredom, restlessness, annoyance ("This is stupid. I'm not reading any more of this"), sleepiness, cravings ("Let's explore the refrigerator"), deep sadness, sexual desire—you name it. The psyche may employ all of these are strategies

*In this chapter I use several synonyms and related terms for *mind* to capture the breadth, depth, and full color of this complex and invisible part of our selves. The words *mind, ego, intelligence, personality,* and *psyche* are not identical in a dictionary or psychological sense, but they overlap. For our purposes here *personality* refers to the broadest and most inclusive view of the self and includes our mind, thoughts, behaviors, and beliefs. Thus *mind* is a subset of *personality*.

to distract itself from the necessary work you are closing in on here.

So stay alert, keep reading, and do the exercises. This is a hero's journey, not a walk in the park. We are standing at the very threshold of inner change and psychological individuation in your life. If you really want to change your life, you will need to change your life—only you can initiate the necessary changes and that begins with getting a leash on your unruly mind.

Here we go!

CASE STUDY

Nancy's Struggle to Trust Her Heart

Nancy is a nurse in her fifties who came in for a fire-talk counseling session with me. She was feeling stagnant in her personal life, unsatisfied with a husband who paid no attention to her, and she was seeking new direction in her life. She had tried marriage counseling and recently had a brief, exciting affair with a man who had gone back to his wife. Nancy was devastated: she thought the new man was going to be her ticket out of an unhappy marriage.

Unlike my client Keith in the prior chapter, Nancy did have a sense of what she wanted ("more fun in my life, dancing, companionship, a soul mate"), and she had a full range of emotion available to her. But when I encouraged her to honor the longings of her heart, she stiffened and looked at me and said, "'The heart of man is deceitful among all things and desperately wicked, who can trust it?' Jeremiah 17:9."*

It was as if an evangelist had suddenly taken over Nancy's body. Then the light drained from her eyes, and she slumped in a deflated posture of defeat and shame. Nancy said, "The one time I followed my

*Nancy was quoting the King James Version of the Bible, which translates the two key Hebrew words *achov as* "deceitful" and *anush* as "desperately wicked." But these words have different meanings based on context, history, and translation. The Hebrew could more carefully be translated as, "The heart is complex and fragile, who can know it?" The very next verse in Jeremiah reads, "I, the Lord, search the heart, examining the affections to give to each one according to his ways according to the fruit of his practices." If our hearts are so wicked, why would God bother searching them?

heart, I had this affair, ended up getting hurt, and now I'm back with my husband feeling as miserable as ever. That's my punishment."

Nancy had confused her emotional needs and physical desires for the deep and sacred center we are calling the heart. And now she was rejecting *all* of her instincts, heart tones, and personal aspirations as being shameful and unreliable. I learned that Nancy had been raised in an authoritarian church where the pastor was God and individuals were discouraged from personal soul seeking, meditation, or contemplative forms of prayer. (The compassionate heart-centered teachings of Jesus seemed missing from her religious education.) But most significant was the fact that Nancy had been sexually abused by her own father. This meant that from an early age she had been groomed to *not* feel or trust the most instinctual good and bad feelings of her own body, mind, and heart.

The heart of which we have been speaking in this book is not concerned with who you are dating, married to, or divorced from. It is not concerned with romantic love or the poetic meaning of "heart." It is concerned with your sacred center and the great force of life yearning to come more fully alive in the world through you as a power-filled shaman of your life.

How do you know when you are being called to the spiritual adventure of the hero's journey and not experiencing a passing mood or creating an excuse for avoiding responsibility? Bill Plotkin (paraphrasing Joseph Campbell) notes five qualities and two practical tests for discerning an authentic call from Spirit:

1. An authentic call will feel like the opposite of an escape. It will feel more like facing something difficult, unknown, or frightening that summons you, like stepping out into a night storm.
2. The call is oddly familiar, though unexpected, like déjà vu but even more disorienting and inexplicable.
3. You have a strong sense that the chapter of life you have been living is suddenly over, whether you wanted it to end or not. What had been meaningful to you becomes strangely emptied of value.

4. The call is almost always unexpected and unwanted, as if life has grabbed you by the collar and is tugging you forward, volunteering you for a task you were not seeking.
5. As an encounter with Great Mystery, the call is typically accompanied by powerful emotions and a numinous sense of the sacred and holy.
6. Test the call by not acting on it, ignoring it, and laughing it off. See how that works. If you are ignoring something real, alive, and growing in you that is sacred, you will know it (as it would be akin to trying to ignore a pregnancy).
7. Test the call by beginning to act on it, moving your life toward it. See if the feeling of rightness grows stronger, over the background noise of fear. The fear may also grow, but the two will be different. Moving toward the call will feel right like you are growing nearer to your true home; the fear will be like that of a child feeling lost or too far from home.

With this clarification and much support, Nancy began walking a courageous healing path in our sessions, learning the difference between the voice of her authentic heart and the abusive voices of doubt and shame that had been programmed into her head as a child. With this grounding in love-based reality, Nancy looked at all her options, chose to return to her husband as an interim move, and began her heroine's journey of getting to know and honor her beautiful soul for the first time. This was no easy road for her. It meant making a descent to discover her deep feminine goddess self, to become intimate with *her* body, creativity, values, and power for the first time.

HIDDEN FROM VIEW

The Unconscious Personality

We humans are so proud of our intellect and reason, our scientific method and our vast technology. We see ourselves as logical, dispassionate thinkers in full mastery of our thoughts and actions. But if you have ever attempted to meditate, you know that your mind is completely out of control much of the time. Thoughts quickly arise out of nowhere and careen around in our heads like billiard balls on a hard break, bouncing off each other and the billiard table bumpers. Underneath these thoughts are powerful but unconscious emotional patterns, unseen yet fully active in your psyche like strong tides or undercurrents flowing under a placid ocean surface. Occasionally you get a glimpse of these unseen thoughts or belief systems, like when you have a strong emotional response to someone you've just met and know nothing about: "She's insufferable." "He's a total jerk." "Lazy teenagers."

It's difficult to see what's really going on in our head and heart most of the time. The great insight of modern psychology is that we have an active yet *unconscious* part of our personality running quietly behind our awareness, like the operating system of a computer. It's comprised of our past experiences, social programming, anxieties, and ego defenses. C. G. Jung, the great psychoanalyst, believed this unconscious part of our personality actually comprises the bulk of the human psyche: our conscious thinking self is only a small part, similar to the visible portion of an iceberg, while the huge mass of it, the unconscious, is below the surface, invisible.

Fig. 7.1 Iceberg view of the human personality

Thus in Jung's view the human personality consisted of two main parts: the smaller part we are aware of called the conscious personality (above the water and visible) and the larger part we are unaware of called the unconscious or subconscious personality (below the water and invisible). We can become aware of our conscious personality and the related "voice in our head" of inner thoughts, commentary, opinions, and judgments. This voice in our head likes to believe it is running the show, like a small child riding a very big horse. But it's the unconscious part of our personality that is influencing our conscious thoughts and behaviors much of the time. If that horse gets startled or threatened, the child will be carried in directions not of its choosing!

Further complicating the accuracy of our perceptions, our mind will actively filter out (or project onto others) any information about our self that conflicts with our self-made image, our ego persona. These filtered-out or shunned aspects of our personality are what Jung called the shadow self and are so unappealing to the ego that we *project* them onto others.

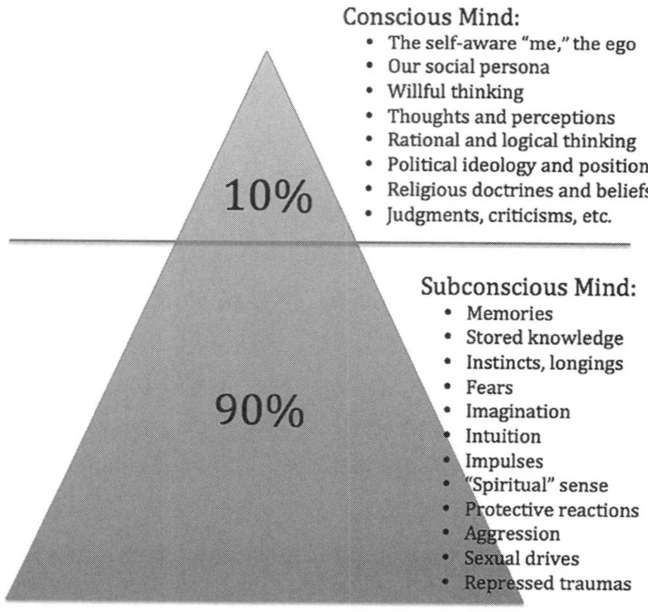

Fig. 7.2. The conscious and subconscious mind

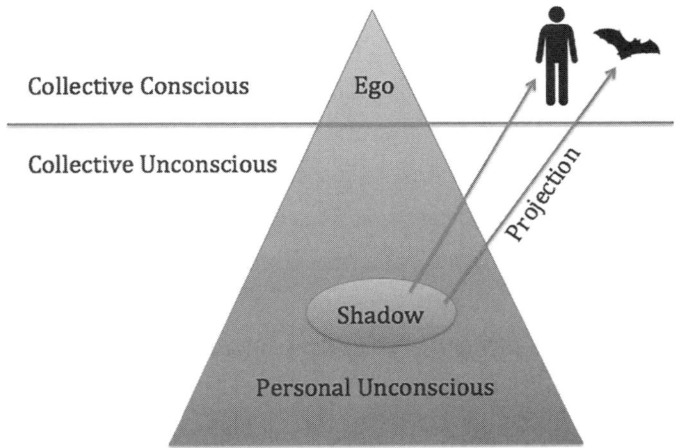

Fig. 7.3 Projecting the shadow personality onto other people and creatures

For example, I dislike people who act like they are special in dress, manner, or self-expression. *They are so stuck-up,* I think. But guess who actually believes he is special in dress, manner, and self-expression? Me!

We can also project our negative shadow onto nature: seeing evil or danger in dark caves, spooky forests, swamps, snakes, bats, and spiders. We are surely projecting our shadow when we see an aspect of the created world as evil.

The diagram in figure 7.3 illustrates how we can project our shunned shadow aspects onto other people and creatures.

HELP OTHERS, HURT YOURSELF

The Brawl in Our Heads

From the moment we awake in the morning our mind is on full alert, scanning for tasks to do and social duties to live up to. We hit the ground running with urgent thoughts ringing with importance. "I have to call Susan . . . Amy needs her lunch and gym shoes . . . Dave needs the contract by 9:00 a.m. . . . The house is a mess . . . I need to go shopping . . . The cat needs her medicine . . . I need a gift for Shawn's wedding."

This commotion of a thousand things keeps us weak and running in short-sighted living. Trying to help us sort through these demands is a whole committee of voices in our heads that range from the reasonable and strong to the completely infantile and helpless.

Our thoughts are like mosquitoes buzzing around in our heads, and the effect is what the *naguals* of Toltec shamanism call the *mitote,* meaning "the smoky mirror." In the Toltec creation myth, when the gods created humans out of white corn (flesh) and red corn (blood), the final product was so successful that the humans had knowledge, intelligence, and wisdom that nearly rivaled that of the gods. In order to keep humans in their proper place, the gods decided to obscure the humans' vision so they would not be able to see beyond what was in front of them. They created the mitote, a fog of smoke that blinded them and prevented them from seeing beyond it. The Smoky Mirror exercise in this chapter is a reference to this Toltec myth.

If we are reacting to the mitote all day, we never get to the really vital matters of living. *When I get these chores done then I'll go for a relaxing walk,* you tell yourself. But the chores are never finished, and you never go for the walk. Or you are too tired to go for the walk. Or you go for the walk, but spend the whole time thinking about the chores you need to do when you get home. You miss the purple coneflowers you are passing by, the joyful children down the block, or the serene river flowing past the park. Sadly, we can fill our day with good works for others yet walk Earth as an empty soul ourselves, betraying our angel mission on Earth. At the end of the day, you've lost the game.

Final score? Chores and Good Works: 179. Self-Care and Personal Growth: 0.

You may be thinking, *But isn't caring for others good for the heart?* Sure, but there's a balance. Even a dog knows when to rest, eat, and play. Shamanic work is about responsibility to your *soul,* not just to your family, work, or church. I know a devout Polish Catholic man who divorced his wife because she was having an affair—not with another man but with her church. "She spends all her time at the parish, helping in the office, with the school, with funerals and fundraisers. She is never home," he lamented. "She misses our daughter's games and doesn't want to go on family vacations because she says they need her at the church." There's a big difference between serving the Lord and serving an unhealthy ego that needs to be needed.

In shamanic work, the way you follow the Heart Path is not by getting all the chores done first. The way to leave the house is to *leave the house,* unfinished chores and all. When you do this, you learn a shocking thing: the house does not collapse into filth and chaos without you. Your family members and friends do not die without you. You feel a little stronger on the inside, more free. Some of the chores become less urgent, and a few even disappear from your concerns. Their importance was an illusion of anxious thinking and social expectations . . . like a dream.

The Heart Path asks you to consider an important question: What part of your living is a dream, and what part of it is real? The Toltec shamans said *all* of our living is a dream, until we wake up to the true invitations and power of our heart.

THE MIND'S RELIABILITY PROBLEM

Although we trust the reliability of our thoughts and assume we are rational people, it turns out that our thoughts can be one of the least reliable sources of information. Our thinking patterns are designed to shore up our fragile sense of self and defend against any threats to that cohesiveness. Our self-image may be positive ("I am a good mother") or negative ("I can't do anything right"), but either way, the mind is a formidable gatekeeper, like a security guard frisking anything that would enter the door of awareness and pose a threat to that self-image. It will modify or outright deny entrance to information that does not fit our self-image. This is where things can get really crazy: if we have a negative self-image ("I can't do anything right"), we will defend *that* and sustain it by minimizing our positive accomplishments or compliments from others.

This problem is compounded by the individualism of our society:

our mind assumes every situation is personal; it's all about me. If someone behind you honks his horn, you assume he is honking at you, and you become angry. But the driver may have been honking at a friend or accidentally bumped his horn. Much of what we perceive can be highly flawed interpretations of what is actually going on.

Recently I did a workshop for the Michiana Gerontology Institute. After my talk I found two of the participants' written evaluations had been left behind on their chairs. On the 1–5 rating scale for my presentation, one evaluator had marked all 5s, indicating "excellent." The other had written in a large scrawl across the entire page "waste of time."

I had to smile. This was a very good lesson in not taking the opinion of others, positive or negative, too seriously.

We think our beliefs are formed logically from our unbiased perceptions. But our perceptions are highly influenced by our beliefs. If you believe all white people are racist, or all black people are lazy, or all Hispanic people leave junk in their yards, you will be quick to see supporting evidence for your bigotry but slow to acknowledge evidence to the contrary. If you believe your boss is a fool, you will notice his foolish behaviors and dismiss his wise or effective ones.

This helps sustain your belief of "I am unhappy because my boss is a fool" and prevents awareness that, say, you have a completely stagnant life and won't go back to school because you are afraid of failure. Your perception of your actual boss—a man with talent and a daughter in the hospital—is an incomplete fiction.

When we take a hard look at our own minds and observe our individual thoughts and the negative belief systems they constellate into, we begin to see the hell we have been creating for ourselves and for others. This painful awareness is the beginning of our liberation.

TOLTEC MIND-MANAGEMENT TOOLS

In 2003 a Mexican surgeon named Miguel Ángel Ruiz (Don Miguel Ruiz) published *The Four Agreements: A Practical Guide to Personal*

Freedom. A synthesis of ancient Toltec wisdom, the book has sold seven million copies in the United States alone.[1]

Ruiz was raised in rural Mexico by a *curandera* (healer) grandmother and a *nagual* (shaman) grandfather of the Toltec tradition. The Toltec were "men and women of knowledge," a society of pre-Aztec scientists and artists centered at the ancient pyramid city of Teotihuacan near Mexico City. Of the many shamanic traditions, Toltec wisdom is particularly effective at healing the mind-based sources of our suffering; the Four Agreements are four simple but powerful rules for doing this. Mind-based sources of suffering differ from more heart-based ones, which concern lack of vision, lack of energy, lack of supportive relationships, and/or lack of the inner power necessary to move forward.

The basic premise of Toltec shamanism is that humans live in a dream of distorted perceptions that obscures our true angel nature and that of others. As children we were domesticated through punishments, rewards, and the opinions of others to believe we were "good" or "bad," "artistic" or "not artistic," "intelligent" or "not intelligent," and so on. These opinions were internalized and became like tyrants in our head, endlessly judging everything we think, feel, and do according to these inner beliefs or agreements. This creates unnecessary suffering, anxiety, sadness, self-doubt, and jealousy that have nothing to do with who we really are: beautiful angels of goodness, power, and divine light. Ruiz calls this whole faulty system of perception "the Dream of the Planet; a true dream of Hell."

The art of the Toltec is learning to wake up from this distorted, secondhand dream of hell that we are living. With great intention, we see the negative belief agreements we have been judging ourselves with and create a new dream of heaven for our life that brings us joy rather than unhappiness, heaven rather than hell. We do this by going through our inner agreements one by one and choosing what we want to keep, change, or delete from our belief systems.

Here is my own summary of the wisdom contained in *The Four*

Agreements; they are four powerful tools that should be in any journeying hero's backpack.

The First Agreement: Be Impeccable with Your Word

Every word we speak or hear is like a seed of love or hate, and our minds are fertile ground for these seeds. When we speak against ourselves or plant seeds of fear in others, we spread our personal poison everywhere. To break the spell of negativity, we have to make a new agreement based on truth and practice it each day: "I am impeccable with my word." Impeccable means always using the power of words in the direction of truth and love.

The Second Agreement: Don't Take Anything Personally

Everything that others do is a projection of their own reality, their own dream. When someone says you are hurting them, it is not you: they are hurting themselves with thoughts that arise from old wounding patterns. The countermeasure is a new agreement: "I will not take anything personally." There is no need to believe what other people say, good or bad. You can live with your heart completely open because no one can hurt you. You can say, "I love you" without fear of rejection or ridicule. You can say yes or no without guilt or self-judgment.

The Third Agreement: Don't Make Assumptions

We assume everyone sees life the way we do, feeling and judging as we do. So we assume others know what we think and want and will react like we would to criticism or threat. But we all see life through a fog of chaos in the human mind, which causes us to misinterpret things. Our assumptions make us feel safe, whether or not they are true. So we have an agreement, "It is not safe to ask questions." The countermeasure is to ask questions until you are clear on what the situation is really about. You have the right to ask for what you want, and others have the right to say yes or no.

The Fourth Agreement: Always Do Your Best

We believe we need to be perfect in order to be loved and approved (i.e., to be safe), but trying to be perfect at all things all the time is impossible. This causes unnecessary guilt, self-abuse, worry, and regret. The countermeasure to needing to be perfect and approved by others is to simply do your best, all the time. If you do your best, then you cannot judge yourself with guilt or blame. Your "best" will change from moment to moment, when you are sick or injured, tired or grieving.

USING THE FOUR AGREEMENTS

The way to use the Four Agreements to deactivate your dragons is to practice them every day. Over and over, watch your words for integrity. What kinds of seeds are you putting in your mind and in the minds of others? Over and over, catch yourself taking things personally and remember the situation is not all about you or intended to hurt you. Start asking for clarification before you make an assumption about another's comment or behavior, and ask for what you want and need. Drop the useless attempts to be perfect and just start doing your best, depriving your inner judge of anything to judge you on. And then you can begin to sit back and smile, having learned to be skeptical of the stream of voices in your head and all around you.

In my own life, the Second Agreement, "Don't take anything personally," helped me immediately. Where I used to feel stung by a comment from someone else and about to react or shut down in my old silent treatment, I now say, "Hey, wait a minute. This actually isn't about me. It's about *her*. It's just her dream, her beliefs about her life, about me, and the whole world. Ohhh." That simple pause and shift in my usual perception-reaction cycle is often enough to stop the normal cascade of emotion and drama. Then I can listen with love, and without defensiveness, and decide if there is anything I want to do to help this unhappy person in her pain. In 2011 Ruiz published a sequel, *The Fifth Agreement,*[2] which is "Be skeptical, but listen." This means to be skeptical about all the problems, the drama, and the negative emotions that are offered to us in this life and ask, is it really the truth?

EXERCISE

The Smoky Mirror

It's difficult to have clear perception and thinking with an inner judge leaping around in your mind. It's like being in a smoke-filled room trying to see yourself clearly in a mirror. Toltecs call this the smoky mirror problem. Our judgments are like a thick smoke or fog obscuring the truth of who we really are: mirrors of the sacred. This exercise helps clear out the smoke of our inner judge.

1. Make a list of every person that is annoying to you: family members, friends, coworkers, neighbors, people in the news.
2. For each person, write down exactly what this person does that is so annoying. Notice your judge at work on each person as you do this.
3. Notice any patterns you see in the type of behaviors you're listing.
4. For each behavior pattern noted above, now write down instances where you have seen this same behavior in yourself.

Continue to notice throughout each day how you judge others and yourself and how often you do this. ("There she goes again, meddling in other people's business!") This exercise will help you get behind the self-inflicted behavior of creating unnecessary judgments and clear up your view of what is really out there and what is happening to you.

EXERCISE

Recapitulation

Recapitulation is a classic Toltec practice of recollecting one's life down to the most insignificant detail in order to see the wounding events of one's past, and then changing the emotional damage that resulted. The term *recapitulation* was first used by Carlos Castaneda in his book *The Eagle's Gift.*[3]

To do this, you identify and then review your old agreements one by one, "disagree" with the negative ones, and rework each agreement into a positive new belief system. For the Toltecs, this could involve an extended two-year process of deep self-review. It's a real warrior-shaman practice of marching directly into shadow territory, like a Navy SEAL team going into hostile territory and locating and extracting an enemy leader. As with all shamanic practices, we approach this work from our strong side as an agent of the Great Spirit, not from our anxious, wounded, or victimized side. Here's the process.

Step 1: Identify the Old Agreements

1. Draw a time line of your entire life from birth to present in five-year increments.
2. On the time line, note all the key places you lived and spent time: houses, schools, church, where you hung out with friends.
3. Now note the names of the key people you knew during those five-year intervals: your main friends, enemies, lovers, neighbors, coworkers, church relations, and classmates.
4. Looking at the time line, pick one person or experience that hurt you. You can start anywhere.
5. Write down exactly what she or he said or did, or what happened that caused so much harm.
6. Write down your emotional response to this.
7. Identify your specific belief or agreement that resulted from this in one sentence. For example: "I'm not good enough." "I'll never please my father." "Men cannot be trusted." "David is a jerk." State your agreement aloud. Then write this down on an index card; one card for each agreement you identify. Use as many cards as you need.

Step 2: Disagree with Your Old Agreements

1. Now shift perspective. Get into that other person's heart and mind. State that person's point of view aloud and write it down.
2. See how the person's behavior to you was from his point of view or from his own sense of being wounded, or from his fears, and as such, how it had *nothing to do with you.*
3. Make a decision to forgive the person for this incident. As you know, this

does not mean forgetting the harm, feeling emotionally happy or good about the other person, or saying that she "deserves" to be forgiven. Instead, this is all about you, to release you from years of bondage to old pain and judgment. You are making a clear-headed decision to *walk away from that old story of you,* the story where you are a helpless victim. You are going to create a new story where you are a hero.

4. You are now going to *disagree with your old agreement* and send that old agreement back to its source. To do this, take the agreement you wrote on the index card and attach that old agreement card onto some talisman, like a stick or a piece of wood. You can decorate that talisman as you wish, to fully embody the pain and hurt of that old situation. Be creative and add as much detail and effort as you wish. Then create an outdoor sacred fire (in a fire pit, or your outside grill), call in your spirit helpers and ancestors, and *burn the talisman in your fire.* Stay and watch the entire card and stick be consumed and turned into ashes. This may take a while, but the waiting and watching is part of the deep transformation. You are not in a hurry.
5. When the talisman has completely burned to ashes, carefully remove the ashes of your agreement talisman and bury them in a deep hole in Mother Earth. Say a prayer of thanks to Mother Earth for taking back this pain, and offer up some tobacco, sage, or a small gift.

Step 3. Create New Agreements as an Artist of the Soul

1. Compose a new agreement for each of the old ones, one that transforms each of the old beliefs into new, positive sources of power and truth (see examples below). These are not generic self-affirmations ("I am good and I love myself") but tailor-made positive agreements for your life.
2. Write each new agreement on a separate index card. Here are some examples:

Old Agreement	New Agreement
I cannot trust Bob and must avoid him.	I am a power-filled person. I can go wherever I want, when I want.
I should not speak my mind; it will make other people mad.	I speak my truth with confidence and clarity whenever it serves me.

3. Practice your new agreement cards each day. You are creating a new mind-set. This is not simplistic "positive thinking," an ineffective form of wishing where you attempt to bypass your shadow or layer happy thoughts over dark and fearsome beliefs. That doesn't work. Rather, we are fully facing the darkness and engaging with that, while also visioning the light and moving toward that.

When I first worked through this recapitulation exercise in the fall of 2009, I ended up with an inch-thick stack of index cards, each one representing an old agreement I wanted to change. On one side I had written the old agreement, and on the flip side I had written the new agreement. I tested myself by first reading each old agreement and seeing if I could generate the new agreement from memory.

In this way I quickly learned which cards needed more study and focused on those. Every morning throughout that winter, I stood in my backyard, did my Four Directions prayer with sage and chanting, and practiced the recapitulation cards. I faced west when releasing the old agreements, and east when welcoming the new ones. It worked. One agreement at a time, I literally *changed my mind*. Now I instantly see when an old agreement is trying to creep back into the house of my thinking, and I am able to stop, challenge the old agreement at the door, and quickly turn my thoughts around.

So the bad news is: most of our suffering is self-created. But the good news is: the opportunity for happiness is also self-created. Shamanism provides powerful practices to observe and stop the illusory dream of the self-made ego and wake up the authentic power of the heart. The Trappist monk Thomas Merton spoke bluntly of this need to end the influence of the false self so that the real soul can shine: "Be careful when you pray to the Holy Spirit for help. Because what the Holy Spirit teaches us is how to die. It's the only show in town."*

---

*This quote paraphrases James Finley, wherein Finley was sharing a conversation he had with his mentor Thomas Merton while both were monks at Gethsemani Abbey, Kentucky.

⊙ ⊙ ⊙

In this chapter, we have looked into the cave of our dragons and instead of actual dragons, discovered dragon-shaped movie screens playing back to us the flickering home movies of past traumas and negative agreements given to us by others. Though we still see and feel them intensely, most of the dragons are not real anymore. We just keep dutifully replaying the fearsome movies. With the tools of ancient artists of the soul like the Toltecs, we are now learning the tools to pull the plug on the old movie projectors, break the dream state given us by others, and teach our ego-illusions "how to die" by practicing the Four Agreements: by being impeccable with our word, observing our words, and asking whether we are planting seeds of fear or of love in our minds and the minds of others; by no longer taking anything personally, remembering that difficult people and situations are not about you or intended to hurt you; by no longer making assumptions, asking instead for clarification when you encounter a confusing or harsh behavior, and asking for what you want; by no longer striving to be perfect but instead just doing your best, which deprives your inner judge and others of anything to judge you on; and finally (the Fifth Agreement), by being skeptical of everything: the stream of voices in your own head, the drama all around you, the negative emotions and threats of frightened people, the contents of this book, the stories in the news—*everything* you perceive around you.

Listen for the unmistakable truth of love and the unmistakable lies of fear. Follow the love and create more love on Earth as a shapeshifter who can create his or her own dream, a dream of heaven rather than the dream of hell that is always "playing now at a theater near you."

With the next chapter we move into the third major section of this book, shapeshifting. Chapters 8–10 will shift our emphasis from just understanding what's been holding you back (the descent phase of the hero's journey) to helping you take action to change and move forward in your life. Within this major section, we will devote one chapter to each of the three broad strategies for acquiring shamanic power: mindfulness of the body and Earth (chapter 8), transforming fear in the mind (chapter 9), and releasing the full spiritual abilities of the heart (chapter 10).

In the next chapter we will define mindfulness, see the power of mindful living, and also see how modern life pulls us away from that power. We will then learn several simple but effective practices for restoring mindful living using your physical body and the world of nature around you as reliable anchors in the present moment. And we will begin all this with a story about a single volcano out in the Pacific Ocean.

Are you ready to visit the Hawaiian Islands? Read on.

PART III

◎ ◎ ◎

Shapeshifting

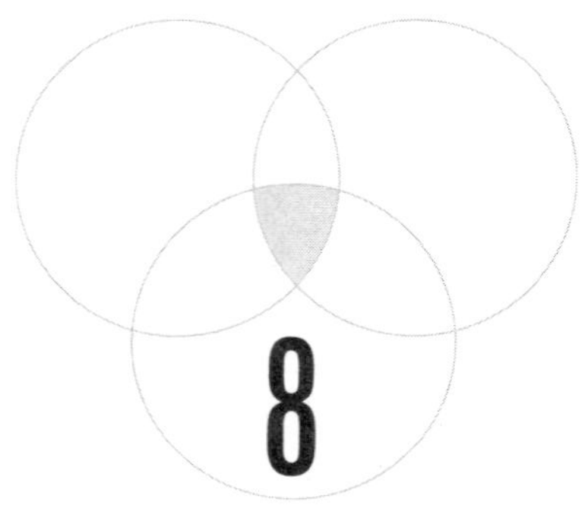

8

Power from the Body and Earth

Many people live habitually as if the present moment were an obstacle that they need to overcome in order to get to the next moment. Imagine living your whole life like that.

Eckhart Tolle, ABC News interview

A LESSON ON POWER

The Hawaiian Islands

For years I thought the eight main Hawaiian Islands had each been formed by separate volcanoes. But during a trip to Oahu a friend set me straight: There is only one volcanic hot spot on the ocean floor erupting lava. The hot spot is located in the middle of the Pacific Plate, a vast slab of slow-moving rock that is part of the outermost shell of the planet.

During periods when the plate remains stationary over the active hot spot, the continual flow of lava emerges in one place. The lava solidifies and builds up an underwater volcanic mountain. Eventually the rising peak of the live volcano breaks the ocean surface to become an island. But as the tectonic plate slides over time to the northwest, it pulls the entire mountain island off the hot spot—like a frying pan being pulled off a burner—and its active volcano goes dead. A new volcano then begins to form on the ocean floor.

Eons pass and a new mountain rises, emerges from the sea, and becomes another island: Oahu. The whole plate shifts again, and Molokai is born. Right now, the youngest and easternmost Big Island of Hawaii is being pulled off the hot spot, and next to it, deep on the ocean floor, a new volcano is already forming, which will someday emerge from the sea as the next Hawaiian island.

This geologic story is a perfect metaphor for how shamanic power is gained and lost. As long as your attention is aligned over the "hot spot" of the present moment, you have maximum power available for action and change in your life, like the frying pan simmering directly over a stove burner, ready to cook. But if your attention is pulled off the hot spot of the present moment into past regrets, current distractions, or future worries, you lose your power. You cool down, lose vitality, and become as stagnant as a dead volcano.

Fortunately, we are not volcanic islands. We can pull our attention and our living back onto the burner of the present moment with the mindfulness practices that I am about to introduce to you. The most powerful of these are those that use your physical body and the "body" of the living Earth as anchors. But first let's define mindfulness, explain why this book on shamanism focuses on mindfulness practices, and take a closer look at why nature and the human body are so helpful in achieving a mindful state.

MINDFULNESS

The Third Strategy on the Path to Shamanic Power

The heart-opening and mind-management practices we have studied so far are essential, but both need to be grounded in the present moment to result in any meaningful action. That's what this chapter is about: focusing both your heart and your mind *here,* in the now, at the same time. Mindfulness is the third main requirement for walking the Heart Path.

Mindfulness is an umbrella term for any practice that helps actively focus one's mental attention on the present moment. Sitting meditation, yoga, centering prayer, labyrinth walking, and tai chi are some examples of mindfulness practices.

Mindfulness was not taught in traditional cultures because it didn't have to be. Our ancestors were plenty "mindful" just trying to stay alive in the wild. Yet shamans still used preparatory rituals for focusing attention before commencing healing work. These included the drumming, rattling, chanting, ecstatic dancing, smudging with burning herbs, and/or calling in the ancestors and the helper spirits.

Let's begin with an easy mindfulness exercise now. We will journey up to Earth's atmosphere for a satellite's-eye view of the dynamic aliveness of our planet's weather systems.

EXERCISE

☼ Observing NOAA Weather Systems

On the website of the National Oceanic and Atmospheric Administration (NOAA), you will find a time-lapse video loop of weather systems for both your own region and the full forty-eight contiguous United States.[1]

Spend some time gazing at the shifting images of current weather systems as they move across the North American continent. Then imagine that you *become* those shifting systems and merge with their ever-moving, swirling flow. Become the wind itself, the literal breath of the planet, and ponder a few of your human concerns from this higher perspective. What is "yesterday" for the wind? What is "tomorrow" for a weather system?

I'm Busy: Why Bother with Mindfulness?

Mindfulness practices seem a waste of time to a lot of people. Why not just get down to business and commence the shamanic healing work itself, like a Western doctor marching into the patient's exam room, asking questions, and then prescribing a medication?* Why *is* mindfulness so important, and why is it so difficult for us to make it a priority?

Mindfulness is important because it is essential; a lack of it often manifests as our being unsuccessful in life. I've seen many people in health care, ministry, counseling, and athletic or fitness settings all fail to reach their goals because of the inability to stay focused in daily life. Some of my own clients leave their therapeutic sessions with a clear self-care plan for changing their lives, but they never take action. They are intelligent, well-intentioned, and good people. But they cannot get anything important done because they lack the mindfulness to stay on course and thereby attain the personal goals they have set. They are busy, hardworking—and completely ineffective at life change.

One reason that it's difficult for us to focus on mindfulness is because we have nearly eliminated the practice of it from our daily lives. Former Apple and Microsoft executive Linda Stone describes the current epidemic of continuous partial attention (CPA), a state in which one's attention is on a primary task but also monitoring several background tasks just in case something more important or interesting comes up. Our open-plan office designs, classrooms that cluster students in face-to-face pods, and the bleating TV screens that hang in every restaurant and doctor's waiting room and on every airline seat also discourage mindfulness. Even in my quiet massage office, sessions would get interrupted by incoming text notifications on clients' phones. Our distractedness is so habitual that a 2014 University of Virginia study found a majority of people (primarily men) would rather administer a painful electric shock to themselves than be alone in silence for more than a few minutes![2]

Our attention to nature is so broken that we are harming ourselves,

*It is worth noting that modern medicine is least effective at treating illnesses with spiritual and emotional components: depression, loss of purpose, anxiety, soul loss, stress, grief, relationship dysfunction, chemical and behavioral addictions, eating disorders, and so on. These matters of soul cannot be healed with medication and technology alone.

our children, and Earth, unaware that we are even doing so. Author Richard Louv coined the phrase *nature deficit disorder* (NDD) to describe the medical, emotional, and spiritual problems that result from our disconnection from nature.[3] In urban areas today, even when we do manage to get outside our buildings and vehicles, we no longer hear crickets, coyotes, or prairie songbirds; we hear car alarms, aircraft, jackhammers, police sirens, and the piercing backup alarms of construction vehicles.

Given these conditions of modern living, mindfulness is not just a helpful spiritual practice; mindfulness is a radical social act. Author and TV newsman Dan Harris calls mindfulness "the public health revolution story of the century."[4]

THE CHAIN THAT BINDS

Examining the Stream of Our Thoughts

In chapter 7 we examined the unconscious mind to see how our thoughts can stop us on the Heart Path. In this chapter we will examine the wandering mind to see how that too can derail our progress.

If we could actually see the stream of our thinking, it would look like a long chain, with each link of the chain being an individual thought. Research on the mind shows that we have twelve to fifty thousand individual thoughts each day. Of these thoughts, 95 percent are *completely redundant,* and 49 percent are focused on the past or the future. In other words, we have very few new or creative thoughts, and half of our waking lives we are not even "here" in the present moment with the actual people and situations around us! Instead, we are chained to the past or stuck in the future.

In his 2014 book *10% Happier,* author Dan Harris writes about the shock of observing his own chain of thoughts for the first time when he began to learn meditation. Harris says that having to sit still and observe the repetitive voice in his head was "like being kidnapped by the most boring person in the world." When he complained to his meditation teacher that his thoughts kept wandering away from the present moment and returning to his problems, the teacher asked Harris bluntly, "Which is more exciting to you: present reality or memory?"[5] Harris, a fast-talking, overcaffeinated TV anchorman for ABC News, realized the present reality usually seemed too boring for him. But the power of the present eventually caught up with Harris when he had a panic attack in front of five million television viewers during a broadcast of *Good Morning America*. After that, he took up the mindfulness practice of meditation to reduce his anxiety and spinning thoughts.

How present are you in the actual moment-by-moment unfolding of your daily life? Here is an exercise that helps you identify the pattern of your thoughts to see if they are more focused in the past, in the present, or in the future.

EXERCISE

☼ Observing the Time Zone of Your Thoughts

1. Consider ten things you tend to think about, worry about, or otherwise dwell upon often. Your children? Your partner's health? Your pending bills? Your job situation?
2. Write down a short title for each of these ten worries.
3. Now indicate whether each concern is rooted in a past experience, an issue occurring in the present moment, or a concern about some future matter.

   For example, "I never should have bought that car" (past). "This pain in my tooth is really bad" (present). "If Mother doesn't stop smoking she is going to get cancer" (future).

Did you notice any pattern here? Know that your mind has to work overtime to sustain any thinking that is located in the past or the future because *the only situation you are ever facing is the present moment*. Awareness of this liberating truth is the basis of Zen meditation, where the goal is to have as much of your waking day as possible focused in the present, in the "just this" of each moment.

Obviously, we have to plan for future events and recall the past from time to time. The point is to do this selectively, only as needed, and then promptly return to the present moment rather than get lost in endless worry or fantasizing about the future or lamenting about the past.

HOW TO TURN A SITUATION INTO A PROBLEM

A big benefit of mindfulness is being able to tell the difference between a real situation that you need to deal with and an imagined problem. The latter can pull you right off the Heart Path and into the ditch of useless worry, regret, or self-doubt.

Spiritual author Eckhart Tolle makes a very helpful distinction between a "situation" and a "problem." A *situation* is something that is facing you in the present moment: a flat tire, pain from a toothache, cold rain on your head. A *problem* is a situation accompanied by a negative thought judging that situation as "bad" and *all about you*. Here are a few examples:

Situation	Problem
It is raining.	My picnic is ruined!
He didn't call.	He didn't have the decency to return my call!
I was there; she was not.	She let me down again!

Challenging situations arise in our lives all the time. But when we add negativity and personalize the situation as "all about me," then we convert a mere situation into a personal problem and introduce needless suffering into our lives. Not only is that painful, but it sucks available time and energy away from our Heart Path.

In extreme cases, our negative thoughts can completely take us over for periods of time (recall a time you were unable to *not* think about a person you were very upset with), and we lose contact with—dissociate from—our very bodies and everything around us. Mindfulness helps pull our thinking back to the original situation—what is really happening—and disentangle our wounded ego from the mix.

This all has big implications for our relationship with the living Earth because if you can dissociate from the reality of your own body and surroundings, then you can easily dissociate with the physical condition and needs of the larger Earth.

The point here is not to create doubt about your mental state. The point is to build motivation for living a more mindful life, day to day. This is difficult work, and some people, like myself, seem to need a prolonged crisis to really see the light.

THE DAY I LOST MY MIND

In 2009 I had an experience of being taken over by my own negative thoughts—for four months! The hospital I worked at was laying off employees due to the recession. Many coworkers and several friends had already lost their jobs, and it seemed that no position was safe. In the middle of this uncertainty, a new vice president, "Doris," was named to head up the department I worked in. She sent me a one-line e-mail saying she wanted to meet with me. As lead massage therapist, I assumed this was a routine chance for Doris to introduce herself and learn about my program.

I was proud of my work: I had spent five years building the massage program into a popular hospital-wide service. My patient satisfaction scores were high, and post-massage evaluations showed the clear therapeutic effects of massage on patients' pain, anxiety, nausea, and hopelessness. Massage helped patients (and family members) to heal, particularly in high-stress specialties like oncology and intensive care.

But when I walked into Doris's office for the meeting, she said, "Frankly, I don't understand why we have a massage program in this hospital. Who authorized this?" I was stunned. She continued, "And I don't see massage therapy listed in our hospital strategic plan or budget." I explained that the program had grown organically from the ground up, with the support of my manager and individual nursing unit directors. It was paid for from the budget of each nursing unit I worked in. But Doris wasn't interested in that. "I'll need to get back to you on this," she said, and that was it. I asked if she wanted to meet with the patients or directors who supported the program. "I said I'll get back to you," she repeated and ended the meeting.

I was shocked and confused, then angry, and finally worried. For the next four months I went to work not knowing if I would have a job at the end of the day. My enjoyment of my work plummeted. I was distracted while working with patients. I avoided Doris in the hallways and considered quitting to find another job before I was fired. I was unhappy at home and irritable with my family over nonessential expenses like eating out or gifts for the holidays.

I had completely lost my spiritual center.

One day in the spring a lower-level manager named Kris called me in. *This is it,* I thought, *I'm going to lose my job.* I braced myself as I entered her office. But she pointed to an architectural blueprint spread out on her desk and told me the hospital was designing a new complementary medicine area. I was going to be put in charge of designing and running the massage therapy suite, and Kris wanted to know what sort of amenities I would like to order: new furniture? A sound system? Artwork and plants? Kris saw the expression on my face. "No one told you about this?" she said. I nearly hugged her. I wasn't going to lose my job.

But as the reality of my still-secure job settled in, a troubling new awareness came to me. As far as I knew, my job had never actually been *insecure*. Had Doris even followed up on her stated concerns? The blueprints implied the new massage suite had been approved months earlier. *All that drama about losing my job was an illusion,* I realized. *The suffering I endured and then inflicted on my family . . . I created in my own head!* I saw that my anxious mind had taken a simple, factual situation (a new administrator questioned the authorization of the massage program) and created a huge personalized drama of bullying, threat, and betrayal: *She doesn't like me. She wants to get rid of me and all my work.* I had been living in a jail cell of my own making.

This experience really affected me. In the days that followed I began to notice other ways my anxious mind would turn a simple disappointment or unexpected situation into a personal problem. For the first time in my life, a small but helpful gap of awareness opened up between my *thinking* and my *actual life*. Through that gap I glimpsed what I had been doing to myself: creating fear and then keeping it alive. As Don Miguel Ruiz advises in *The Fifth Agreement,* I became skeptical: I began to distrust all of my negative thoughts.

FIND YOUR BODY AND YOU FIND THE PRESENT

We have seen how our thoughts may not be our most reliable guides on the Heart Path. This is where our bodies turn out to be such an effective partner in mindfulness practice. Unlike our minds, which can be careening around time and space like a kite in a gusty wind, our physical bodies can *only* exist in the here and now of the present moment. Anchoring our attention in the body is a reliable and stabilizing point of reference for the mind, like connecting a kite string to a stake pounded into the ground.

Three Simple Ways to Return to Your Body

Here are three "shamanic" ways to step into the power of the present moment using your body's natural connection to nature and the sensory world.

Get outside. Simply walk outside. Open your senses. Draw your attention to some natural thing and hold it there: a tree, a birdsong, a breeze, a cloud, an aroma, a weed growing up through the sidewalk. Say hello to that other thing. This breaks the trance of your self-focused thoughts and opens the heart of curiosity and connectedness to nature.

The first thing I do every morning is get out into my backyard and look around. I am always surprised at the immediate calming effect and the dynamic movement of life all around me. Even in the dead of winter, fresh tracks in the snow reveal the busy activities of rabbits, cats, raccoons, squirrels, birds, and mice moving around my yard at night.

Drum or rattle. The mind is attracted to intense energy. A shout, a flash of light, a dog bark, or pungent aroma (*skunk!*) will instantly snap your attention out of the trance of your worries and into the present. Shamans discovered long ago that steady drumming or rattling snags the thinking mind and holds it in a kind of suspended state so the heart can vision without intellectual interference. The shaman's drum is her gateway or portal to the spirit world. Try it: drum or rattle for a period of time, experimenting with different rates or beats per minute and see which feels most natural and sustainable for you. Feel the percussion in your body; let it resonate at a very deep level. Notice how at some point your thinking mind just slips into neutral and you are just there with the sound of the percussion.

Smudge. A smudge is a short purifying ritual using the smoke from smoldering dried herbs such as sage or cedar. Smudging is often done at the beginning of longer ceremonies to welcome and cleanse participants. It doesn't matter what herb or incense you prefer; the earthy aromas hook the mind and draw attention back to the present. (I smudge myself and my computer keyboard and screen before sitting to write each morning to help me focus and remember that my work is sacred and needs to be kept in service to others.)

Help from Your Inner Mama Bear

Let's say you do encounter a real and threatening situation in the present moment, something you do need to deal with *right now*. Good! Because unlike the past or future, in the present moment you have special survival powers available to you. As a large animal with a huge brain, we humans have an arsenal of evolutionary skills for dealing with threats and opportunities. In a real crisis your inner warrior, predator, and stalker will all be available for action.

For example, you may normally feel like a meek pushover, until some bully threatens your child and—BOOM! Here comes Mama Bear roaring out of the woods. When your physical strength, intellect, and spiritual powers are all lined up in the present moment, you have a fierce and powerful team of allies at your service.

Mindfulness practices have helped me discover two truths about my old habit of worrying about the future. First, if a future concern does eventually arrive in the present moment as a real situation, it is never as awful, complex, or powerful as I had feared. Second, I usually know what to do then, because all the facts—the entire situation—is now right there in front of me. This is always more manageable than the endless and unknown what-ifs of a future worry. In the case where the situation is still not fully clear then I have something I can do about that too: getting more information. That locks in the power of the present, when I take the action step of investigating further.

Sweat Lodge on a Roof

The traditional Amerindian sweat lodge ceremony powerfully connects breath, body, and soul in the present moment. In the heat of the dark lodge, the hot air rising from the glowing stones, the water in the steam and the sweat, the earth in the wood, soil, and body all blend together to create intense presence and shift consciousness from thinking to feeling, body, and breath.

I do not teach the traditional sweat lodge ceremony in my programs out of respect for the Native people who regard it as sacred to their own ways.* But having participated in many sweats I now recognize other activities that had similar qualities and effects on me: the final miles of running a marathon, riding an endurance bicycle race, even loading

*Sweat ceremonies led by non-Indians have been a particular point of bitterness for some Indians who know the ceremony is corrupted when fees are charged and harm is caused by unsafe practices.

dishes into the steamy maw of an industrial dish machine for hours at a time. At some point the heat, exertion, and repetitive movement shifts the mind into neutral and something else takes over. This is *flow,* the state described by athletes, musicians, and others during peak times of creativity and movement. I even experienced this one summer on my roof.

Years ago I was roofing my house in full sun on a hot August day. The heat was so extreme the asphalt shingles were melting under my work boots, smearing the gritty surface as I climbed the sloped roof. I drank liter after liter of sports drinks, sweating it out nearly as fast as I could take it in. The work was very repetitive, and at one point I fell into a trance of rhythmic movement and breath. *Place the shingle. Grab the nail gun. Bam, bam, bam. Turn around. Pick up a shingle. Place the shingle. Grab the nail gun. Bam, bam, bam.* Over and over. Up and down the ladder with bundles of new shingles on my shoulder. The hours passed. I felt power filled and deeply alive, using my animal powers of balance and strength with little conscious thinking or planning.

At some point I reached the peak of the roof and stood there amazed. I had laid several hundred square feet of shingles alone, completely absorbed in the moment-by-moment alchemy of heat, sweat, breath, and asphalt. Although I was not participating in a spiritual ceremony, I experienced exactly the same shift into body and breath that a sweat lodge can induce.

Consider a time when you have experienced a shift in consciousness as a result of exerting physical effort: hiking in the heat, working in a laundry, standing in a factory line, baking in a hot kitchen all day. Although many people avoid physical exertion, assuming it only gets worse the harder you work, athletes and laborers know that you must go *through* the apparent barrier of physical crisis to break through to the flow state on the other side. The barrier turns out to be an illusion, a mere veil, a nonsolid attitude that is like the gatekeeper of a more pure state of transformative power. Many Americans know nothing about this state. They do not know there even is a flow state on the other side of physical endurance, that the very thing they avoid is the portal to the thing they seek.

BECOMING MINDFUL OF YOUR BODY'S ENERGY CYCLES

Ship captains, surfers, and the military all coordinate their activities with the predictable tides of the ocean. Why use a huge crane to lift a ship for hull repairs when the next high tide will do the same thing? Why launch a beach invasion through dangerous coral reefs when a high tide will carry landing craft safely over the same reefs without harm? Like the changing tides of the ocean, we have high and low tides of energy in our bodies, hearts, and minds. To maximize your power for following your vision, you need to coordinate your efforts with your peak times of physical energy, mental clarity, and spiritual vision.

This has been a more recent discovery in my life. In childhood I began each day with my mother marching into my dark bedroom, turning on a bright light, and forcing me out of bed for school. Mentally startled and physically unbalanced, I stumbled through my morning routine utterly unprepared for the day. I dragged my sleepy body to the bus stop, and then years later to the job, and then later to my own massage office for the convenience of clients who "could only meet in the mornings"—forcing myself to function as best I could. I was getting enough sleep, but mornings were simply not my best time to be interacting with people. But later in the day—any day—I would notice a curious thing happening. As the afternoon arrived, I found myself really coming alive, and by early evening I would be completely on, with energy, alertness, sociability, and creativity. I could easily handle problems, juggle more tasks, be more assertive, laugh, work, and create. I could stay up until two or three in the morning when others had long nodded off to sleep. Yet for forty-five years I was trying to go to sleep during those very same hours of my natural aliveness because that was the consensus behavior and values of my society: you get up for work by 8:00 a.m., and go to sleep in the evening by midnight.

I now align my daily routine to my natural energy cycle, and the results have been dramatic. I do not schedule clients in the morning.

When I first awake I stick to nonsocial activities like writing, walking, prayer, chores, and connecting with Earth. In the afternoons I do more physical and social activities such as chores, building projects, house repairs, and running errands. In late afternoon when the predictable drop in energy arrives, I don't fight it: I take a nap. But when I awake, I am then ready for six to eight more hours of straight-on work, creativity, or play. I save the late afternoons and evenings for what is most important to me: creative and spiritual work, seeing shamanic clients, shamanic journeying, visioning, and art projects. I match my external activities to the rhythms of my internal energy, not the other way around. At various times during the day, I will even stop and ask myself, "What activity will best suit my physical energy and mental state right now?"

I have even noticed that I am physically stronger during my peak times and activities. For example, immediately after a client fire talk or teaching a workshop (when I am feeling especially energized and soul-satisfied), I can lift more weight and run farther or faster than normal. There is no biological explanation for this, but there is an easy spiritual explanation: I am in my power.

EXERCISE

☼ Tracking Your Daily Energy Tides

Turn to appendix 2 now, where you will find a detailed journaling exercise to help you discover your own hidden power reserves by pinpointing the time(s) of day and activities during which you are most energized and productive.

Well Nice For You, But . . .

At this point you may be thinking, *Well, nice for you, you're self-employed, but I don't have the freedom to choose my schedule. I have to go to work at 8:00 a.m.* Or, *I have to get up at 6:00 a.m. for my kids.* Or, *I have to work the night shift.*

I, too, have worked jobs that began at 8:00 a.m. I have children that needed me up at 6:00 a.m. I cared for my terminally ill mother at all hours of the day and night. And I worked the night shift for many years as a security guard, a janitor, and a hospital chaplain.

I was not born self-employed, and I did not create a self-directed life overnight. It took years, and every single step toward my vision involved some new challenge or difficult decision about leaving something valuable behind. Like my house. When I was working full-time as a chaplain in the 1990s and realized I wanted to go back to graduate school for my master's of divinity degree, Regina and I looked at our budget and saw that we could not afford the loss of my income and still continue to make our mortgage payments. With her blessing, we sold the house, a small but expensive little home in a "good" neighborhood. We moved to a fixer-upper in the inner city (which most friends considered a "bad" neighborhood) that was one-third the cost and had three times the land, with our two little girls, then aged five and three. That turned out to be one of the best decisions of my life.

Over the years I have made many changes to my work hours, household routines, and relationship habits to keep moving toward my vision. I had to come out of the closet, so to speak, with my heart and say to others, "Look, this is who I am, this is how I operate, and this is what someone like me does."

Ultimately, I had to quit my twenty-year, fully vested career as a hospital chaplain so that I could shift to my growing passion: shamanic healing. I didn't do that overnight, either. First I doubled up, keeping the day job while adding a few clients and teaching a few shamanic workshops in the evenings. This was difficult and required sacrifices elsewhere, but it established a foothold for my new shamanic work. Then I began to slowly cut back on my day job: to three-quarter time, then to half-time as my shamanic work increased. The cutbacks worried my wife, who was also working full-time and concerned about our family income, but I explained patiently (and repeatedly) what I was doing and why I was doing it. The cutback on hospital hours provided more time in my day for workshops and shamanic clients. When

I decreased my hours at the hospital to part-time, I had to pay a higher monthly health insurance premium for our family coverage, but I didn't care. I was coming alive, which was priceless.

At some point, several years later, I realized I was within striking distance of a daily routine focused around my shamanic practice. I took a deep breath, quit my day job (still remaining on call for some months), and began the new life. The clients came, the workshops filled up, the money followed. Now I can't believe I waited so long to make the change. I have followed this same basic process of reeducation and job transitioning four different times in my life. My heart has always found a way, whereas my anxious mind had only been able to say "no way."

NATURE
Your Ally in Mindfulness

Simply being out in nature promotes mindfulness and quickly awakens our soul self. "Nature does the work," I tell participants in my outdoor programs, "by opening the heart." This is the power of a wilderness vision quest ceremony, which uses stillness, fasting, prayer, and the extended connection with nature to alter ordinary thinking and allow the emergence of a vision from deep within. Even our indigenous ancestors needed the solitary wilderness experience to break from their ordinary social consciousness and connect deeply with the spirit for guidance.

This is why nature and actual outdoor experiences are critical to both the shamanic Heart Path and healing our wounded planet. In nature we are not just enjoying the beauty of a sunset or the calming effect of mist on a lake. In nature we are in *school:* we are being given lessons on our forgotten essence as spiritual kin to our surroundings. Each fern, raccoon, centipede, and raindrop is a family member in the web of life. You cannot learn this intellectually; you have to see it, smell it, and feel it experientially to really understand that it is true.

The immediacy of our animal nature is the key ecospiritual awareness we have lost in urban living. We don't seem connected to or dependent upon anything natural anymore. Instead we are connected to our iPhones, Facebook, and Amazon.com; we feel dependent upon Shell Oil, Comcast, and CVS Pharmacy.

To help you reconnect with your deep nature, here is a type of mindfulness practice based on a Buddhist walking meditation called *gatha* walking.

EXERCISE

Gatha Walking

The word *gatha* is a Sanskrit word meaning "song" or "verse." The contemporary Buddhist monk Thich Nhat Hanh has popularized traditional gatha verses as a mindfulness practice that can be recited while going about your daily activities like walking, washing your hands, or doing the dishes. "A gatha can open and deepen our experience of simple acts which we often take for granted. When we focus our mind on a gatha, we return to ourselves and become more aware of each action. The gatha brings our mind and body together."[6]

The following is a gatha walking exercise Hanh teaches his students.[7] The exercise is done at a very relaxed, strolling-the-park pace. As you walk, you say each verse in rhythm with the natural in and out of the breath. The farther you walk, the more deeply you are drawn into the body, your surroundings, and the present moment.

"As I walk (breathing in) . . . the mind will wander (breathing out).
With each sound (in) . . . the mind returns (out, etc.).
With each breath . . . the heart is open.
With each step . . . I touch Earth.
(Repeat)

This meditation does it all: it opens the senses, returns your mind to the present moment, shifts your attention to the heart, and grounds your body in Earth.

I remember the first time I tried this gatha meditation. I was walking home from my hospital work on a hot summer day. My mind was crawling with the day's patient encounters and problems. I took off my shoes, and with a very slow pace that matched my gait to each phrase, I began repeating the lines above. This had an immediate calming effect as I could feel my tangled thoughts releasing, like cats being let out of a bag. With less turmoil in my head, I then became more aware of my body and its sensations and surroundings: the heat of the asphalt under my feet, the sounds of birds, the traffic over on Lincoln Way, kids shouting down the block, and the mixed aromas of the street, of alleyway garbage bins, flowers, and barbecue.

At one point, when I got to the last line, "With each step . . . I touch Earth," the asphalt section under my feet seemed to lift ever so slightly to meet my left foot as I stepped down on it. Then the asphalt rose ever so lightly to meet my right foot as I stepped down on it. Left foot (street pushhhing up) . . . right foot (street pushhhing up). . . . I was astounded. With each step, I felt *met by Earth:* supported, held up. I was still walking Lindsey Avenue with its empty liquor bottles and crushed Newport cigarette packages, but under all the battered asphalt was the living Earth reaching up to support me and help me walk forward.

WHAT DOES THIS HAVE TO DO WITH HEALING EARTH?

Throughout this book I have made the rather grandiose claim that walking the Path of the Heart will benefit the larger community and even the whole living Earth. Can that be true? What do I mean by that?

By this point you have seen how being calm or upset affects more than your private inner world. Our invisible thoughts (chapters 6 and 7) turn into real behaviors in the outer world so quickly that most people aren't even aware they're doing this. The science of neurobiology tells us that every emotion or thought we have, good or bad, triggers the release of a corresponding hormone (chemical messenger) into the bloodstream. And that chemical messenger soon travels to *every single organ and cell in your body,* creating a specific physical reaction (stimulating or relaxing, tightening or releasing, "fighting" or "flighting") in your muscles, your liver, your stomach, your kidneys, your brain, your heart. And that physical reaction then enters the world through your corresponding behavior, be it agitation, calmness, aggressiveness, joy, silence, lethargy, and so on.

So the issue is, what are your private thoughts—what is your mind—causing you to bring into the world? Joy or negativity? Gratitude or complaint? Hope or despair? As you walk through your community, are you leaving behind a fertile field of kindness and love, or a toxic spill of negativity and fear? You are like a boat moving through the water. What are you leaving in your wake?

Your private thoughts have very public consequences.

The ultimate public impact is what we are leaving on Earth itself. We humans are small organisms living off the resources of a very large planetary host, and there are only two ways to do this: as a beneficial organism that enhances the condition of its host, or as a parasite, which, according to the dictionary, is "an organism that grows, feeds, and is sheltered on or in a different organism while contributing nothing to the survival of its host."

Thich Nhat Hanh writes beautifully of the ecospiritual consequences of our footprints on Earth: "Our walking is usually more like running. When we walk like that, we print anxiety and sorrow on the Earth. We have to walk in a way that we only print peace and serenity on the Earth. Be aware of the contact between your feet and the Earth. Walk as if you are kissing the Earth with your feet. We have caused a lot of damage to the Earth. We bring our peace and calm to the surface of the Earth and share the lesson of love. Every step makes a flower bloom under our feet. We can do it only if we do not think of the future or the past, if we know that life can only be found in the present moment."[8]

WISDOM FROM BODIES WITH DISABILITIES

In appendix 2 you will find another Earth-based mindfulness walking exercise that I teach my students called One Perfect Step. In this exercise, you pay close attention to the sensations and movements involved in taking each step, while coordinating your breath and body. (Try this exercise before you continue reading.)

I am grateful to my friend Jenny who, in helping me outline this book, reminded me that people with disabilities may not find these walking exercises very easy to do. Jenny has cerebral palsy, and although she can, with much effort, walk, she fatigues easily and gets very physically tense in the process.

When I asked Jenny what alternative body-mindfulness practices she might recommend for the physically disabled, she smiled. "You know, Jeff, we are the *original* mindful-of-our-bodies people. People with disabilities don't have to work very hard to be mindful!" She explained how she sees her own intense body awareness in a positive way, then added, "I love to swim. I find water to be very grounding. You don't have gravity in water. For me being in water is to be free. When I go for a swim, my mental state is completely different afterward." Jenny also rides a recumbent three-wheel bicycle that allows her to stay fit, exercise outdoors, and take her dog for a good run in the process. This is a wonderful example of using the problem-solving ability of the mind to serve the real needs of the body and the heart.

MINDFULNESS MAXIMIZES PERSONAL POWER FOR CHANGE

If you want to change your life, you have to *change* your life. This doesn't happen by wishing, worrying, praying, visioning, shamanic journeying, or even reading this book. It happens with action: by *doing something different* with your life. This doesn't have to be a huge or sudden change. But it has to be a real change. "*Any* change," a counseling supervisor told me years ago in graduate school, "is a therapeutic intervention. It counts."

Your power to change is in the present moment. It is *only* in the present moment. Begin to do something differently *now.*

We've seen that our own thoughts can stop us from the change we desire, so if we're waiting for our thoughts to change first ("I guess I really *can* do this"), nothing may ever happen. Our habit-and-security-preferring mind will never, ever be 100 percent convinced that change is safer than known routine. So we have to start with our behaviors first—changing our actions—not our thoughts and beliefs. "Fake it until you make it," as the twelve-step recovery saying goes. That is, pretend like you really believe you can change your behaviors and do it, before you really start to think about whether or not things will work out. Eventually, your mind will have to admit, "Well, I guess, I can do this after all."

This takes courage. It's a hero's journey, my friend, not a walk through the mall. If you are not in your power and are distracted by regrets about the past or worries about the future, even a few barriers to change will stop you in your tracks and keep you there. The mindfulness practices in this chapter, coordinated with your peak energy tides, will position you for maximum success in what comes next: harnessing the full power of your mind and the full power of your heart to create the kind of life you really want to be living.

In the next chapter we will learn a core shamanic practice for transforming each of your dragons into a servant of the heart. We will do this by returning to the individual dragons you laid out in chapter 6, and then conduct a direct shamanic conversation with the living spirit in each dragon. I will share the case of a married couple I helped to examine their relationship dragons to show how their dragons could be harnessed to lead them forward in their marriage. Then we will return to your own dragons and have them explain to you directly what their core needs are to point you forward in a specific direction for lasting change in your life.

But first we will travel to the high Andes Mountains. We are going to listen to an ancient South American prophecy about the eagle and the condor. That prophecy holds the secret to the proper relationship we have been seeking between the mind and the heart.

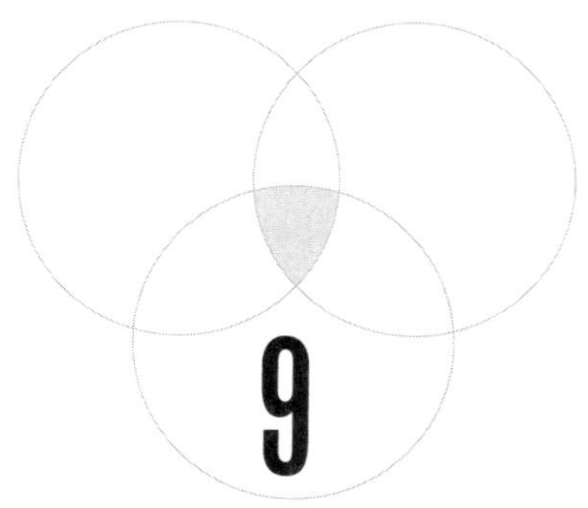

9

Power from the Eagle Mind

How do you slay the dragon? Follow your bliss! Don't be afraid to follow it.
You say, "Oh, I couldn't be a writer." That's your dragon!
Then in saving yourself you save the world. The influence of a vital person vitalizes.

Joseph Campbell with Bill Moyers, *Joseph Campbell and the Power of Myth,* documentary

HARNESSING THE MIND TO PULL FOR THE HEART

You have learned to anchor your attention (your power) in the present using your breath, body, and Earth itself. We are now ready to reenter your dragon's cave to harness your mind to become obedient to the callings of the heart. This is a difficult portion of the Heart Path to perceive clearly. But you are a shaman of your life—*one who sees*. And what I want you to see right now is a beautiful metaphor for the proper relationship between your mind and heart.

So look up above you now, far up into the sky. Do you see that magnificent bird soaring on the wind? It's a condor, from the high Andes of South America, and it carries the heart of healing for both yourself and the world.

Eagle and Condor: A Prophecy for Our Time

In North America the archetypal bird is the bald eagle. With its piercing eyes, battle-ready talons, and handsome stature, it embodies the American psyche. But in South America the sacred bird is the condor, which personifies the heart of the Andean people in art, mythology, and spirituality. The condor is the largest bird on Earth that is capable of flight and is the national symbol of Argentina, Bolivia, Chile, Colombia, Ecuador, and Peru. The eagle and the condor both play lead roles in an ancient South American prophecy that illustrates the proper relationship between the heart and mind.* The prophecy of the eagle and the condor comes from the Q'ero people, modern descendants of the ancient Incas.[1] Similar prophecies can be found in other indigenous cultures throughout the Americas, such as the "prophecy rock" of the Hopi Indians.

This prophecy foretold that around 1490 CE, human society would split into two separate ways of being: the Eagle People and the Condor People. The Eagle People were people of mind, materialism, and the masculine spirit; the Condor People were people of heart, mysticism, and the feminine spirit.

This split would begin a five-hundred-year period or Pachacuti, during which "the world would be turned upside down." The Eagle People

*The *Star Trek* television series presents a popularized metaphor for the same relationship between heart and mind. First Officer Spock is the science officer, the "man of mind" with his logical, emotionless mental database of scientific information. Captain Kirk is the "man of heart," the passionate, courageous leader who breaks with protocol and logic as needed to outwit enemies with his unconventional and spontaneous directives. Together, Kirk and Spock make a powerful team. But Kirk is the captain, not Spock, and Kirk leads his ship and crew safely through battles with powerful enemies to explore unknown galaxies, and "boldly go where no one has gone before."

(now understood as the European conquerors) were predicted to dominate with weapons and war and become so powerful they would nearly exterminate the indigenous Condor People. But in 2012, according to the prophecy, a new five-hundred-year Pachacuti would begin during which "the world would be turned right side up again." Then the ways of the indigenous peoples would return, and the eagle and the condor would fly together. But this time the condor would lead the eagle in flight, as only the heart can be allowed to lead our lives and our society. The mind, left to its own ways, can only lead to abuses of power and the separation of people from people, and people from nature.

The Q'ero prophecy speaks only of the potential for this unification of heart and mind, not its certainty. How the story turns out is fully in our hands.

Encountering a Real Condor

A condor once flew just inches over my head and I will never forget it. I was visiting Peru in 2013 to attend a conference on Amazonian shamanism, and after the conference I traveled into the Sacred Valley region of the Andes Mountains. Along the way, I stopped at a wildlife preserve where several condors were recovering from poachers' gunshot wounds.

Condors are not attractive birds at rest. Unlike the photogenic eagle, the condor (a member of the vulture family) has a featherless head, crooked neck, and hunched shoulders. Standing still the bird appears awkward, ugly, and top-heavy. *So this is the great bird of the Andes?* I thought. I was not impressed.

I was instructed to take a seat on a hillside overlooking a small canyon while an attendant on the far side of the canyon prepared to release a condor. From that distance the condor was a dark, nondescript shape perched on a dead tree limb. Another attendant stood right behind me farther up the hill. Then he reached into his bag, pulled out a dead rabbit, and held it up.

Instantly, the condor across the canyon saw the rabbit, leaned forward, and unfolded its wings so wide I couldn't believe it. The wingspan was impossible, nearly ten feet across, and before I knew what was happening, the condor covered the entire distance between us in three powerful wing strokes, swooped over my head like a dark Cessna, and landed with a thump behind me. I suddenly understood: the condor was a living expression of the human *soul,* which is most powerful and beautiful only when it completely spreads its wings and takes flight.

WARRIORS AND HEALERS

The detailed practice you will learn in this chapter is from the lineage of warrior shamanism, which views the healing path as a battle or confrontation with unhelpful spirits that stand in the way of full living. Chapter 10 will introduce practices from the lineage of healer or adventure shamanism, which views the healing path as a harmonizing of opposite but necessary energies needed for wholeness.[2] The Path of the Heart we are learning here draws on the traditions of both warrior and healer-adventurer shamanism.

The tools presented from this point on in the book can be learned in any order, and every person does not need every tool. Like a wise physician, the shamanic practitioner applies only the medicine that will be most helpful given the client's situation and personal readiness. The methods I share in this book are like a set of ordinary hand tools that can be learned and used by anyone. There are additional practices beyond the scope of this book that are more like the electric power tools used only by skilled tradesmen. For example, the deep practices of shamanic soul extraction and soul retrieval take years to learn under the supervision of a good teacher. The use of entheogen plant medicines like ayahuasca and San Pedro are also for journeyers working with skilled *ayahuasceros* and *curanderos*. I will describe these later and provide resources to learn more about them.

As far as the basic shamanic tools that you will acquire here, please know that some healing methods will come to you more naturally than others. Each practitioner must learn his or her own areas of natural strength and weakness, and different shamanic healers do not all use the same approaches for the same problems. My teachers have insisted I learn their healing ways, but also that I bring forth my own shamanic medicine and way of teaching, even if that means modifying their own carefully taught practices.

Now let's pick up a big warrior weapon I learned from my first teacher and get back to your dragons. We have some transformational work to do! As we walk to the cave entrance to learn the new practice, I'll share a fire-talk client case that illustrates the benefits of making a direct shamanic encounter with our dragon(s). As you will see, this was the last thing the woman wanted to do, yet the results were immediate, healing, and empowering for her.

CASE STUDY

Kristin's Angry Scorpion

Kristin is a financial planner who came for a fire talk to discuss her difficulty in setting personal goals and getting a clear vision for her life. She had attended my workshops and knew many of the conceptual tools needed for change, but something else was blocking her way. As I led her in a stone-layout exercise to name her concerns, I noticed she started to become agitated. "I'm *angry,*" she admitted, "but I don't know why I'm getting angry. I just want to shove all this crap aside, these stupid stones, this whole process! What a waste of time!"

I asked her to look around my hermitage space and select some item to represent her anger from the array of natural objects, travel souvenirs, and memorabilia I have scattered all around the room on the shelves and walls. Her eyes landed on a little scorpion souvenir I had brought back from Mexico, hand-made from bent wire. "That scorpion," she said.

"OK," I said, placing the scorpion on the floor in front of her. "This scorpion is your anger. Let's greet that."

"Greet it?" she said. "I've never done that. I'm always trying to make my anger go away."

"Exactly," I said. "So let's do a different thing here and see what the anger might be trying to tell us." Since shamanism believes everything has a spirit (even anger), I told Kristin we were going to try to connect directly with the spirit of her anger. She looked a little puzzled, then hesitant, but was willing to try.

I had Kristin say hello to the bent-wire scorpion and then say whatever needed to be said to it honestly and from her heart. She began a direct dialogue with the anger that arose in her whenever she tried to get clear on a vision for her life. She talked to it, scolded it, admitted she was afraid of it. At one point Kristin paused, looked up at me with an incredulous expression, and said, "Ohhh. It's trying to *protect* me. The scorpion doesn't want me to get hurt if I try a new direction." This recognition of her vulnerability and need for protection, previously unconscious on Kristin's part, completely changed the situation for her, and she was able to move forward on visioning from her heart but now with the anger scorpion sitting nearby as a protective *ally,* like a little guard dog. As long as Kristin honored her scorpion's concerns by incorporating personal safety measures into her plans, she was able to move forward with no difficulty.

Kristin had been on the verge of abandoning a process designed to help her, and she would not even have known why, only that she was feeling "this is a waste of time." Imagine how many times each day we all may miss opportunities for healing due to the unruly and short-sighted voice in our own heads. We don't see the emotional resistance going on (in the wounded unconscious), we only get the agitation and mental reaction at the conscious level ("this is a waste of time"), and we follow that!

THE SHADOW ASPECT OF PERSONALITY

Like the survival instinct that kicks in when we feel our lives are in mortal danger, our minds have a self-preservation instinct that will fiercely resist any threats to self-image or deeply held beliefs, even when that self-image and those supporting beliefs are harming us. Much of our hesitation or avoidance in life can be caused not by actual threats we face but by situations that trigger old protective emotional patterns, whether we are conscious of these old patterns or not. Most of our barriers to happiness are not caused by other people, lack of money, or blocked opportunity but by the negative thoughts or worries *in our own head*.

I remember after my parents divorced, my mother became rude with nearly every male she would meet. One day she became furious at a young clerk in the grocery store for giving her the wrong change, berating him with a venom approaching hatred—as if the man had intentionally betrayed her. To my mother's wounded psyche, here was one more man out to take advantage of her, just like my father. Her mind turned a stranger's simple mistake into a full-blown personal insult, retraumatizing herself and wounding the clerk at the same time.

We will now learn the practice I used with Kristin for talking with her dragon. It is more difficult to do this using a book than by being face to face with a shaman who can see your hesitation or confusion and respond to that immediately. Thus it is important to go slowly and follow the steps below.

EXERCISE

Breaking Down a Dragon

Like a hero of legend, we're going to get a running start and leap right down the throat of your dragon(s). Every culture teaches the necessity of this descent: Jonah entering the belly of the whale (Jonah 1:17), Jesus descending into "the heart of the earth" (Matthew 12:40, New Revised Standard Version), and Luke Skywalker getting stuck in the garbage disposal system of the Death Star.

It is here that you will encounter the spirit of your dragon and transform it into your helper. (This is a continuation of the exercise, Talking to Your Dragons, in chapter 6, where we identified each of the dragons around your circle of mandala art. Go back to that stone layout now or reconstruct it from the photo you took on your smartphone.)

1. Take a mindfulness moment to center yourself in body and breath, grounded on Earth. Shift your awareness to the heart and gut area of your body. We want your answers to come from here.
2. Looking at the arrangement of your dragon stones in front of you, which one feels the most bothersome or urgent today? Give this a few moments to become clear to you. The answer may not be the one you expect, the one your mind is saying you "should" focus on. Let your heart be the arbiter.
3. When you are clear on the primary issue for you today, set that stone in front of you in a prominent position. The other stones/issues remain on stage, but they will not be the focus right now.
4. Take a minute to break this primary dragon down into its component parts, similar to how we did the whole process in the beginning, designating one additional stone for each of its components. For example, if your primary dragon is "worry," you might arrange additional stones beneath it to represent its several components: "Worry I can't get a job," "Worry about Bob's drinking," "Worry about paying for college."
5. Test if you have identified all the components of your primary dragon by asking yourself, "If all these components were resolved or gone, would I then have no more [worry]?" Add additional stones if needed.
6. Regard the new set of dragon stones before you representing all the aspects of (worry) for you. Remember that these issues in the web of your life are not *you*. Dis-identify yourself from these situations. You are the spider of this web. You are the shaman, the shapeshifter of your life—a Toltec artist of the soul.

Getting to the Heart of the Dragon

We will now ask your heart for a good name, a handle for this whole situation.*

---

*This process borrows from the focusing work of Eugene T. Gendlin. See Gendlin's *Focusing* (Maharashtra, India: Everest House, 1978).

1. Imagine you are sitting in your favorite movie theater and up on the screen are images of your main dragon and all its component parts, presented like a collage. Regard these screen images collectively, with your felt sense, and ask for a name—a title for all "that" on the screen, the whole collage. We are seeking a word that captures the whole problem, the crux of the matter, the essence, the aura of the whole thing for you, not just an emotion but a deeper symbol that gets to the heart of the situation. What is all that, "in a nutshell"? What would be the short title of this movie? You can use a short phrase or image in lieu of a single word. Drop the reins of your thinking and allow the best word to rise up from within you. This takes focus but not thought.
2. When you have the right word, the best word, you may feel a slight physical shift, a release, as if your body is saying, "Ahhh, yes. That's it!" If you have two or three good words, test each of them against the images on the movie screen. Only one will be the best fit. This is your handle for the whole movie.
3. Select a new stone to represent this handle name for the whole matter, and label it by writing the handle name on a small piece of paper and placing the stone on that paper. We will call this final stone your *wisdom stone*.

Here are some examples from my fire talks of clients' key barriers and the handle word(s) that the respective clients came up with that best captured what the crux of each *felt* like.

Key Barrier (the dragon)	Handle Name
Fear	Feeling unloved
Chronic medical problems	Trapped under the ice; I can see life, not get to it
Tension	A tight fist
Indecisiveness	Being alone
Tired, no energy	Protecting self, escape, avoid, leave me alone
Marriage estrangement	No communion

Key Barrier (the dragon)	Handle Name
Insecurity	A black cat in the dark
Harshness, being cut off	Left alone to die
Separateness, loneliness	Annihilation, empty, void
Demands of my children	Running with a hornet's nest all the time
No time due to family needs	Fractured windshield of my mind
My stubbornness	The "mountainness" of my problem
Aging	Dogs barking at heels, crows cawing at head
I can't get pregnant	Loneliness, can't share love
Anxiety	Wrecking ball, afraid of being destroyed
E-mails at work	Feeling heavy, clutter, fragmentation

Dragon as Adviser

From this point on, your questions are to be directed *at the new wisdom stone* representing the handle-crux of your dragon. This is an important detail: we are interacting shamanically with the *spirit of the wisdom stone* directly, not with "you" or your intellect. (This is similar to the exercise in chapter 4 where you connected with the spirit of a tree, plant, or animal in that we want the responses to come directly from the energetic soul of the dragon itself.)

So ask your wisdom stone:

- What does it believe is missing or needed in this situation?
- What would help it to be more whole or more healed?
- What would help it to feel better?

As before, allow plenty of time for a response to come *from the stone*. Again, this requires focus but not "thinking." Drop the reins of control and allow a response to arise from the stone. It's very important not to judge or analyze whatever comes up. We want the communication lines wide open. If you get stuck or confused, just back up and remind yourself what you are doing. For example: "OK, the crux of this dragon and its component stones is all about feeling unloved and feeling 'trapped under the ice.' This wisdom stone is unhappy, obviously. It needs or wants something in order to feel better. So I'm asking the wisdom stone, not me, 'What is missing for you? What is needed that would help you feel better, more whole or healed?'"

Here are examples of responses that have come to my clients from their wisdom stones telling them what was most deeply needed:

Tired of being the fortress, holding everything up, wanting a rest.

To feel special, prized, get the notched feather of a warrior.

To feel safe, like I can let my guard down.

To feel like I'm together on the same team as my spouse.

Light, a torch to illuminate all the corners of darkness in my marriage.

To know every moment that all I need and want is right here.

Permission to be tired, exhausted, sad.

The strength to express my concerns to the board of directors. Be okay with small failures. Things are not "over."

The response that comes from your own wisdom stone will arise from a very deep place in you. This process retrieves information from both your unconscious and the spirit world, which the rational mind cannot access. Make a note of the response you get. It may be a single word, a phrase, an image, a feeling or intuition.

We will turn to the final and most important stage of this practice in a moment. But first, a story about a married couple whose personal dragons were in direct conflict with each other.

Not about the Baby

Years ago a married couple came to me with a problem that seemed unsolvable at first. I was working as a pastoral counselor for a Mennonite church, and although I had solid training in pastoral psychology, I knew nothing about shamanic healing. The couple had three children, and the wife deeply wanted to have another baby. The husband deeply did not want to have another baby. He considered her emotional, needy, and unrealistic. She considered him selfish, stubborn, and unsupportive. Barring a huge sacrifice on either side, this looked to be (and felt like) a perfect stalemate.

At the time I struggled to know how to help because I accepted their premise, which was that the conflict was all about a *baby*. But the heart is not concerned with how many babies you have. The heart is concerned with conceiving and delivering its own new life into this world, and this process is not dependent on other peoples' behavior, whether that person is an infant or adult. This is the great confusion of our romantic, codependent understandings of love and parenthood. "If only she/he would ______, then I would be happy."

If that couple came to me now, we would dive into the dragon caves of their belief systems, not their reproductive life. We would take a hard look at their *spirits* of unhappiness. What deep need—to nurture, to be a caregiver—did the woman's desire for another baby connect to? And what fear was behind that desire? For the man, what was behind his resistance to having another child? What fears did he have? Were they financial, related to time constraints or potential fatigue, or broader population and overpopulation issues?

Once we identified those fears, we would then talk to *that*—to the fears *themselves* as spirits—and learn what was missing and what was needed to feel better and move forward from the soul's perspective. Whether or not this approach resulted in another baby is not the point. We would be helping the couple see what their hearts were really longing for and seek a way forward from the soul, not the bedroom.

This is an entirely different approach than trying to get two different people to agree over a fundamental disagreement about family size. And it works because it gets past the filters of the self-interested ego that is so quick to feel injured or taken advantage of and into the unconscious mind. It gets to the universal Heart of Everything That Is.

Your Dragon as a Navigational Guide

The final step of this whole exercise is to seek information from the wisdom stone in terms of an actual step that you should take to address the needs that have surfaced.

So now return to your wisdom stone and take a moment to recall its core deep need that emerged above. Then ask the wisdom stone directly,

- What would be one *small* step forward to meeting the need(s) stated above?
- What would one *nonburdensome,* real action in the direction of that vision be?

These are two ways of asking the same question. Again, drop the reins of your thinking and your usual problem solving. It's very important that the response be from a fresh place and that the steps that emerge be something small and doable. They should not feel like a big chore or duty, which will only increase your resistance to change. The step(s) will likely be something intriguing and energizing, and will make sense to you. For example: "You know, I've been wanting to get my art supplies out of the attic." The step(s) should also be very specific ("I will set up my easel in the spare room") and not too general ("I am going to be more creative"). Following these guidelines will assure success rather than frustration.

Here are some examples of action steps chosen by my clients after each one of them consulted with their wisdom stones using the above exercise:

Enjoy solitude with my dog, by the water.
Take the next step to start my coaching business.
Bring my lovely green chair inside and sit in it.
Say "no" to interruptions from my small child.
Attend to my physical self with yoga.
Pillow talk with my partner before sleep, go walk the dog together.
Each day, ask my husband to tell me five good things about myself.

When your wisdom stone has given you the action step, the small step forward, you have three remaining tasks:

- Write your idea(s) down immediately.
- Select a talisman object to represent the action step forward.

- Place this talisman on your home altar or some other sacred place to be a placeholder for the work you have done and will continue to do.

At this point you may return to your other main dragon stones and select another dragon to work on, repeating this whole process and systematically getting to the wisdom teaching of each and finding a small step forward. Or you may decide to wait and select the next dragon another day.

This deep dragon-wrestling process is a type of shamanic journey for penetrating the unconscious and the spirit world. In this journey you faced a dragon, named it, and opened a communication link with it. With strong intention you broke down the dragon into its component parts, shifting your perception of it as one big impenetrable difficulty to a more manageable collection of smaller component parts and feelings. You found a more nuanced handle name for your problem that reflected its essence. Now able to relate to it with less fear and more curiosity, you treated that essence as a living spirit, a wisdom stone, and asked for its own perspective on what was needed in your life. In other words, you brought the unconscious into your consciousness, traveling between the spirit worlds like a shaman. Finally, the wisdom stone (the spirit of the dragon itself!) instructed you on a way forward, a small but real step on your hero's path.

Know this: your heart, an expression of the Great Spirit itself, has shown you a safe, workable path forward on that particular issue. *Go this way,* your heart insists. Of all the possible reasonable and logical directions you could take, *this one particular step* will be the best step at this time. Take that step, and you will begin to move free of your dragon forever. Ignore it, and you will continue to suffer and stagnate. But you do have to take the first step before the magic of a new life begins to unfold.

You now have a powerful practice for dragon taming. But our journey does not end in a dark cave of domesticated dragons. We will climb back into the sunlight to learn how to release your condor heart and let it soar in the world.

In the next chapter we will define shamanic power and see how this power flows naturally from a clear vision, as in a traditional vision quest ceremony. You will meet a modern shaman whose ability to harness his creative mind and heart literally changed world culture, and read a case study that shows how shamanic fire talks can be used to access this kind of vision and power. We will introduce the vast world of dreamwork, a classic source of shamanic knowing, assisted by the insights of psychiatrist and psychotherapist Carl Jung. And we will help you anticipate both the joys and the pitfalls involved in living a heart-centered life.

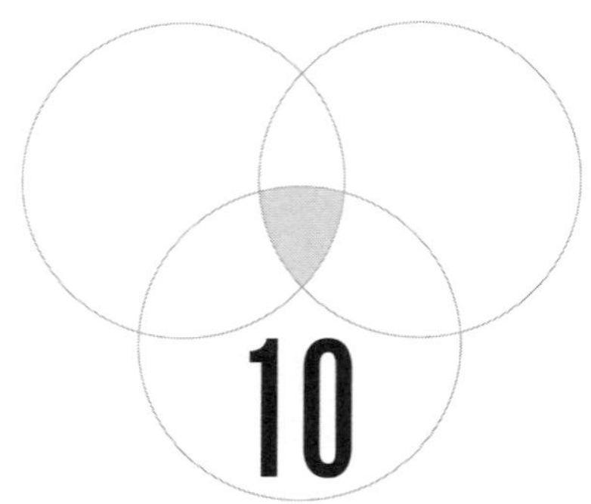

10

Power from the Condor Heart

Pilgrim, pilgrim, pilgrim,
There is no way, there is no way, there is no way.
You make the way, you make the way, you make the way,
By walking, walking, walking.

Peruvian saying

THE POWER OF A VITAL LIFE

It's time for some fresh air and sunlight. Let's hike out of your dragon's cave and climb up to the top of that ridge for a view of the landscape and your life ahead. From this high vantage point, we will explore the meaning and use of shamanic power. Then you will learn several heart-opening practices to help you access and utilize your innate power: shamanic fire-talk counseling sessions; communicating with the characters in your dreams; and a journaling practice of questing for a vision.

Defining Power

The word *power* is important to understand as it relates to the Heart Path. We have mixed feelings about the use of power, which is often perceived to be—and experienced—as power *over* another, as in domination, discrimination, abuse, bullying, or institutional corruption. Religious values such as compassion, forgiveness, meekness, and turning the other cheek are deeply embedded in Christian culture and can seem contrary to the exercise of personal power. In sum, we know what bad power looks like, but we are not always taught to recognize or use good power.

Shamanic power means living a life in alignment with your true nature—your heart or spiritual center. It is not power over others in this world or the spirit world (one definition of sorcery); rather, it is the radiant energy and influence that flows from being naturally yourself without fear.

Power will vary depending on one's unique nature and situation: a salmon is more power filled swimming up a river to spawn than floating in an aquarium. An artistic person will be more power filled creating an art piece than assembling identical components on an assembly line. I am more power filled leading a fire talk or wilderness trip than sitting in a conference room discussing financial reports.

The small backyard cabin I built where I work with clients is filled with artifacts from my life that open my heart and thereby activate my power: photographs, small boyhood toys and treasures, art, stones and souvenirs from my travels, an alpaca wool poncho from the Andes, a *chakapa* leaf rattle from the Amazon, a tumbleweed from the Great Plains, a dried rose from my mother's casket. When you are operating "in your power" in the shamanic sense, you're not flexing your individual power but riding the wave of your gifts in service to your life purpose.*

---

*I recall an interview with the British stage and screen actor Michael Caine in which he described the key to portraying a power-filled person like a Shakespearean king. To paraphrase Caine, he said a real king is calm during a crisis, no yelling, no outbursts, because a real king is the *king:* he does not have to constantly wield power. He is power.

POWER ARISES FROM VISION

In 2009 I had an experience of being power filled during my first wilderness vision quest. I had been in the wilderness for two days and nights, fasting completely from food and water, and I was quite weak but alert. As I watched the sun set from high up on a sand dune, my vision came to me: a deep inner shift and sense that I needed to drastically simplify my life of unsatisfying busyness and too many commitments.*

Here is an excerpt from my journal describing what happened next:

> The changes began immediately. Once I realized what had happened up there on the dune, I slid down the steep bank to the beach, picked up my gear, and marched back to base camp in pitch dark with the energy of ten men. It was really astounding. No food or water for two days, yet I strode through a mile of shoreline surf and then two more miles of deep woods, wide awake and nearly dancing along the black forest paths in the eerie light shaft of my LED headlamp. I was on a mission. I felt pulled forward by a benevolent force toward my new destiny . . .
>
> The surprising cascade of energy and urgency continued . . . Upon return to the mainland I was absolutely on fire to drop every nonessential activity and commitment in my life: committees, volunteer projects, even the public radio stories I enjoyed writing and recording but which were too time consuming. I stayed up late composing resignation e-mails and sending them to all the necessary people.
>
> *This is so easy,* I marveled. *Why didn't I do this before?*
>
> Each time I pushed the e-mail "send" button, releasing another commitment, I felt my shoulders relax another notch, a return of energy, a restoration of integrity, self-respect, and authenticity, and

*The full account of my vision quest can be found on my website at www.greatplainsguide.net, under "Vision Quest" in the menu.

more space opening up in my life. It was like having too many programs running on your slow computer, but as you close each program's window—the computer speeds up! *Can this be?* I wondered. After years of religious imperatives that one should serve, serve, serve, and do for others . . . could it be that the Great Spirit was telling me to do less? I was amazed.

The felt sense of peace and new energy was undeniable. It didn't matter to me what other people would think or say in the days to come. I knew I was on the right track. I had no confusion about this. *What will other people think?* I smiled. *How does that matter?*"

This is shamanic power: The power of knowing who you are inside your own heart with deep certainty. When you combine this inner fire with the heart's ability to create and connect with other people, the mind's power to solve problems, and the body's ability to move in space . . . anything is possible. You step out of the prison that was never there and begin to live the courage of your deepest convictions.

You live *your* life, and no one else's.

Shaman Steve Jobs

Apple founder Steve Jobs was a cultural shapeshifter who saw himself more as an artist and a visionary than a computer engineer. In a 1994 interview he talked about discovering the power to change his own life and the world around him.

> When you grow up, you tend to get told that the world is the way it is and your life is just to live your life inside the world, try not to bash into the walls too much, try to have a nice family, have fun, save a little money. That's a very limited life. Life can be much broader, once you discover one simple fact, and that is that everything around you that you call life was made up by people that were no smarter than you. And you can change it, you can influence it, you can build your own things that other people can use.

> The minute that you understand that you can poke life and actually something will, you know if you push in, something will pop out the other side, that you can change it, you can mold it. That's maybe the most important thing. It's to shake off this erroneous notion that life is there and you're just gonna live in it, versus embrace it, change it, improve it, make your mark upon it. Once you learn that, you'll never be the same again.[1]

Job Number One

As discussed previously but bears mentioning again, some people confuse the Heart Path with being selfish. They remain trapped in stagnant jobs or relationships by a scolding voice in their head that insists others always come first. "My children need me to stay at home," or "My husband wouldn't like it." The people and commitments in our life are important. But they are not more important than your angel mission.

Our number-one responsibility in life is not to meet the needs of our children, partner, aging parents, employer, or church. Our number-one responsibility is to come fully alive as the unique person God created us to be and to live our unique angel mission on the planet. The power to love, heal, forgive, endure, and transform the world does not come from keeping yourself small and uncontroversial. It comes from a mind aligned to the power of the Great Spirit in you, a power that is endless and radiates in all directions. The influence of a vital person vitalizes others. *This* is how we serve. Not under the grim yoke of duty but dancing on the lightness of our joy. As Campbell says, you bring the world alive by bringing yourself alive.

The question facing each of us, then, is not what can we afford, what can we fit into our schedule, or what will others be comfortable with. The question is, How free do you want to be? How free can you stand to be? This face-off between your destiny and your possessions or your social approval rating is a sacred one.

ASSERTING THE HEART'S POWER THROUGH SHAMANIC FIRE TALKS

When people first come to my hermitage, we sit on the floor and they tell me their problems. To be honest, many times I have no idea what the person needs or what we are going to do next. But I do know what my number-one job is: helping the person get clear on his or her heart. So after listening and taking notes for a while, I may say, "Thank you for telling me that. And now we are going to talk about your heart for a while and get to know this 'you' that is seeking a way through this situation."

A client named Laura illustrates this process.

Fire Talk: Laura's Intruder

Laura is a divorced, sixty-two-year-old health-care executive. She came for a fire talk saying she felt unfulfilled, stagnant in her work, and frustrated with the clutter in both her life and large house. But her biggest concern was a frightening "heavy presence" that had begun to visit her during her daily meditation practice. It felt to her like a spirit, and it always approached her from her left side. "It scares me," she said. "I am afraid this spirit wants to move in and control me." A friend had gotten Laura even more upset by telling her it was a demonic spirit that could become violent. Laura began avoiding her meditation time.

I had no idea what Laura's spirit visitor was about. But I did know that every created thing has a spirit. I told Laura we were sitting in a room filled with spirits: the spirits of the land, the spirits of Laura's ancestors, our various helper spirits, and the spirits of the four elements in and around us. We talked about this and my belief that these spirits are not "out to get us." There can be unhappy spirits and spirits that are lost and have moved into our homes like squatters after a trauma or death. But if a strange person shows up in your front yard, you don't have to shoot her *first*. You can say, "Excuse me, are you lost?" You can drop the ego assumption that the intruding spirit wants to ruin your life, and then you can relax a bit, put on your detective's hat, and become curious about the thing. This shifts the dynamics from a futile attempt to suppress, ignore, or avoid the spirit. Doing so takes a calm, grounded presence (mindfulness).

To help Laura get more clarity about the nature of her unwelcome visitor, I had her lay out each of her concerns with stones (as we did earlier in the book). Although the heavy presence was chief on her mind, it turned out she had many other big burdens: her homeless alcoholic son, some family business issues, the stagnant job, her relationship with her partner, and her uncertain future. Laura broke down the heavy presence into four main aspects and named the crux of it all as "the opportunity to turn fear into love." This was an unexpected statement of potential power that came from *her,* not me.

I then had Laura put down a new stone—her wisdom stone—to represent that new opportunity. She then asked the wisdom stone directly what it needed in order to stop interrupting her meditation time. After some reflection Laura looked up and said, "This is what it wants me to get clearer on: What am I really needing at this point in my life?"

"Ah," I said. "So the question is not only about who this meddling spirit is, it's about you. Who are *you,* at this crossroads in your life?" Laura nodded in agreement, and I could tell this new question was just as scary for her as the "intruding spirit." I wondered aloud if the intruding spirit was, in fact, the spirit of her own uncertainty about her life ahead. Laura found this intriguing, and it made more sense to her than her friend's anxious belief in a demonic spirit out to get her.

Based on this information from the spirit, we created the following two-pronged plan. First, to deal with the meddling spirit, when Laura sat down to meditate she would expect the heavy presence to come. She would wait for it with her journal, pen, and questions and turn the interruption into an interview, firmly asserting her power by asking the spirit what was going on. Second, because her meditation time was being disrupted, she would employ her other enjoyable self-care options of biking, yoga, massage, and walking around a nearby lake. With this alternative self-care plan in place, Laura would then focus more intentionally on the big life issues she was facing: retirement, selling her home, and the new opportunities ahead.

"I have a hunch your spirit visitor may become scarce as you move forward on your life plans," I told Laura. She looked visibly relieved to have an assertive self-protection and self-care plan in place and left the session with a smile on her face.

A few days later Laura e-mailed me to say, "My next meditation time was not scary. The spirit did show up, but it didn't bother me. It wasn't much help with answers, but I am doing well, continue to feel lighter, and have definitely felt a shift within myself. I had some vivid dreams about my dad; he wanted me to touch his hand and know he was there. It is wonderful to have my meditation time back." Months later Laura e-mailed me to say she had resigned from her job and was planning to sell her home, move out West to be closer to her son, and seek part-time employment there. The heavy presence was nearly gone.

Laura used her heart as an ally and guide in this process. She had come in frightened and frustrated, unable to figure out the "heavy presence" with her mind alone. By shifting her attention to the deeper needs and invitations of her heart (safety and self-care during a major life change), Laura did three powerful things: she addressed the unwelcome spirit, navigated her way forward, and shifted from a victim role to an assertive shamanic role as shapeshifter of her own life—all without medication, months of therapy, or an unnecessary battle with "demonic spirits."

This case raises the issue of "spiritual emergencies," unusual states of mind that traditional psychiatry treats as mental illness but are actually crises of personal transformation. Paranormal or out-of-body experiences, telepathy, and kundalini awakenings, for instance, do not necessarily precipitate a plunge into insanity.[2] When supported rather than suppressed, these states can be healing and have very positive effects.

I am not minimizing the seriousness or suffering of real mental illnesses such as schizophrenia, bipolar disorder, or borderline personality disorder. The point is that there can be ways other than the use of medication or psychotherapy to respond to spiritual emergencies. The best healers select the least invasive medicine with the most impact. And this includes (for shamanic practitioners) the humility of knowing when a situation needs to be referred to a psychologist or psychiatrist.

ALIGN YOUR LIFE TO YOUR HEART, NOT TO A SOCIAL ROLE

After a client gets clarity on the needs of her heart, we can return to the original problem she came in with, which by then has often become less of an issue (like Laura's meddling spirit above). What should he "do" about his original problem now? Choose the path, relationship, job, or action that most closely supports *who he is*. The medicine is to align one's life to one's heart, not the other way around. Here is where we invite the analytical mind (Mr. Spock) back into the process as first officer to the heart captain (Captain Kirk). *The heart sets the course forward, and the mind makes it so* with its power to plan, enact, and protect the progress.

You're Ruining My Life! Special Challenges on the Path

A special problem can seem to arise when the thing your heart seems to desire most seems unavailable or blocked by someone else. (Recall the woman in chapter 9 who wanted another baby when her husband did not.) This is an indication that you have not yet penetrated to the deepest level of your heart to get clarity on the core metaphor or archetype for your life.

The Great Spirit will not invite an acorn to become a mallard duck and leave the acorn feeling miserable with unfulfilled desires to fly. The Great Spirit invites the acorn to be an oak, the strongest, grandest thing it can be.

I have a client, Audrey, who is a former Roman Catholic sister, now working as a lay chaplain in nursing home ministry. She has remained single and is a gifted chaplain and spiritual guide. "But I really feel called to the Catholic priesthood," she laments. This thought then triggers a landslide of anger and resentment that she cannot be ordained in the church, which she projects on the Catholic priest she works with. But Audrey's main problem is not her ordained colleague, or the male-dominated hierarchy of the church that she rails against. Her main problem is thinking that a clerical role will be her ultimate fulfillment, rather than living out the deeper metaphor for *who she is.*

To put it bluntly, the Great Spirit doesn't care whether Audrey is a priest, painter, pilot, or paramedic. What the Great Spirit cares about is whether she is manifesting *Audreyness,* the fullest expression of her soul in the world. So Audrey and I have worked hard together to uncover the deeper rivers of passion, joy, and purpose that bring her alive: her love for God, her joy in working with the poor, her need for strong spiritual community, her gifts of sharing her faith and the gospel. True, these gifts could find convenient expression in the religious role of a Catholic priest. But the deepest metaphor she has come to about her heart—"a lover of God" and "an oasis for others"—doesn't need a cleric's collar or a bishop's ordination to be released into the world. Audrey doesn't need to be *a* priest; she needs to be priestess and oasis. *That* is Audrey's path and her heroine's journey: doing the hard work to discover how she is to fully be priestess and oasis in the world, ordained or not. And no one can stop her from that journey except Audrey herself.

This is hard work, friends. Living a heart-centered life and declining the seduction of preexisting social roles dictated by convention, prestige, or peer approval is a radical act of social disobedience. Finding your way usually means *creating* your way—cutting your own path through the uncut wilderness. Recall the Peruvian saying that begins this chapter: "Pilgrim . . . There is no way . . . You make the way . . . By walking, walking, walking."

This is the toll we must pay the gatekeeper of joy, to become a psychologically individuated and spiritually mature person and to be a true shapeshifter of your life, an artist of the soul. Although this is hard, it is not impossible. And what alternative is there really? A life of stagnation where you feel like you're a victim? You have nothing to lose by living toward the dream. As famed NHL ice hockey champion Wayne Gretzky says, "You miss 100 percent of the shots you never take."

When I was growing up on the prairie of southeastern Minnesota, I dreamed of one day living in the mountains (I'd never seen any) and pictured my adult self in an idyllic cabin on a creek in Colorado. Where did I end up? In an inner city neighborhood of a struggling postindustrial city in Indiana! But in the process of transforming my weedy backyard lot surrounded by a chain link fence into a landscaped sanctuary with a cedar privacy fence, pond, little hermitage cabin, fruit trees, flowers, birdfeeders, and honeybees, I discovered I didn't really need a mountain cabin by a creek (a particular location). I needed solitude, beauty, and nature. These were my deeper soul needs, not several acres of expensive Colorado real estate. And I created them and "made a way" in the last place you'd expect to find them. Now my family, neighbors, visitors, clients, abundant animals and birds enjoy this same little paradise I created in the middle of the inner-city neighborhood.

If you feel stuck because you are not living the life you're meant to be living, or because your current job or home makes you unhappy, or you are squelching your own desires on behalf of others (the mother who says, "I just want my children to be happy"), I invite you to turn now to the Thirty-Three Questions exercise (in appendix 1). Working through this exercise will help you get clear on who you are at your deepest core and what direction your Core Self is inviting you to move.

USING DREAMS TO LISTEN TO YOUR HEART

Traditional cultures all placed great value in dreams. The Bible is full of characters whose dreams played a key role in their decisions and understanding of God's action in the world. Carl Jung believed dreams are deep transpersonal vessels conveying shared experiences of meaning. Like a shaman entering the spirit world, Jung learned to penetrate his own dreams and actively engage with key images and feelings there for learning, personal growth, and healing.

You can too. The following process for opening up a dream will teach you to unlock the meaning of your dreams like opening the lid of a great treasure chest.

Before we proceed, it is important to understand several key points about working with dreams, which will help you stay on track and get the most out of them. First, a dream is an open, dynamic, living thing that will speak to you on the level of *feeling*. It is not a dead specimen to be pinned down and dissected analytically on the psychological lab bench. Thus we are *opening up* dreams, not pinning them down with one particular interpretation. In working with your dreams, you will explore them by utilizing your felt sense of the imagery and feelings, not by utilizing your intellect. Let go of the notion that there is one meaning to be extracted from a dream. A dream can continue to unfold its meaning for you long after the night you had the dream.

Second, do not assume that the meanings of your dream images are the same as in your waking life—that a dream featuring your old girlfriend Julie is "about" her. The imagery is just the container, the vehicle that carries deeper associations for your nonverbal, unconscious self. To bring this nonverbal information into your conscious awareness, your psyche casts about looking for an image in your experience that captures the essence of what it is trying to tell you. So in working the dream, you will be tracking the *feelings* you associate with and around Julie.

Third, do not assume that the meaning of your dream images are the same as anyone else's—that your dream featuring a snake has anything to do with the snake in your sister's dream. Your inner dream master selected "snake" to hold the essence of the dream meaning for you. Your sister may have entirely different associations with snake.

Finally, do not trust the ego to be a trustworthy guide, for you may often hear that "eww" voice that finds some dream imagery to be distasteful or repulsive. Trust instead the dream master that produced the dream for you as a form of deep intelligence and communication.

Explore the "eww" like any other feeling, and you will be surprised.

EXERCISE

❁ Opening Up a Dream

Here is one approach for opening up a dream.* You are going to record your dreams using a journal or a recording device or the voice-recorder function of your smartphone and then work to get a felt sense of the dream.

Step 1: The Overall Feel of the Dream

1. Keep a journal or smartphone by your bed so you can use it as soon as you wake up. Upon waking from a dream, immediately write down or dictate the dream imagery and all associated feelings. If you don't have time, capturing a few key words or images will help hold the dream in working memory long enough to recall and work with it later on.
2. Stepping back from the dream details for a moment, ask yourself: What is the main thing that struck me about this dream? Write that down.
3. Give your dream a title: "Jeff meets his old girlfriend in the high school gym."
4. Get a felt sense of the dream as a whole and then write down the crux or luminous center of this dream: "Longing for reconnection . . . a soul mate and friend."

Step 2: The Details of the Dream

1. Describe (write down) your whole dream and its images as concretely or poetically as possible. Include all images, even the frightening or disturbing ones.
2. Underline the key or "thick" words you have written: those words that seem to have particular warmth, depth, energy, pull, or power for you.

---

*Much of this approach comes from my first shamanic teacher and Jungian scholar C. Michael Smith.

Step 3: Tracking the Feeling Associations of the Dream

1. Looking at each of your underlined words, consider what associations you have with that image or feeling. Write those down on a new page.
2. Consider the last few days and weeks of your daily life. Ask yourself, "What in my recent life feels like that metaphorically?" Write that down.
3. Using these associations as guides, piece together a few sentences or paragraphs that make sense for you at this time in your life.

Step 4: Honoring the Dream Invitation

1. What feels invigorating, intriguing, or suggestive about this dream for your life ahead? We are seeking the invitation at the heart of your dream for you: some new attitude, action, or way of being in your life. Although the content of our dreams can vary dramatically the purpose of our dreams is always the same: healing, acknowledging, growing, liberating, full living, wholeness, and completion.
2. What is one small way you could honor this invitation of your dream or move forward along the path suggested by it?

CREATING YOUR OWN RED BOOK OF DREAMS

In 1913 C. G. Jung began recording his dreams and visions in a series of personal journals. This was the same year as Jung's difficult break with his mentor and friend Sigmund Freud, a split that triggered a long period of struggle and introspection that, at times, bordered on psychosis. After the outbreak of World War I, Jung realized his visionary experiences were entwined with the greater cultural moment around him, and he began adding commentary and detailed full-color illustrations to his journals. The result is a massive, red, leather-bound volume he titled *Liber Novus* (Book of the New), which was published after his death under its popular title *The Red Book*.[3]

Jung considered those early years of struggle, journaling, and visions "my most difficult experiment."

> The years . . . when I pursued the inner images were the most important time of my life. Everything else is to be derived from this. My entire life consisted in elaborating what had burst forth from the unconscious and flooded me like an enigmatic stream and threatened to break me. That was the stuff and material for more than only one life. Everything (I wrote) later was merely the outer classification, scientific elaboration, and the integration into life. But the numinous beginning, which contained everything, was then.[4]

You can create your own Red Book of your dreams and visions and illustrate and comment upon them over time just as Jung did. Purchase a quality journal or artists' sketchpad and use pen, colors, paint, markers, or collage to illustrate key images and insights. This is not just to record the dreams in a collection but also to allow them to remain active as a source of revelation to you.

I have been amazed how vision imagery from my early shamanic breathwork sessions continues to simmer and breathe as dynamic symbols for my evolving life and work. For example, a central lighthouse motif at first helped me with a personal understanding of my Core Self and spiritual center. But that same image has turned out to be a perfect fit for the counseling and public speaking work I do. "Helping people find their way, in the dark, using all my powers," is the personal mission statement I arrived at using the Questing for a Vision exercise below.

EXERCISE

❋ Questing for a Vision: The Journaling Version

A vision quest is a sacred ceremony used by some Amerindian societies for clarifying a sense of vision and purpose for one's life. Traditionally done alone in a wilderness setting, it involved several days of fasting from food and water while opening one's heart to the Great Force of Life and to Mother Earth. It was understood that clarity on one's spiritual center was needed early in life before attempting to answer secondary questions such as: "Should I marry this person?" "Should I move?" "What role should I seek?"

In the indigenous lachak path of the Central Andes this involved working in the three *pachas* of the Andean shamanic cosmology: the physical realm of body and Earth (*kaypacha*), the interior/unconscious/underworld realm (*ukupacha*), and the realm of the great force of life, of spirit (*hanaqpacha*).

Not everyone is able to make a traditional wilderness quest, so I offer an intensive journaling version I call the Written Quest (see appendix 1).* In addition to being a good alternative for those who cannot do a wilderness quest, it is helpful for any individual who wants to start working on clarifying the purpose of his or her life.

The journaling quest will help you find your place in three arenas of life: your geographical place, your place in the life cycle, and your place in the human community. Like the wilderness version, the written quest involves opening your heart to Mother Earth and to the human community. You explore within yourself while remaining firmly grounded in physical space and time. I completed the written quest during the winter following my 2009 (wilderness) vision quest, and it provided much additional clarity on both my personal life and my public mission, which I now call the Great Plains Guide Company, "Spiritual Outfitter for Life's Adventure."

WHAT HAPPENS WHEN YOU BEGIN TO CHANGE YOUR LIFE

Doing the detailed inner work in this book and appendices will open your heart and increase your power, like a shamanic soul retrieval. As you recover this vital energy, you will find yourself restless for change

*The Written Quest was developed by the Taoist teacher and focusing trainer Kye Nelson and refined by C. Michael Smith.

and less content living out of alignment with your center. You will find it harder to be with others who are resigned to stagnation, complaining, and self-victimization. Your restlessness is a positive shift, not to be confused with unhappiness or doing something wrong. It is the same restlessness experienced by a pregnant woman in her final days before childbirth, impatient to release the new life inside her. It is the urgency of the artist with an image in his heart, burning to be transferred onto canvas or clay. It is the discontent of a Gandhi, Mother Theresa, or Martin Luther King Jr., who has a dream for social change. For each of these people, a tipping point occurred where life could no longer remain the same. Action had to be taken.

What happens when you start making actual changes and moving forward in your life? *Resistance.* Expect it, it will come. You will experience resistance from other people in the form of confusion, questions, concerns, and even criticism. If they are living fear-based lives, your love-based changes will threaten their own life choices and beliefs. You may receive warnings about your future or accusations that you are becoming selfish, detached, or even ungodly.

Even in publishing this book, I faced resistance from people I respected. Since my primary purpose was to have an immediate resource for clients and workshop audiences, I planned to self-publish the book first, then seek a traditional publisher for the long term. But two publishing professionals and one of the top-selling authors in the field of shamanism strongly recommended against this. "Be patient," they said to me. "Traditional publishers will not consider a book that has been self-published." "There's no market or money in self-publishing." I decided to use the principles in this book for guidance and did a shamanic journey to meet with the spirit of this book itself to see what it wanted. The book came to me as a multicolored, book-sized butterfly sitting on a stone in the jungle, slowly opening and closing its "wings" (the two covers of the book). I explained my dilemma to the book spirit, which listened, and then promptly took off in flight. The message was unmistakable: *I want to fly. Now.*

I self-published this book. When it unexpectedly became Amazon .com's "#1 hot new release" in its category two weeks later, I took a screen shot of this status from the book's Amazon.com page and sent it to the one publisher I had submitted the manuscript to but had not heard back from. Two days later, I had a publishing offer. The first book-advance check I received from Inner Traditions/Bear & Company covered the entire cost I had incurred in producing the self-published version and I earned thousands more in the interim months from the online sales of my self-published book. My spirit guides had showed me how to do what some experts said was impossible. All I had to do was listen, and honor their invitations.

Although the outer resistance to your heart's path is difficult, it's the inner resistance that can be most daunting. You are leaving the secure harbor of convention and habit in your life and sailing away from shore, out into the wide-open sea of possibility. Like a true explorer, at some point you will realize that you can no longer see your way back to shore. And at a further point you'll realize you could not get back to shore even if you wanted to; your only choice now is to keep moving forward. This is a sobering moment. This is no game.

During this phase of your journey, you may feel very alone at times. Friends who were not ready for a fuller life have stayed behind, and other brave visionaries who set sail before you are out living in exotic new lands and hidden from view. This is the *voyage* stage of your journey, the odyssey known to all spiritual sojourners and artists. The medieval mystics called it "the dark night of the soul." The author Stephen King called it (writing a novel) "like crossing the Atlantic alone in a bathtub." There's no glamor about it. Just hard work, day after day, rowing forward as you strive to keep to your compass heading while waves and wind hit you from all directions.

But magically, you will be provided for. Each day you find what you need for that day in order to keep moving forward: the sun warming your face, rainwater to drink, fish that occasionally leap into the boat, helping tides, tailwinds, even dolphins or whales for company.

Each day your rowing muscles become stronger and your heart grows in strength and conviction. You will encounter other seafarers new and old, searching and experienced. *You are living.* Moving forward.

At some point you will realize the sea journey itself has become the life, the main thing. You have become a sea journeyer and you are living that life, by sailing, sailing, sailing.

IF YOU WANT TO CHANGE YOUR LIFE, YOU HAVE TO CHANGE YOUR LIFE

A few times in my life I have found myself standing in the doorway of a long-sought opportunity, and from that doorway I had an unobstructed path to the very life I was sure I wanted to live. Yet in those moments I hesitated. The most recent example of this was in 2013, after my mother died. For years I had wanted to commit to serious writing time but had dismissed the desire as nonessential and unaffordable. It takes me hundreds of hours to turn out a good short piece of writing (not to mention an entire book), hours that I'm not seeing paying clients or leading workshops. And much of the time I did have available had been focused on caring for my mother, who was declining with Parkinson's disease.

After my mom died, I discovered she had left me an unexpected gift. She had quietly invested her nurse's wages in mutual funds over the years, and after all of her estate bills were paid off, I realized I had enough of an inheritance left over to actually cut back my client load for a while. I could devote half a day to writing and was free (for several months at least) to do what I'd said I'd wanted to do since college. Write! All systems were go, and I could do exactly what I always urge my clients to do: "Follow your bliss!"

And yet I hesitated.

It finally dawned on me what was going on. If I was going to be a writer, I could no longer be a man who *wanted* to be a writer. My ego self has a strong attachment to envy and longing for things I cannot have, and the "story of Jeff" included "the man who longs to write." I had a strong investment in melancholy that my ego did not want to lose! Good grief.*

Even after realizing this, I continued to self-sabotage my new opportunity. I did this by creating distractions from writing. For several weeks I found projects that interrupted my writing progress: shoveling snow, cleaning the refrigerator, repairing a lamp. "I finally have some time," I told myself. "Now I can get to that broken lamp." I was doing useful things, but I was not writing. And the heart doesn't give a damn about clean refrigerators or electric lamps.

I realized what I was doing and began a new ritual to get me back on track. When my feet hit the floor in the morning, I walked directly outdoors, got my bare feet on Earth, and shifted my consciousness to nature mode by using whatever was available: sun, rain, wind, snow, bird song, blowing leaves. I lit some dried sage and let the pungent aroma take me back to my vision quest and shamanic community ceremonies. Then I went directly to my writing nook, turned on my laptop, and began to write. No shower, no breakfast, no morning newspaper, no checking e-mails or Facebook, no distractions. (Just coffee.) And it worked. As soon as I shifted into my creative mode, the writing spirit immediately had me. Everything else fell away, and hours would pass before I realized my rear was sore and my stomach was growling for food. By then I had many words on the page and could take a break.

This kind of joy and energy from finding your path also makes it more obvious (and unpleasant) when you stray off that path and lose your power. For example, when I shifted my attention from the creative process of writing this book to the equally necessary task of *selling* it

---

*I learned much of this about myself years ago while studying and later teaching the Enneagram, a personality-typing system of nine interconnected personality types. The origins of the Enneagram are disputed; many believe it to be rooted in early Christian or Sufi mysticism.

(i.e. publishing, distributing, and marketing) my energies completely fell off. Even though I was closer to my goal than ever I found myself resistant, uninspired, and slogging through the technical matters of manuscript file formatting, optimizing search term keywords, puzzling over copyright issues and distribution channels, and erecting a social media platform. Only months later with those tasks behind me and the book selling well was I was able to turn my attention back to a new creative task, writing a long-dreamed-of first novel. Then bingo, the missing energy and focus returned. I was back on the beam of my power, purpose, and medicine.

In this chapter you have learned the difference between your job or social role and your Core Self. You have learned how to break open your dreams, create your own Red Book, find your core of aliveness, and quest for a vision.

You now have the basic tools to find, empower, and release the great condor of your heart. You can explore its vision and longings, nurture and protect its growth and talents, and soar high up and out of the dark valley of the dragons.

With your heart thus released, you are now ready to learn the core practice of traditional shamanism, the *shamanic journey* into the spirit world. Everything in this book has led to this point: the doorway to the Heart of Everything That Is. Learning the art of shamanic journeying will open a whole new realm and resource for healing, vision, inner guidance, and life navigation for you.

In the next chapter we will define what a shamanic journey is and distinguish it from other forms of spiritual and energetic healing. You will learn the practical uses for shamanic journeying and some of the methods used around the world for achieving the altered state of consciousness necessary to journey in the spirit world. We will then lead you on an introductory guided shamanic journey using a script to help you stay on track during the experience, followed by another guided journey to help you establish your shamanic departure station in the spirit world. This will be your jumping-off point for later unguided journeys of your own design.

Ready to jump off into the spirit world? Let's step through that shaman's doorway now!

Hang on!

PART IV

◎ ◎ ◎

The Shamanic Journey and Return

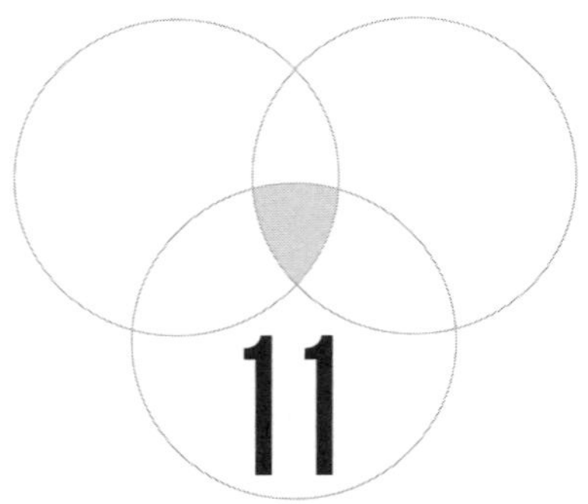

11

The Guided Shamanic Journey

In my thirty years of teaching shamanism around the world I have taught over ten thousand people how to do shamanic journeys. I have never met a person who could not journey. However, I have met many people who tried journeying many times before they felt that something was happening.

Sandra Ingerman

SHAMANIC JOURNEYING

Practical Help for Real Life

The shamanic journey is the central defining practice of shamanism and distinguishes the shaman from other spiritual and energy healers. Journeying is used for advanced healing work such as soul retrieval and psychopomp (assisting the dying and deceased), as well as for ordinary day-to-day needs.

To illustrate the practical applications of shamanic journeying, here are some of the personal needs I have addressed with journeys:

- Deciding whether to leave my hospital career to pursue private practice
- Receiving assistance in creating a university course (story in chapter 2)
- Understanding clients' core problems and needs
- Finding a path to reconciliation with my sister
- Understanding the nature of a newly diagnosed leg tumor
- Seeking the cause of a chronic eye twitch
- Responding to a marriage conflict
- Receiving help in interpreting a powerful dream
- Receiving vision and energy to move forward with writing projects
- Guidance in making difficult end-of-life decisions for my mother
- Gleaning insight into old emotional patterns related to childhood bullying
- Assistance in managing changes in income and finances
- Reconnecting with my extended family
- Obtaining help in articulating my business mission and focus
- Interviewing characters from a nighttime dream
- Reconnecting with my grandfather, A. G. Nixa, who died when I was four

Journeying to seek information (divination journeys) is but one function of the shaman in his or her community. In her book *Shamanic Journeying: A Beginner's Guide,* Sandra Ingerman recommends that people journey for other purposes as well, such as addressing the spiritual dimension of illness, dream interpretation, journeys to connect with the natural world, and journeys for creating ceremonies.[1] You can journey alone or in groups with others, sharing experiences afterward for an integrated approach in addressing larger, global issues such as climate change.

Shifting Consciousness to Soul and Spirit World

Every human society has beliefs and practices to help humans connect with the spirit world, the sacred nonordinary realm that transcends ordinary reality and the natural world. The spirit world is, by definition, the world inhabited by spirits; it goes by many names and just as many understandings of its nature, purpose, and how one is to "get there."

Many world religious beliefs and spiritual practices are shared with shamanism. These include the singing of sacred songs, retelling (or rereading) stories of the founding heroes, lighting of a sacred fire or candles, water blessings, the burning of incense or herbs, calling out or praying to the divine and to ancestors and saints, questing for a spiritual vision, worship ceremonies, specialized priest or healer roles, seasonal celebrations, and life-stage rituals or sacraments at birth, puberty, marriage, and/or death. Mystical traditions like shamanism emphasize direct experience of the Absolute, the Infinite, or God as contrasted with a mediated experience through a priest, sacraments, or a holy book, or through theological reflection or philosophy.

Various methods are used in shamanic cultures to access the spirit world by altering ordinary consciousness. These can include drumming or rattling, ecstatic dance, chanting, fasting, sweat lodge ceremonies, evocative music (like Sacred Breathwork), and entheogenic plant medicine. These different practices all are used to the same purpose by the shamanic practitioner to capture and hold conscious attention long enough to allow for a shift in perception and access to transpersonal states. The power of the shamanic state of consciousness lies not only in the realm the journeyer is going to but in what it allows the journeyer to separate from: limited ego consciousness and the dream of the mind, the mitote of distracted, fear-based modes of thinking (as discussed earlier).

The Purpose of Shamanic Journeying

First and foremost, the shaman is a healer. People come to a shamanic practitioner because something is wrong: physically, emotionally, or spiritually. Emotional problems may include issues with moods or relationships. Spiritual problems may include issues with a lack of vital energy or life purpose. Thus does the shaman enter a shamanic state of consciousness with the specific intent of gathering information to relieve suffering and/or provide guidance. The information acquired during the interaction with spirit guides, power animals, ancestors, and lost souls allows for a rebalancing in four key relationships: with one's own soul, between self and others, between human beings and nature, and between created beings and the spirit world.

The focus of any particular shamanic journey depends on the needs of the situation. The shaman may travel to the past to consult with her own ancestors for the healing of generational wounds. She may visit the future by following the momentum lines of her present life forward to gain insight and to change the present course.[2] The shaman is like a skilled database administrator, where the database is the entire living realm of transpersonal intelligence and information, the akashic field that is the substance of the cosmos. The term *akashic field* was coined by Hungarian philosopher of science Ervin Laszlo in his book *Science and the Akashic Field: An Integral Theory of Everything.*[3] Laszlo posits the *akasha* (a Sanskrit word meaning "ether" or "space") as a cosmic field of information that forms the substance of the universe itself, a quantum vacuum of fundamental energy and information that informs not just the current universe but all universes past and present collectively known as the metaverse. The akashic record is a permanent compendium of the life experiences and reactions of every human and animal being since time began.

SERIOUS BUSINESS

The shamanic journey is very focused and workmanlike. The practitioner may prepare beforehand with fasting or prayer and by interviewing the client and calling in power animals and spirit guides. Then the shaman begins a power dance or song, and when she feels fully connected with her power, she will begin the journey in whatever manner she prefers—drumming, rattling, and so on. The shaman calls out to her spirit guides, states her intent for the journey, and then the journey unfolds. She journeys rapidly and efficiently, finding or being led to the location, characters, or information in the spirit world that she is meant to work with.

Once the shaman has acquired what was sought, she thanks her power animals and guides for the help proffered, perhaps leaving a gift for them before returning to ordinary consciousness. This whole process can be accomplished in just a few minutes or take half an hour or more.

The point here is that the shamanic practitioner is "on the clock" during the journey, and works as purposefully as any carpenter, surgeon, or laborer. The shamanic journey is not a game. Instead, the shaman is engaged in a sacred practice, not touring the spirit world for an entertaining out-of-body experience. In fact, "the shaman is fully in her body during the journey," says Sandra Ingerman. "You bring your body with you into the spirit world."[4]

Achieving this level of skill takes focus, repetitive practice, and good coaching. When I met with my first teacher, he would often ask, "Have you been journeying?" He was making it clear that serious shamanic work such as soul retrieval for others was not to be attempted without years of experience and a certain level of skill in journeying. I found this to be true when I began doing soul extraction and soul retrieval work later on in my practice. Journeying alone for my own purposes, the experiences went well and I got rather confident in my journeying skills. But the first few times I had a client lying next to me awaiting a return of his soul(!), I felt very self-conscious and distracted and struggled to keep my focus during the journey. The problem was a combination of performance anxiety and my ego interference. I was forgetting that "I" am not doing the important work during a shamanic journey. Rather, my helper spirits are doing the work.

GUIDED AND UNGUIDED SHAMANIC JOURNEYS

Anyone can successfully experience a shamanic journey. Although some people take to journeying quite quickly, many of us require practice for our journeys to become consistent and focused. The difficulties usually relate to our conscious mind overthinking or holding preconceptions of what the journey should look like.

For this reason, it can be helpful to learn by beginning with a structured or guided journey rather than an unstructured one. A guided journey is a script that is read aloud by someone else. Or it has been prerecorded so that you may listen to it alone. The script leads you step by step through the journey's imagery and makes it easier to follow the journey's story and intent. The advantages of the guided journey are the same as using training wheels on a bicycle: you receive an immediate experience of riding. The disadvantages are also like training wheels, in that limits are placed on mobility and user control.

An unguided journey begins with setting a clear intent ("I am asking my spirit guide how to respond to the Seattle job offer") but then detaching from desired outcomes and allowing your guides to lead you through the whole process. An unguided journey unfolds spontaneously within the guidelines of your intention for that journey.

In the guided journey, you are told much of what you are to see and do.

Many books on shamanism provide instructions on undertaking shamanic journeys, but the instructions prove to not be very useful in that they tend to function as general prompts for the first-time journeyer. ("Then, pass through your transitional tunnel, go through the light portal ahead and find yourself in the spirit world. Explore this area, then look around for a power animal and ask its name.")

This approach can leave the new journeyer completely adrift or stuck at the "pass through the tunnel" stage. Even with another person drumming and giving clear instructions, beginners can have difficulty with their journey experiences. They may give up, thinking, *This is too hard,* or *I don't have the talent to do this work.*

The real fact of the matter is, however, that anyone can journey. So we will begin your training with a whole chapter here devoted to guided journeys.

In the exercises to come, you will see a fair amount of repetition at the beginning of each journey. This repetition is deliberate and important in carving out a familiar and predictable path into nonordinary consciousness. (Things will get unpredictable enough once you are in there!) Eventually you will be able to shift consciousness easily and enter the journey world without so many preliminaries.

You may listen to audio track 1, Guided Skeletization Journey, in conjunction with the following exercise.

EXERCISE

☼ A Guided Skeletization Journey

What follows is a script for the guided skeletization journey. If you have online access to the accompanying audio track for this journey, you can simply listen to the author's narration of the journey on the audio track (see How to Use the Audio Tracks Accompanying This Book on page 258 for the online link). If you do not have online access you can have someone read the script aloud to you.

I encourage you to enter into this journey exercise as intended, not just skim through the script below for information to see what it's about, as if reading a cooking recipe without working in a kitchen. The spirit world can *not* be accessed with the intellect—that is to say, on the level of information or reason alone. If you want to comprehend and experience the shamanic spirit world, you must enter it, not read about entering it.

If somebody is reading the script aloud for you, it should be read slowly and purposefully to allow you (the journeyer) to follow easily through the imagery without feeling rushed. There should be a natural, unhurried, strolling-the-park pace in the reading of these guided journeys. No drumming is necessary during this first guided journey. As noted throughout this book it is important to drop the reins of conscious thinking during the journey and allow whatever imagery, feelings, or intuitions that arise to come. The actual imagery here is not that important. It is only a story structure to help shift conscious awareness. The more important thing is feeling your way through the journey. So if the narration instructs you to "imagine going down a tunnel" and instead you find yourself moving down an escalator or ladder, go with that. The main thing is to feel yourself going down, rather than the means of getting there.

This journey will involve a classic motif in shamanic initiation known as "dismemberment." Common in Inuit, Siberian, Australian, and South American shamanism, the initiate experiences being physically ripped apart by a large animal or spirit. The journeyer's scattered body parts are purified of illness or self-limitation and then reassembled with new powers of strength and spiritual vision (e.g., the eyeballs are reversed so the initiate can "see on the inside"). This body- and ego-dissolving experience is important to help us move beyond the perceptual limits of our conscious mind. I learned the gentler *skeletization* journey below as an apprentice, and we will use this same journey here to help you disconnect from ordinary consciousness and experience yourself as pure spirit or soul.*

To prepare for this journey, locate track 1 of the accompanying audio tracks or arrange to have someone read aloud the entire script below (in italics).

When you are ready to undertake the journey, ensure that you won't be distracted by cell phones, pets, or other people. Lie down in a comfortable position and cover your eyes to allow for complete darkness. (Even dim light stimulates ordinary waking consciousness in most people.) Begin by taking several deep breaths, drawing your attention to your physical body and your breathing. Then begin to listen to this script:

> *Imagine you are walking a wooded path at twilight. The stars are all above you, a full moon is rising, and you can easily see the path ahead of you. Your senses seem very alert tonight, magnified in power. You are surrounded by the pulsing sound of crickets. See the wind moving*

---

*From a guided journey created by C. Michael Smith and used at Crows Nest Center for Shamanic Studies.

through the swaying branches above and feel the breeze on your face. With your nose you smell the earthiness of the soil, damp wood, and moss. Your gaze notes every tiny insect crawling through the maze of delicate flowers and decaying leaves on the woodland floor. Off in the forest, you hear the hoot of an owl. Feel the aliveness of this whole scene all around you, above you and under your feet. . . . [Pause.]

As you walk along, the path emerges from the woods at the edge of a small, beautiful lake. The surface is calm, shining with pale light from the moon above, and radiates a luminescent turquoise from deep within. Wade into the water, which is warm, welcoming, and crystal clear. You dive in and swim down, down, to the center of the lake, where you find a hole in the bottom. It's a tunnel. Swim down through the tunnel, which levels off. You swim easily, breathing magically, and moving through underwater grasses and small schools of darting fish. Then the tunnel turns upward, and you swim up until you break the surface. You find that you are in a small underground cavern. Swim over to a ledge and climb up there. In the luminescent, flickering light from the water, you can see the cavern walls and ceiling all around you. Take a moment to look all around you. . . . [Pause.]

As you sit on the ledge you sense the presence of a friendly, positive energy in the cavern. This is the presence of your spirit guide: your ally and helper. You may sense the presence of other helper spirits. As your eyes adjust, you may see them as luminescent points of light or sense them as energies that twinkle and float about like fireflies. The spirit helpers come over to you, and before you know what is happening, they painlessly split your skin from your head down to your toes and slide it off of your body in one big piece. They carry the whole skin away limp and lifeless, like a pair of heavy coveralls, and set it on a flat rock. Next, the spirit helpers return and peel off each of your muscles: the big muscles of your arms, legs, back, and chest, then the smaller muscles of your neck and hands, feet and toes. They take each of these muscles and lay them down on the rock as well.

Next, the spirit helpers come and remove all your internal organs, one by one: your intestines, stomach, liver, and kidneys. They lift out your heart and lungs, attached together. They carefully pop out each of your eyeballs from their sockets—Pop! Pop!—and set them down at the side. Surprisingly, you realize you can still see and perceive somehow, without your eyeballs. You are fully aware of what is going on. Finally, the spirit helpers come and lift off the top of your skull, reaching in and lifting out your whole brain with its spinal cord still attached, dangling down like a long wet tail.

You are just bones now, a complete skeleton. You touch your dry leg bones with your skeleton hand and hear your finger bones clicking on your femur bones. You look down and see your empty rib cage, your backbone, your open hipbones, your arm bones, and your leg bones. But now the spirit helpers are back, disassembling even your skeleton quickly. They peel off all the connective ligaments then remove your arm bones, then each of your leg bones. They detach each of the ribs from your spine, and finally, they lift your skull completely off the top of your spine. For a moment, the whole set of bones is held up in front of you, made to dance in a comical way—a skeleton marionette! Then the helpers carry all the bones over to the ledge and drop them into a pile with a clatter. They're all there: bones, bones, bones. Nothing but dry bones. . . . [Pause.]

At this point you realize that you are still fully present and aware, there in the cavern. You are fully conscious of what is going on and can still feel your aliveness, the deep sense of "you" that exists behind all the individual parts of your body. You find you can move your attention and location around inside the cavern. You skim across the water. You move up to the ceiling, and down the walls. You are aware of everything in the cavern at once. You are in no single place, yet you are everywhere. You feel expansive freedom and joy. You have no physical aches or pains. You have no anxiety, no worries. What is there to worry about?

Who am I now? you wonder. Without that body lying over there?

Beyond my brain and nervous system? Who or what is even asking these questions? It is you: your spirit, your essence. You are formless consciousness. That is what is aware, asking these questions, experiencing all of this. Your pure essence, your soul.

You are the source-erer of your life. You create the kind of life you want from this core consciousness, to be the kind of creature, the kind of creation you want. No one ever told you or showed you this: that you are not merely a brain inside a body covered with skin. You are spirit first and foremost. You are the animator, the puppeteer behind that body. You are not merely a body that has a soul. You are soul. You are the maestro, the magician, the shaman of your life. You can create, change, and shapeshift your life where and when you wish. And when your body wears out and becomes skeletized again one day, this is no big problem, no catastrophe. You can let it go with gratitude and move into a new form, whatever that may be.

Enjoy this awareness for a while. Feel the freedom of your deep and beautiful soul self, this luminescent new power. This is your truest self. . . . [Pause.]

And now the helper spirits begin to reassemble all your body parts. They start with your bones: each one is picked up, lovingly washed in the luminous water and dried off, then reassembled with its mates. The vertebrae of your spine are restacked from the tip of your tailbone up to the top of your neck. Then your twelve pairs of ribs are reattached to the backbone. Click, click, click! Your skull is cleaned, polished, and set back on top of your spinal column. Your hand and arm bones are expertly reassembled and reattached to your shoulders. Your foot and leg bones are reconnected and attached securely to your hips. Your ligaments are securely reattached and snugged up between each of the bone joints, holding your skeleton firmly together.

Now your organs are returned. Your brain and spinal cord are rinsed, reenergized, and slipped back into your spine and skull. Wow! That's an electric sparkling feeling, as your whole nervous system comes back online. Your eyeballs are brought back, all shining and clear, and are slipped easily back into their eye sockets. You roll them around; they work perfectly. Now your internal organs are all replaced one by one, in exactly the right places: your heart and lungs, stomach, liver, kidneys, and intestines—everything nestled in together.

Now your muscles are returned. Your big thigh muscles, your arm muscles, and your back, shoulder, and neck muscles are all back in place. You can now roll your head around, flex your arms, and wiggle your toes. Everything is working smoothly, ready for action. Ready for doing things, moving things, lifting and loving and creating things in the real world. Finally, your skin, the protective envelope of your entire body, is returned to you. It's all scrubbed and glowing, flexible and ready to protect your inner organs from the elements. You are now whole again: body, mind, and spirit all reunited.

You stand up on the rock ledge in the cavern, back inside your body, cleansed and refreshed. Your body is tingling with energy and pure potentiality.

You thank the spirit helpers and say good-bye, and then turn and dive back into the luminescent water. You swim down through the long tunnel of grasses and tiny fish, and then up and up, through the hole at the bottom of the lake and back up to the lake's surface. You swim to shore, climb out, and there you stand, under the full moon on a warm evening, surrounded by the sounds and aromas of the living forest. You gaze up at the stars with new appreciation and new awareness of your timeless, expansive soul self.

You head back into the woods along the moonlit path; walking with new energy and a light step to return to this place, back to this room. You are alive and filled with gratitude for this experience of your essence, your pure spirit self. You are a soul person. You are a maestro, a conductor, a shapeshifter. You are the Great Spirit walking and moving in your body. And now slowly, gently return to your own room here and your ordinary consciousness. Wiggle your toes, open your eyes, and sit up when you are ready. Welcome back to the middle world.

Take a few minutes after this journey to journal or draw any memorable experiences, sights, or insights that you may have gleaned from it. What was it like to sense a "you" capable of perceiving and moving around without your physical body? And then to be fully reconnected and back in your body? This experience is a glimpse into the spirit world of shamanic consciousness and of our learnings and journeys to come.

A Word about Journey Imagery

Initially it can be helpful to have concrete images like the ones provided in this guided journey to break through the normal overthinking and potential skepticism of what you are experiencing. However, in the unguided journeys in the next chapter, you will have more freedom to travel spontaneously in the spirit world, without training wheels.

Now that you know how to move your awareness around, free from your body and intellect, you are ready to embark on another journey.

You may listen to audio track 2, Guided Departure Station Journey, in conjunction with the following exercise.

EXERCISE

❋ Journey to Find Your Shamanic Departure Station

The shamanic teachers I have worked with all taught journeying skills by beginning with a journey to a sacred garden. Students are told to imagine a lush natural environment with plants, water, trees, flowers, and perhaps a log or large stone to sit on. This garden then becomes their "departure station" for future journeys, akin to a futuristic space station orbiting Earth that astronauts use as a home base for further journeys out into space.

This fertile-garden imagery (an archetypal feminine motif) felt forced to me and never worked very well. Eventually, I came upon an image that worked better for my imagination, a rugged expanse of prairie out in the Great Plains of the western United States. I'm drawn much more to open places like this and could easily feel my way around this setting, which I pictured as a simple campfire of dry mesquite wood surrounded by distant hills, scrub brush, and the wind. *This* was my natural heart-opening place, which is the whole point of defining this setting for yourself. Like an artist or poet, the shaman seeks imaginary spaces that will arouse the heart. The arousal is *everything,* so it is important that your departure-station imagery works for you. You will discover your own starting place in the next exercise.

We will be entering the spirit world through some natural opening in Earth, a classic shamanic practice. Take a few moments to think of some real opening that you know: a cave entrance, a pond, a natural spring, a badger hole, a narrow canyon, or even a manhole. (After I visited an abandoned cinnabar mine in Terlingua, Texas, its vertical mineshaft entrance showed up in my journeys as the new portal.) Your entrance portal can be any size because your spirit can go anywhere. The main thing is that it holds some fascination for you, a sense of mystery that you feel drawn in to when you are there.

Hold that image in your heart, and we'll return to it shortly.

You will commence this journey as before, by lying down, covering your eyes, and listening to the script below. One difference is that we will add drumming or a drum track to this journey. I have narrated the entire script along with drumming on the accompanying audio track, so if you have access to the online audio tracks please locate track 2 now. If you don't have online access, you will need to have someone drum at a steady beat for you as they read aloud the entire script (in italics) below. Or perhaps one person could drum and another could read aloud.

This journey's imagery begins at the same wooded path at twilight but leads you farther down the path, through your favorite opening in Earth (as you have defined it above) and into the spirit world for a short exploratory visit. This repetition helps create a familiar mental path (and corresponding neural pathways) for your future unguided journeys.

This journey will last from ten to fifteen minutes. Start the drumming now.

Begin by setting your intent: "I am journeying to find my shamanic heart-opening place, my departure station in the spirit world."

Now imagine you are walking the wooded path at twilight . . . (until you arrive at the small beautiful lake in the woods. This time you will not jump into the water.)

As you stand at the edge of the lake, you notice the flickering light of a campfire on the far side. You are drawn to that light and you walk around the edge of the lake toward the fire. When you arrive you realize the fire marks a small primitive campsite at the foot of a rocky bluff. Someone has been tending a cooking fire, and there is a rustic clay pot near the flames.

As you look around, you will see the opening into Earth that you are familiar with. Walk over to that place. This is not a hole into ordinary dirt, stones, and roots. It is a shaman's portal into the underworld, a passageway into a magical realm that you perceive as lying deep below the surface of ordinary reality. Lying at your feet you will find a long coiled cord of gold and silver strands. Tie the loose end of the cord securely around your ankle. The other end is anchored deep into the bedrock of Earth. This cord is your way back to the present time. If you should lose your way in the underworld journey, just reach down, feel the cord, and find your way back to this place. You cannot get lost.

Now move into your passageway. You can make yourself as small as needed to fit through. Once inside, you notice a dim passage, tunnel, or chute that drops downward. Look around and get clear on that imagery, and then move back out of the passageway. Practice this a few times, going back and forth through the entrance.

Now remind yourself of your purpose: "I am going to find my shamanic soul place and departure station in the spirt world." Enter your opening in Earth a final time and now move down that passageway. Continue moving. It may be short or as long as blocks or miles. It may be straight or undulating. Just keep moving as the passageway carries you down, down, down. Eventually it levels off. As you come to the end of the passage, you will see a bright light ahead and a circular entrance to that light. This is your portal to the spirit world, the "hole in the roof of the underworld." Allow the drum to carry you through this portal now and move into the light. You may experience yourself falling momentarily, or tumbling, or just landing on the ground.

When you emerge you'll be in a landscape or dreamscape of some sort. It may be fairly clear or it may be a shadowy realm like being in a fog or cloud. Be patient, things will settle in and become clearer in time. For now, just relax and look around. Orient yourself to the outlines of this soul place, your journey-departure station. Look all around. Is this a natural place, outdoors? Is there a structure of some sort? See if there are other people, animals, objects or beings around.

You may not see anything visually, yet still be able to feel the presence of your surroundings intuitively or telepathically. This is good. It's all about the feeling of the place. At this point you are just observing and exploring so be attentive, without thinking, and allow the drumming to carry you. See what comes to you. Often imagery or perception can emerge out of the fog or just suddenly be there as in a dream. Shamanic journeys can have an element of surprise or serendipity to them: you are expecting one thing, and something completely different arises. Things often come in symbolic form, not literal images or expressions.

If you feel completely adrift, in the dark, or stuck at some point, just relax and repeat your intent: "I am seeking to find my sacred dream space for journeying. Help me to experience it more clearly." You are learning to function in another reality—the shamanic spirit world—which can feel like being in a timeless dreaming state. In future journeys this place will be your shamanic journey stage, the jumping-off point from which to explore your whole spirit world. Enjoy what you can see or feel on this short journey without judgment or thinking. . . . [Pause a few minutes for more drumming time.]

We will now return to ordinary reality. Make your way back to where you first emerged from the circle of light, the hole at the top of the underworld. Go back through the portal and the long passageway, and emerge up by the campfire near the lake. Leave a little tobacco offering in the fire, and return back around the lake on the woodland path, to this room. Open your eyes now. Wiggle your fingers and toes, and sit up when you're ready.

As before, take a few minutes to note in your journal anything you saw, felt, or experienced during this journey. In a shamanic journey there are no unimportant details. Notice the primary sensory mode you used. Was it mostly a visual experience of some images, scenes, or symbols (clairvoyance)? Was it more a sense of hearing words or voices (clairaudience)? Perhaps it was a felt sense in your body, a physical awareness of what was going on (clairsentience). Trust that your mode of experiencing the journey was the right one, without second-guessing this. The details of your shamanic departure station will continue to come to you, and with each journey, it will get more focused and detailed. Some people have highly detailed locations; others are very minimal and simple.

Repeat this journey several times in the days to come, if needed, to get more clarity on your soul place. It will become like your shamanic home away from home.

You have now experienced two guided shamanic journeys. Good work! You first experienced yourself as pure soul apart from your body, and then journeyed into the spirit world to identify a personal base camp for further operations.

The next step in our learning process together is to journey out from this base camp to take your first unguided or "open" journeys in the spirit world. Here's where all your learnings will come together, as you learn to move in and out of the spirit world at will, seeking and finding what you need to know in your life.

In the next chapter you will go on a journey to meet your power animal or spirit guide, a classic shamanic helper. I will share resources for learning more about the innate powers of this guide you meet, and share examples of spirit guides as portrayed in world myth, literature, and film. You will read an excerpt from my personal journal of a shamanic journey I used to obtain help in caring for my terminally ill mother.

We will consider what the spirit world is, and then explore a shamanic understanding of the transpersonal Mind, a consciousness that far exceeds the anatomical brain or the psychological mind. You will then make a second shamanic journey into the shamanic upper world to meet with an ancestral spirit from your own lineage. And finally we will address the common questions and problems that people encounter as they learn this art of shamanic journeying.

Ready? Good! The spirit world awaits.

Let's go!

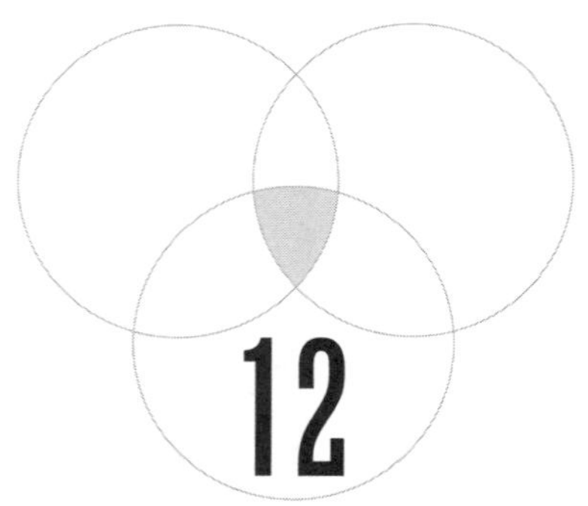

12

The Unguided Shamanic Journey

The imagery we encounter during shamanic journeys, the power animals, the spirit guides . . . you may ask, "Are we making all this up?" Yes. You're making it up. But you're not making it all up.

C. Michael Smith

RETRIEVING A POWER ANIMAL OR SPIRIT GUIDE

A spirit guide (or helper spirit) is a broad term for the various assistants you will meet and work with in shamanic journeying. These include power animals, guides in human form, and the guardian spirits of trees and other created things in the natural world. A number of my guides are deceased humans, including the Trappist monk Thomas Merton (as we have established), my friend Will, and an old Indian man who meets me in a desert kiva. While journeying in the Peruvian Amazon in 2013,

I met the spirit of the jungle in her common form as a great anaconda. The obtaining of one's primary or chief guide is so important that the journey to meet a power animal is considered a soul retrieval in itself and one of the primary healing ceremonies of classic shamanism. Other primary healing practices include soul extraction, soul retrieval, and spirit depossession work.

Whether your guide is in animal, human, or spirit form, during shamanic journeys it will function as your primary helper in navigating landscapes, seeking out information, and helping with your dragons. In advanced shamanic work, spirit guides (not "you") do the primary work of seeking out and helping to retrieve lost soul parts for others. Over time you may acquire a whole array of different spirit guides, each with its own specialty. But you will always have a primary guide who plays a key role in most of your journeys. The other guides will come and go as needed.

A word about expectations for the power animal you will meet. If you already have a favorite animal or totem that you identify with, the spirit guide that comes to you in this journey is probably not going to be that animal. For example, I have clients who might say, "Oh, I just love wolves. They're so strong and independent. People say I have wolf energy, and I have wolf art all over my house." This is not a power animal in the shamanic sense. In shamanism you don't get to select your power animal; the animal chooses you.

Receiving a guide is a form of healing and rebalancing: a mini soul retrieval of lost or unrealized spiritual energy in you. So like a good doctor the guide that comes to you will be bringing what you need, not necessarily what you want. It will likely represent a power you are *not* strong in or even aware that you need.

For example, the power animal that comes to you may be a mouse (hardworking detail-oriented energy) or even a snake (symbolizing the power of self-transformation). Do not judge this: the spirits know what you need more deeply than your ego self does.

I have always identified with the poetic migrations of Canada geese:

how they sense the call to leave home, fly thousands of miles to faraway lands, and must find their way back home again. Thus, I thought my power animal might be a Canada goose. But what came to me in my first journey to retrieve a spirit guide was a buffalo, a rather unpoetic one-ton mass of fur, muscle, hooves, and horns. I now see that Buffalo was exactly what I needed for my journeys and life changes to come: a no-nonsense, self-sufficient, four-season powerhouse that could knock down walls and shove aside distractions of fear and self-doubt.

You may listen to audio track 3, Unguided Spirit Helper Journey, in conjunction with the following exercise.

EXERCISE

❂ Journey to Retrieve a Spirit Guide

You will begin this exercise by journeying to the same shamanic departure station you identified in the prior chapter. Once there, you will call out for your spirit guide to join you. But this time you will be mentally guiding yourself through the imagery, while audio track 3, your partner, or another recorded drumming track provides the drumming for you.* Most recorded shamanic drumming tracks signal the journey is ending with a pause and "callback" of staccato beats that allow time for the journeyer to return gently to ordinary consciousness.

Traditional and modern shamanic healers typically drum for themselves during shamanic journeys, which gives them complete control over the drumming rate, volume, duration, and so forth. Traditional shamans physically move or dance around during their journeys while drumming, their eyes half open and partly covered or curtained, assisted by helpers to prevent injury in their altered state. This can all be a bit much for the novice still learning

---

*You can search your favorite mp3 music source (iTunes, etc.) for "shamanic drumming" tracks and purchase those. You will find a whole array of drumming combinations (single, double, or triple drums) and instruments (drum, drum with rattle, drum with rattle and didgeridoo) to choose from. Experiment and find out which instruments and rhythms are the most helpful to your journeying.

the basic conceptual steps, so I suggest you don't drum for yourself in these early learning exercises. Later on, by all means experiment with what works best. At this point in my own work, after preliminary drumming to bring my attention back to my body and present moment (see chapter 8) I put the drum down and switch to simple rattling during my shamanic journeys. Once I am deeply into the shamanic state of consciousness I often put the rattles down and continue my journey in silence because I don't need them anymore. No one told me to do this. I just learned what worked best for me after trying different combinations over hundreds of journeys.

Below are the steps to this journey. Read them several times carefully so you can remember the progression during the journey itself. Most of all, stay clear on your intent for this journey: to meet your spirit guide or power animal. Then put the script down and lie down and cover your eyes. If the accompanying audio tracks are available to you, turn on audio track 3 now and commence the following journey. (Alternatively, have your partner begin drumming or turn on another recorded drum track as you begin the journey.) This journey should last between five and ten minutes.

1. **Begin your journey as before.** Walk down the woodland path, proceeding around the lake to the campfire. Then go through your chosen entry into Earth, down the passageway, and through the circle of light into the shamanic spirit world and your familiar departure station.
2. **Call out for your spirit guide.** Once you are settled in at your departure station, call out with your imagination, "Spirit guide, please come to me!" Do this and wait. Open all your senses, your heart, your intuition, your seeing, and your hearing. See what happens. A spirit guide will often come to you from your right side or you may sense it approaching you from behind. It may come into "view" or you may only sense its presence. It may come and then go several times (a bird swooping over your head), as if teasing you. Your guide could be anything: an animal, person, bird, reptile, waterfall, or the sun.
3. **If the guide does not seem to come, call again.** Be firm and clear with the spirits. If needed, call a third time: "Spirit guide, please come to

me!" Be patient. Drop the reins of control and striving for a result. Expect nothing, yet receive everything.

4. **When the guide appears, ask, "Are you my guide?"** It should respond with some clear affirmative gesture. (The spirits do not usually communicate in words.) Ask it to reveal its name to you. If it does not respond, ask again with firm authority. This is important: the shamanic journey is *your* show. The spirit guide serves you. If you do not get a response, send it away and tell it: "You cannot be my spirit guide." Start the call for your spirit guide all over again.
5. **Make certain the guide responds to your commands**. If the guide is yours, it needs to respond to you. Test it by telling it to move to your left and right, up and down, near and far. It should move instantly as you command. Ask it, "Do you vow to serve my whole self and protect it?" You should receive a clear positive response in some manner, such as seeing it nod or sensing a telepathic yes or sensing a feeling of safety and protection.
6. **See if your guide has anything to give you.** Perhaps a gift or some power object that would help you in your life right now. Make sure you are clear on what it may be giving or showing you. If it is not clear, make it clear with your guide until you are satisfied.
7. **Thank your guide for coming.** That's all you need to accomplish for now, so thank it and tell it you will be returning for future journeys. Ask it to wait for your return. Leave it a small gift or give it a hug. As with any important relationship, you want to nurture this one. Your guide will be doing some important work for you in the future. You don't want it wandering off.
8. **Return back the way you came.** Go back up through the portal of light, through the tunnel, and back up to the campfire. Leave an offering of tobacco and return to this room. Open your eyes. Sit up.

As before, write down everything you remember about this journey and your spirit guide. You may prefer to use nonverbal modes of recording like drawing, painting, or collage.

About the Characters in Shamanic Journeys

Once you have identified your spirit guide or power animal, take some time to learn more about it. Ted Andrews's book *Animal Speak* is a popular resource for the symbolism associated with particular animals.[1] A more scholarly work covering animal and nonanimal symbols in mythology, dreamwork, psychology, and anthropology is *The Book of Symbols: Reflections on Archetypal Images*.[2] You can also conduct a Google search of your spirit guide, entering such key search terms as *shamanic imagery buffalo,* or *power animal snake,* which will yield countless additional perspectives for you.

These reference guides should be considered *supportive* sources because the primary authority on what your power animal represents is you. Your journey imagery draws from your own memory, experience, and personal associations. Trust that your helper spirit has been selected by your psyche as the best "package" to hold the necessary meaning for you at this time, using imagery and symbolism that only you can fully appreciate and unpack.

Although shamanic journeying may be a forgotten art, we have modern expressions of spirit guides and power animals in modern culture. For example, in Charles Dickens's *A Christmas Carol,* Scrooge is visited by three spirits who come to him late at night in dreamtime. They take him on dramatic journeys and show him unacknowledged realities about his own character in the past, present, and future. In the Christmas classic film *It's a Wonderful Life,* the despairing lead character George Bailey is escorted around time and space by his "novice angel" Clarence and shown an alternative past, present, and future world without him in it. In the *Wizard of Oz,* Dorothy is literally knocked out of ordinary consciousness by a blow to the head during a tornado. In her altered state, she meets three helper spirit archetypes: one representing her unrealized courage (Lion); a second, her intelligence (Scarecrow); and a third, her heart (Tin Man).

The shamanic journey process is like embarking on your own journey to Oz with your own personal companions. The information that comes to you is for your life and no one else's, so there is no place in this process for self-criticism or comparisons with the journeys of others.*

A JOURNEY FOR HELP WHEN MY MOTHER WAS DYING

Several years ago I journeyed for help to find guidance and support during the final months of my mother's end-of-life decline. Here are my journal notes from that experience that will illustrate how my spirit guides helped me in a practical and deeply meaningful way.

> January 27, 2013, 6:00 a.m. I'm still in bed. Just hung up the phone from Mom's doctor who called from the hospital to say she won't be going back to the nursing home today. Again. Her vitals are down, she still has an infection, and he's going to start more powerful antibiotics, which I know will cause other problems.
>
> I think my mom is dying. She is eighty-four, has Parkinson's disease, can't walk or even stand now, and is getting more confused. She's been spiraling downward: a fall here, an infection there, a hospitalization, more medications, PT, a partial recovery, repeat. It's heartbreaking. For forty years she was managing the care of other patients and assisting Mayo Clinic surgeons as a charge nurse in a thousand-bed hospital in Rochester, Minnesota. Now she can't even remember her own meds, has food stains on her blouse, and seems miserable. When Mom's upset she tells me she just wants me to "let her go." Yet on her rare good days she seems OK, is pleasant; we laugh, and she enjoys my visits.
>
> I'm feeling conflicted on whether to continue aggressive medi-

*Journeying as a group will often produce uncanny synchronicities of imagery and archetypal meaning. Also, it can be very helpful to share the journey experience with one or more listeners for supportive feedback (not advice or interpretation). In my shamanic training, we would always share the mandala art we generated after Sacred Breathwork journeys, which were extended, two-hour affairs, typically done with a group.

cal care for Mom or shift her treatment to more comfort-oriented palliative care. I have worked my whole career as a hospital and hospice chaplain. I am very skilled at helping other patients and their families through these same difficult waters and I know the medical, legal, and spiritual issues at stake. Yet I am feeling conflicted as a son and caregiver myself now. I decide to do a shamanic journey to consult my spirit guides.

Still in bed, I put on my recorded drum track. I close my eyes and begin the journey. I first arrive at a naval base that I recognize from dad's black-and-white home movies of the Korean War. There's a huge Navy ship waiting with an honor guard of soldiers at the gangway; one of the soldiers is my dad. I give him a hug, but where's my mom? After waiting a while, I call my spirit guide for help. My buffalo power animal, Phil, instantly appears. "I need to find Mom and figure out what to do." He nods, and we leave the ship altogether and climb into an old 1950s black sedan.

Phil takes me to an old, dark, dimly lit barroom in some back street. All the patrons in the bar are shadowy figures dressed in monks' robes, the cowls up over their heads. No one is talking or moving much in the bar. It's a very worn-out, defeated place, and the feeling reminds me of Mom's nursing home. Phil leads me into the back of the room, and there I discover my mom, in her white nurse's uniform, sitting alone at a table. She is young and beautiful, radiant in her pristine outfit and her starched white cap. But she looks sad, as if she were waiting for someone who never showed up, so now she is just politely waiting, forever.

I approach her and she looks up. "Hi, Jeff."

"Mom," I say, "what are you doing in here? Let's get out of here. This is no fun; it's beautiful outside today."

"Well, I don't know," she says. She is hesitant, yet has no good reason to stay. "Mom, there's a whole bright world out there. Better than this." These are just spontaneous words that come out of me. She still hesitates.

I encourage her to get up, and she says, "Well, if you think so."

Mom gets up and we walk out the front door together. Outside the light is bright, almost blinding. Birds are chirping . . . blue sky . . . aromas of flowers . . . life is moving all around us. Mom's white uniform is even more radiant in the sun. She is trim, fit, just immaculate. It's stunning.

Mom is still alone, so now I call out to invite Mom's closest friends to the scene. Instantly, we are surrounded by familiar faces. Her friend and nursing colleague Ruth and other nurses I remember. I see Joyce, the disabled woman that Mom drove to church every Sunday for years. My grandma and grandpa, Mom's parents are there, leaning in from the crowd with proud smiles. It's like Mom is a dignitary in a parade, and everyone wants a hug or handshake from her. She is embarrassed but enjoying the attention. I realize that all the people there have died in past years. My uncle Don and Aunt Ann who was Mom's best friend . . . and oh, yes, Aunt Ann was also a nurse! And there are all of Mom's bridge friends, seated at card tables nearby, looking up with big smiles, as if they are saying, "Hey, look who's here! It's Muriel!" It's a great big collection of friendship and love for my mom. It's wonderful.

I plan to have a talk with Mom about her medical condition and see what she wants to do about that. But before I open my mouth, she has moved forward, right into the crowd, on her own. She is walking away from me quite purposefully, arm in arm now with Grandma and Grandpa, Aunt Ann and Uncle Don. She stops, turns, and waves to me like a young woman heading off to college with close friends. She is not sad to leave home; the whole world lies ahead of her. She is smiling and happy, so pretty and poised, like she was in photos from her younger days.

As my mom walks away, I feel relieved and grateful, not sad or anxious. It's a fitting welcome for her. "Bye, Mom," I say, quite stunned by the whole experience. I realize I have received my answer for this journey.

> I thank all the spirits gathered and Phil, my buffalo guide, and I return through the journey portal to my real bedroom. I get dressed and call my mom's doctor. "No more hospital admissions," I say firmly with a clear heart and mind. "I want to talk about hospice care for Mom." The doctor is supportive, and he orders a hospice consult the same day. Within hours Mom is receiving much more attentive nursing care, new oxygen therapy, and better pain management. I receive additional support from the hospice staff and even a chaplain visit for myself. At night I notice a little smile on my mom's face as she sleeps. She is resting comfortably for a change and is apparently relaxed and happy. Two weeks later, the morning of Valentine's Day, my mom died peacefully in her sleep. The night before she died, my sister, my daughters, my wife, and I were all able to be with her and surround her with love and well wishes.

I received a healing in this journey that I did not realize I'd needed. I had been focused on getting information, on the "what to do" with my mom's medical care. But I also needed reassurance about less worldly things, like whether she would be OK after she died, whether she would feel alone or cared for, happy or sad. These latter concerns were not matters of medicine, theology, or ethics (which I am well equipped to handle). These were matters of the heart—the worries of a boy for his mom—and I would not have found that kind of information or deep reassurance anywhere else.

This journey in the nonordinary world of spirit reminded me, and literally showed me, that I was not the only person available to help Mom and that she would be much happier out of the "monks' bar" of pain and isolation in the nursing home. The deeply felt sense I received of my mom's happiness and support in the upper world freed me to do what was needed in the middle world of hospitals, nursing homes, medications, and technology. Since that shamanic journey, I have never had a single regret about my decision to shift to hospice care, nor doubted its rightness for my mom or myself.

Curing and the treatment of physical pain is the business of medical science. But healing is the business of spirit, and shamanism can access a much deeper medicine than is available from a pharmacy.

WHAT IS THE SPIRIT WORLD?

What are these spirits we encounter during shamanic journeys? What is the spirit world? We don't know. We can make comparisons to the personal unconscious or the collective transpersonal realm of universal consciousness. We can use a modern computer metaphor and say that journeying allows us to access the virtual cloud-storage realm of shared intelligence; the akashic records dating to the beginning of time.

It's easier to define the world we are leaving during a shamanic journey than the spirit world we are entering. We are leaving the small world of the self-made ego, the encapsulated, carefully packaged "me" defined by family, work, social roles, jobs, and linear time. In shamanic journeying, we are stepping out of small mind to access Big Mind, and once we acknowledge that world, it responds to us.

The Mind Is Bigger Than We Think

Recent discoveries in brain research are expanding our understanding of neurobiology and human consciousness in ways that help us make important connections between what scientists are learning and shamans have always known. In the conventional view, the mind is synonymous with the biological brain. We assume the mind is "inside" our brain and that our brains generate thoughts in the same way that a car alternator generates electricity. Given that human brains are larger than those of other animal species, we reason that humans are more intelligent than other species. This assumption conveniently serves the dominionist view, which sees human beings as the highest and most valuable expression of all life-forms. In this view, nature exists only to serve human needs and ambition and justifies our collateral harm to the ecosystem. (See additional discussion of this in chapter 13.)

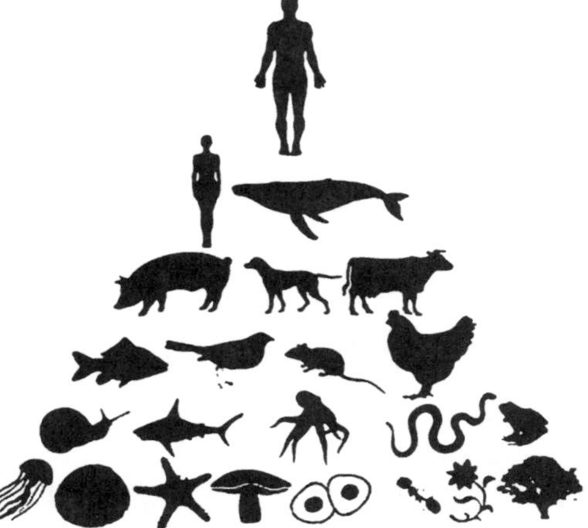

Fig. 12.1 Dominionist view: humans as superior to nature.

This understanding of the mind is incomplete. From a contemporary scientific perspective, the brain is the entire neurological system, including the spinal cord, all peripheral nerves, every nerve cell and neurotransmitter, and the whole endocrine system with its constant flow of message-bearing hormones. These additional components are found *everywhere in the body,* not just in the brain, and particularly in the enteric (gut) nervous system. The stomach and small and large intestines contain 100 million neurons combined and carry the very same neurotransmitters found in the brain. Ninety-five percent of the neurotransmitter serotonin in the human body, for example, is found in the gut, not in the brain. Our gut mind *thinks,* has its own form of intelligence and consciousness, and responds and plays a large role in human perception and feeling ("I have a gut feeling about that"). The gut mind can even operate independently of the brain: if the primary vagus nerve connecting the gut and the brain has been severed, the digestive system can still function effectively on its own.

One view of why shamanic journeying is so effective in opening consciousness is because it intentionally moves awareness down out of the brain and conceptual mind into this felt-sense intelligence of the heart and body. It is in the whole body, not just the brain, that we fully access our ten-thousand-year-old indigenous self, that place of deep awareness, instinct, and survival. It is through our bodies that we are most directly related to the nature all around us.

Unbound by the anatomical brain, the mind is not even bounded by the body. Quantum physicists tell us that the brain functions not like a generator emitting thoughts (the old understanding) but more like a radio receiver, capturing information from the environment and greater universe and decoding it down into useful information for the individual. This transpersonal "quantum mind" is a nonlocal and multidimensional field of information and intelligence extending out from every cell in our bodies into our surroundings and beyond to the farthest galaxy—a shared cloud of memory and intelligence within which our individual human lives and our planet are dense forms of energy suspended in the cosmos. As in the mythic jewel net of Indra (see chapter 2), we are each localized ruby expressions of the infinite consciousness, discrete creatures that simultaneously reflect through ourselves the light and consciousness of every other ruby expression in the web of life.

This modern discovery of the quantum mind and the interrelatedness of all things takes us right back to the cosmology of our ancestors, in which humans were not seen as superior beings perched atop a god-ordained food chain but rather as coequal creatures, kin-spirits of the same Creator with external forms no more or less valuable than any other creature in the great hoop of interconnected life.

Fig. 12.2. Quantum view: the mind is nature.

This shared, quantum mind-consciousness may be what the shaman is accessing during a shamanic journey. It is easy to see how this quantum mind would be a more complete database for effective and long-term decision making than the small-self human ego. It contains the dynamic consciousness of all forms of life, not just that of humans and human institutions.

The Shamanic Upper World

In my journey for help with my mother's care, I began by journeying "down" into the lower world, which is the realm of our instinctual and subconscious intelligence. (Recall our summary of the three-world shamanic cosmos in chapter 2.) There I came upon the image of the Navy ship at dock and was taken to the dark monks' bar by my buffalo guide. But as the journey progressed, it appears I was led to the upper world (the realm of universal spiritual consciousness and ascended beings) with its brilliant light and crowd of deceased family members and friends.

You can journey directly to the upper world if you wish, simply by setting the intent to do so (see below). Some people are more naturally drawn to journey "up" rather than "down." In stories from our popular culture, *Alice in Wonderland* begins with a lower world journey, with Alice falling down the rabbit hole. But in *The Wizard of Oz,* Dorothy is carried to the upper world of Oz by a tornado. Both worlds hold important information, helpers, and healing. The nature of the information held in each world is different however, and that is why students of shamanic healing are taught to choose their entry points accordingly.

To visit the upper world, you use your imagination to create a means of ascent that connects your middle-world reality to heavenly reality. So instead of imagining an opening or passage down into Earth, you might imagine a rising staircase, ladder, column of smoke, whirlwind (Oz), beam of sunlight, chimney, rainbow, tree, vine (Jack and the beanstalk), or a hot air balloon. In my journeys, I seem to prefer riding an eagle, condor, or great white owl to the upper world. As you rise up, you will have the sensation of reaching and then passing through some permeable threshold dividing the middle and upper worlds: a fog layer, cloud, membrane, or celestial ceiling of sorts. If you find yourself stopped in normal clouds, on the moon, or a planet, you are not in the upper world yet (these are still middle-world realities). Just keep moving upward with whatever means you can find. You will know you have arrived when the feel of the place changes, not just the appearance.

Just as a lower world journey is not a trip into the "ground," a journey to the upper world is not a journey into "outer space." The upper world is a particular realm of consciousness, an ethereal realm of transpersonal, enlightened beings and nonphysical space. Some experience this place as a crystal palace (Dorothy's emerald city), a void, or even complete darkness. Or it may be filled with brilliant light and different colors. (I have experienced it as a featureless yet vibrant setting that I can move around in, akin to the blank blue-screen backgrounds used for special effects in film and video productions.)

Regardless of its appearance, once you are in the upper world, explore it and ask for a helper spirit to join you to assist you in your journey.

In the end, your spirit guides will take you where you need to go. After thirty years of shamanic healing work, Sandra Ingerman says, "A lot of the time I don't know 'where' I am in my journeys—upper or lower worlds—I just go where I need to go. And I never tell people what worlds I am going to visit for them. I trust my helping spirits."*

You should take several exploratory journeys at this point in your learning, to explore the landscape of your departure station and strengthen the connection with your helping spirits there. Strong helpers result in strong journeys. Weak or vague relations with your helper spirits will result in unfocused or sloppy journeys. The following exercise will help you strengthen your general journey skills and introduce you to a new helping spirit.

---

*From Sandra Ingerman's teacher training program at Sonoma, California, September, 2015.

You may listen to Audio Track 4, Unguided Ancestor Journey, in conjunction with the following exercise.

EXERCISE

✺ Journey to Meet an Ancestral Spirit

Now that you know how to journey and have acquired a spirit guide to assist you, you have the basic tools to swing the door of shamanic inquiry wide open. From here forward you can ask your guide for help with *any* question, situation, person, place, or perspective to help you in your life and relationships (see the Troubleshooting section below for suggestions on how to frame your journey questions for more productive results). This is the key to success in any journey: your guide(s) needs to be doing the work of the journey, not "you." You summon your spirit guide and instruct it to show you what is needed, or what stands in the way, or to retrieve whatever information you seek, rather than striving to deduce a solution with your normal thinking consciousness. It's like a ballroom dance with your spirit guide. You dance together, but your guide needs to have the lead and you need to follow that lead.

A common starting point for new seekers is a journey to meet with the spirit of one of your own ancestors, to become better acquainted and seek the spirit's help on your path. We will do that here by sending your new spirit guide or power animal to find and introduce you to one of your own ancestral spirits.

Here are the steps for this unguided journey, which should sound familiar by now:

1. Prepare yourself for the journey with your clearing-the-heart mindfulness practices.
2. Call in the four directions and get powered up with your own drumming, rattling, dancing, or chanting. To complete the following steps of this journey you can access the fourth audio track that accompanies this book, "Unguided Ancestor Journey," or drum for yourself or have someone drum for you or use a recorded audio track of plain shamanic drumming. If you choose to listen to the audio track, it will outline the steps of this entire journey for you, so you won't need to read the remaining steps

below. You can just start the audio track when you're ready to begin the journey. Experiment with different methods and see which approach works best for you.

3. Set your intent for this journey, which in this case is to meet with an ancestral spirit. You will ask that spirit to show you a special power you have inherited, or to show you an issue that needs healing in your ancestral line.
4. Set a small alarm for fifteen minutes. This is simply a beginner's practice to help you stay focused by knowing that the journey time is limited. Eventually you will not need an alarm or callback beat (included in most recorded shamanic drumming tracks).
5. Sit or lie down. If you are drumming for yourself, begin now. Or ask your drummer to begin drumming or start the generic shamanic drumming track.
6. See or feel your entry point into the spirit world. Journey to your shamanic departure station and then call for your spirit guide to join you.
7. Tell your guide that you want to meet one of your own ancestral spirits. Ask your spirit guide to take you to the ancestor's home. Drop the reins of your conscious thinking and allow the experience, image, feeling, or intuition to come to you. Be patient. If you get stuck, repeat your intention to your helper spirit.
8. When you meet the ancestor, be respectful. You may recognize the ancestor (a grandparent or other kin) or the ancestor may be new to you (an elderly woman, a farmer, a soldier, a healer, a peasant, a princess). Introduce yourself, and ask to be shown a special power that you have inherited through your ancestors. Alternatively, you could ask to be shown an area that needs healing in your family lineage. Be specific about what you want so there is no confusion about the symbolic response you receive. As the journey unfolds, actively engage with your spirit guide and the new ancestral spirit, clarifying and asking for additional information whenever you need it. Relax, be curious, and have fun with this process without thinking or analyzing.
9. When your alarm or recorded drumming track signals it is time to conclude the journey, thank your ancestor for the visit, and leave him or her some gift.

10. Return to your departure station. If the journey seems unfinished you can always return another time.
11. Write down or otherwise record everything you can remember about this encounter. If you were shown an area of healing needed in your ancestral line, this will be a productive area for you to make additional journeys to in order to find out more and seek a way for healing that issue in your own generation. You might be shown a special ceremony, be sent additional spirit guides for your life, or be shown other information that will help you. You don't have to know what to do: use shamanic journeys to ask your spirit guides to show you what to do.

Just as you used this journey to visit your ancestor(s), you can make future journeys to meet other key characters. You can journey to meet with the spirits of the land that you live on (this would be a middle-world journey out into the ordinary world around you). You can journey to meet the spirit of an element: fire, water, air, or earth. You can journey to meet Mother Earth, or your inner shaman or your inner "Lord of Madness" who knows your shadow side and your illusions. You can journey to meet the Great Spirit itself. You can journey to meet the spirit of *anything* you are curious about or seeking help from.

TROUBLESHOOTING

Sandra Ingerman tells her new shamanic students about meeting a ninety-four-year-old Ulcchi healer who had been practicing shamanism since he was seventeen years old. "As a healer, I still consider myself a baby," he told her. Ingerman then turns to her students: "So, it's 10:00 a.m. on Monday. Relax. You're not going to be journey experts by the end of the day." With this same warm spirit of realism and support, here are a few tips to help you with the challenges common to new journeyers:

- Nothing happened.

Nada. Zilch. You listened to the drumming, waited, and just got more and more frustrated. My advice? Relax, drop your expectations, shift your thinking and striving into neutral, and try again! While some people seem to take to the process like a fish to water, others do not. I wasn't at "nothing happened" my first journey but close to it. I had a few vague, fleeting images I probably made up . . . and then it was over. Shamanic work awakens unused modes of perception, and this can be like waking up from a very deep sleep or a drugged state. It takes patience, and the ego just wants you to go back to slumber. Remember that a shamanic journey is not like watching a movie, and your experience may not be visual. The optimal state during the journey is to be alert but not thinking, and thinking includes making negative judgments about your performance. It's not a performance. It's an encounter with a different realm of consciousness and a different way of knowing.

One other possibility here is that seeing nothing *is* the answer to your journey's intent. "I just saw all black." So journey on that: ask your spirit helper to help you engage with and explore the blackness or void and learn from it. Your spirit helper should be doing the work in the journey, not you.

- My mind was too busy; I couldn't stop thinking.

Distracted thinking is the normal condition of our entire society, so first of all, forgive yourself. Your busy mind is a *focus* issue, not an indication that you can't learn to journey. To avoid mental distractions, you just need to prepare more carefully before you begin. That was the whole purpose of chapter 8's mindfulness practices.

In this book you are not just learning how to journey; you are learning how to let go of thinking and break the trance of ordinary consciousness. It's like when you first learned to ride a bicycle or to juggle—the more you thought about what you were doing, the worse it got. But at some point you just relaxed, and the next thing you knew, you were riding a bike or juggling. "Oh," you may have said, "this is easy. I just do it."

Go back to the mindfulness exercises we discussed earlier in chapter 8 to first get your attention and your body in the same place before you begin your next journey. Preparation is everything. You cannot skip this step and snap from driving your car or working on your computer to deep shamanic consciousness with a few drumbeats. Shamans in the wild danced and chanted for *hours* before journeying. (Ingerman tells of how fussy some indigenous shamans can be about their readiness to journey, only agreeing to begin if their drum feels ready, if the spirits feel ready, if Earth feels ready—people could wait hours for the shaman's help!) So take the time to transition into the shamanic state. If your attention is caught up in thoughts, just return your attention to your breathing and the drumming. Allow the drumming pulse to be your boat, lifting you above ordinary mental consciousness into a higher and wider sea.

- My power animal just stood there and refused to help.

Our helper spirits mirror back to us what's going on in our own life. If your power animal is tired or doesn't seem to feel well, they are role-playing you and presenting you a question about your own life. Power animals and spirit guides are *spirits:* they do not have an ego and do not get sick, tired, or emotional. If your guide is sluggish or unmotivated, consider how your guide's behavior is a reflection of your own life and allow that to be a teaching for you.

- I was able to journey but did not understand the response I got.

This is why we emphasize having a very clear question or intent for each journey so the response is helpful. I recommend asking only one question per journey, and the best questions begin with the words *who, what, where, or how.*[3] "Should I?" questions are not ideal ("Should I marry this person?") because you may receive a yes response and assume this means you will have a happy marriage, when the spirit guide may be more interested in your spiritual growth through painful life lessons! A better question in that situation might be to ask, "What will I learn or experience if I marry this person?" If the response you get is, "You will learn about betrayal," then you'll have a better understanding of what you're getting into. One of my teachers discouraged using "when" questions ("When should I go back to graduate school?") because the spirit world is a timeless realm and the response you get may not pertain to the chronological time you operate in. This is the classic problem with using spiritual prophecies to predict human history and calendar events.

It's important to remember that the imagery you receive is a carrier symbol for some deeper reality. The vision itself is neither the point nor the end of the journey—it's just an invitation to understanding. "See this?" your spirit guide is saying. "What you seek feels like *this*. Pay attention to *this*." Your job is to unpack the imagery and experience after the journey, similar to the dreamwork exercises we did in chapter 10.

- Am I making this up?

As mentioned earlier, my first teacher answered this common question by saying, "Yes, you are making this up. But you are not making it *all* up. You are using your creative dream maker to construct an imaginal bridge to the real spirit world." We consciously set that bridge up—initially: the entry into Earth, the tunnel down or ladder up, the portal of light are aspects of your shamanic departure station. But what comes back over that bridge you are *not* making up. You don't need to take my word for it: see for yourself what happens. You will find time and again that you are surprised, delighted, or startled by the information and interactions that come to you in these journeys. By their quality you will know that you could not have consciously generated this information or wisdom. This is not to imply you are not deeply involved in the journey, but that you are not the only thing involved in the response.

During my first wilderness vision quest, I was expecting a response that would help me reorganize my busy schedule without having to really change my priorities, decisions, or lifestyle. Instead, the vision I received was to simplify *everything* and get rid of *all* the activities. This response could not have come from my conscious mind because my conscious mind was a coconspirator in creating and sustaining the problem itself. Ultimately, "Am I making this up?" is a fear-based question of the small, rational mind that knows nothing about the heart and spirit world.

If you get distracted by critical thoughts that insist you are making your journeys up, just agree with that voice and continue on. Say, "Yes, I'm making all this up" and get on with the journey. Arguing with a voice of blindness is a waste of time.

- I fell asleep during the journey.

Then you need more sleep. Your body and soul were bringing you what you needed most during the journey time—rest! Our conscious minds have an endless ability to disregard the needs of our physical bodies. I do not journey when I am tired because I start to fall asleep, too. Next time, get a good night's sleep or take a nap before journeying and pick a time of day when you are less likely to doze off.

- My journey wasn't very productive.

Some journeys are more productive than others. After journeying for a year or so I noticed there were certain times of the day when my journey efforts went better than other times. Late at night I almost always had good results, but in the afternoons I rarely had a productive journey. Try different times of the day to see what works best for you. Many people find they journey well first thing in the morning or right before bed, when the veil between the worlds is thin.

Another factor relates to how urgent the issue is that you are seeking help with. When I am facing a real need in the present moment (making a decision about my mother's medical care), the journeys tend to be quick, clear, and helpful. When I am pondering a less urgent issue or some future concern (such as "I wonder if I should sell the house after I retire in ten years"), my journeys tend to be more wandering, unclear, and less helpful. A fellow shamanic practitioner once said to me, "I think the spirits respond to *need* not desire." This was a very insightful comment, fully in line with the mindfulness emphasis of chapter 8. All our shamanic power (and that includes your spirit helper's power) is available to help with the now, and only the now. Not with the next month's duties or the next year's imagined problems.

- I am afraid to journey.

Some people do not trust their hearts—or anything else—of their own deep personhood. They have been conditioned to deny their own needs by hating themselves and focusing only on the needs of other people. One student of mine was unable to journey (or even try a simple breathing meditation) because his pastor told him that such introspective practices open the door to deceptive satanic powers. The student had learned to not trust anything of his own natural inclinations. Instead, he had been taught to only trust the sanctioned religious practices of his particular denomination such as verbal prayers to Jesus alone and the study of select Bible verses.

This is fear-based living. It is often rooted in the trauma of relationship loss, abusive or authoritarian systems within the family, and the conformist thinking of some schools, organizations, and churches. Fear like this does not heal or bring hope into the world. It only spreads more fear and is the real "demonic spirit" attacking our hearts. The medicine for this kind of fear, according to the Bible, is love: "There is no fear in love, but perfect love casts out fear; for fear has to do with punishment, and whoever fears has not reached perfection in love."[4]

If you are not placing your trust in your own heart and intentions, then you're placing your trust in someone else's heart and intentions whether you know it or not. Every shamanic journey in this book instructs you to call on the help of loving, compassionate spirits. There is no problem, ever, when this is your intent. Negative or "evil" energies need fear, secrecy, self-doubt, and darkness to survive: they cannot persist in the brilliant light of love, exposure, confidence, and clear thinking. So as Michael Harner (and the Fifth Agreement) recommends, be skeptical! Don't trust this book, or anyone else, until you see the results. Run your own experiments on these practices, and if they don't work for you, don't use them. Conversely if you do experience a little peace or healing after a journey, if you get some useful guidance or information that feels right and works, acknowledge that too. Follow the healing, the peace, and the love you get in your life, not the fear.

THE IMPORTANCE OF SHAMANIC COMMUNITY

The Path of the Heart is a hero's journey, a life odyssey, not an insurance policy. You will still take risks in life, make some mistakes, and experience setbacks, pain, and uncertainty. But these are not problems to be avoided or some indication that you have lost your way. Rather, these are normal experiences of a mature and authentic spiritual life on a *journey*. Of being alive.

Still, it is important not to undertake this journey alone. Spirit guides and power animals are one thing, but we need human support and wise human teachers as well.

You can find respected, well-trained shamanic practitioners in your area through an Internet search (for example, at www.shamanicteachers.com). With good teachers you will also find good community, other like-minded people on similar journeys of healing and self-exploration.

If you are willing to seek out support, you will find it. There are large and growing communities of people walking the Earth-honoring path of shamanism, for example:

- Networks of shamanic healers and teachers (like the Shift Network, "a global movement of people who are creating an evolutionary shift of consciousness" at www.theshiftnetwork.com)
- Shamanic radio shows (like *Why Shamanism Now?* with moderator Christina Pratt, at www.whyshamanismnow.com)
- Shamanic conferences (like the International Amazonian Shamanism Conference at www.vineofthesoul.org)
- Online newsletters (like Sandra Ingerman's monthly *Transmutation News* at www.sandraingerman.com/transmutationnews.html)
- Shamanic chat groups (like at www.shamanscave.com)
- Shamanic blogs (like my www.Urban-Shamanism.org)
- Shamanic Facebook pages (see Crows Nest Center for Shamanic Studies)

With the shamanic journeying skills you have now begun to learn, you are well equipped with the basic tools for walking your Heart Path. You are almost ready to head back out into the world. But first we must talk about the return, the final completion stage of the hero's journey. In this, we will prepare you for making the return back into daily living and highlight several areas of modern society that are in great need of your personal gifts to the world.

In the final chapter we will look at the return as the ascent, the movement up and out of the darkness of heroic struggle and personal transformation into the light and activity of the ordinary world. It is the return *of* you but also the return *from* you, the giving back to the world.

It is not difficult to get back to the ordinary world, but the reception you receive may be another matter. Thus we will look at the inevitable resistance you will experience as you return with your gift to your family, your community, and your world, from people who did not ask you to give them a gift or even know they needed one. I will share examples of what the return has looked and felt like in my life.

We will then shift to opportunities for healing the woundedness I see in various areas of our day-to-day lives. These are arenas I have either lived or worked in that will benefit from the healing and empowering tools of shamanism. We will look at the needs of children, elders, the medical and legal profession, faith communities, my own non-Indian white demographic, Native Americans, and Earth itself. The discussions will stimulate you to use your new shamanic medicine in your own life and in areas of interest and influence.

The return is where the personal becomes the communal; where one's inner work becomes a benefit for the larger community and world. This is what it's all about.

Let's make our return, together!

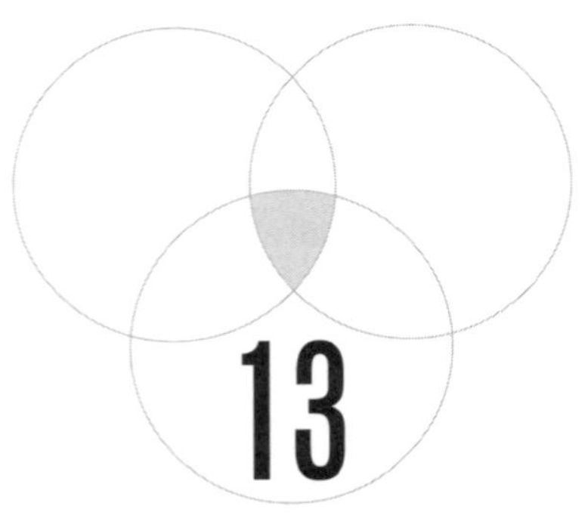

13

Bringing Your Song into the World

When a great ship is in harbor and moored, it is safe, there can be no doubt. But that is not what great ships are built for.

Clarissa Pinkola Estes, author of *Women Who Run with the Wolves*

THE RETURN

The Final Stage of the Heart Path

In this chapter we bring it all together with the return, the final stage of the hero's journey along the Heart Path. The return is the rising, the ascent back to the ordinary world with new vision and clarity about your power and place in the world. Here is where our narrow focus on your personal life becomes exactly the opposite: a gift for the whole community. It is where the mythic hero returns with a boon for his village, where your individual treasure becomes *medicine* for the people.

The shamanic understanding of medicine is much broader than our modern definition of a medication or other treatments from the field of biomedical science. For native people it can mean the essence, power, potency, or spirit of a thing as in turtle medicine or plant medicine. This power can be embodied in a person, place, event, object, or natural phenomenon. For our purposes here, your medicine is the special gift you have acquired through all this work on the Heart Path: your insights, healing, liberated power, and purpose.

Your medicine will not merely be some social role or activity per se but a new way of *being* in the world. It will be your inner response to the very thing you have been struggling with all these years. This is because the thing you have personally been struggling with turns out to be an unmet need in the larger world. For example, the bereaved mother whose child was killed by a drunk driver creates Mothers Against Drunk Driving. A man who escapes gang life returns to the neighborhood and helps at-risk youth. An artist creates a series of paintings about her recovery from abuse. A failed cattle rancher and wildlife biologist buys a small herd of wild buffalo and creates the Wild Idea Buffalo Company to help restore his life and the prairie ecosystem.[1] This book is part of my own return, written to share the tools that helped me come alive after years of anxious wandering.

Expect Resistance

Making the return within one's actual family and community is not easy. Even Jesus found that a prophet is not without honor "except in their hometown, and among their own kin, and in their own house."[2] Connecting with your heart and aligning your life to match your authentic self does not mean friends and family will all rejoice, particularly if they prefer unchanging routine and social convention. Your relationships may get rocky for a while.

For example, people ask me, "What did your wife think of all these changes you made?" Well. When I returned from my vision quest in 2009 and began simplifying my life, dropping external commitments and (eventually) leaving a twenty-year hospital career, my family was puzzled. My wife was initially resistant to my changes, and my mother, a career nurse, did not understand at all. But I didn't take their concerns personally (the Second Agreement) because I knew their reaction was from their own worries about financial security and social norms and acceptance. Since then my wife and daughters have come to support my new life and benefit from it. I am less stressed and much happier. Our financial life has reorganized around my new priorities, and I have even taught classes on shamanism at the Catholic college that my wife works at and my oldest daughter attended.

My family's support is very important to me. But maintaining their approval is no longer a prime factor in determining the course of my life. Rather, the primary factor is being authentic to my spiritual core. "This is who I am," I say to my loved ones. "And this is what someone like me does. Do you love this me or not?"

Recall that the first phase of the hero's journey is "leaving home." "This does not mean you must betray your preexisting responsibilities," writes Bill Plotkin. "It doesn't necessarily require you to quit your job, sell your house, leave your marriage, or end friendships. It can be done without abandoning your children. . . . What [leaving home] does require is that you *surrender what no longer supports your exploration of your deepest nature*. You will discover soon enough which roles, relationships, activities, and possessions get in the way of that exploration: you are being asked to radically simplify your life."[3] (Emphasis added.)

It is difficult to live in a relationship, family, or community where others disapprove of your deepest decisions and way of being. So a big part of the Heart Path is finding an additional (or alternative) support community and being selective about who you share your new vision with while you are still in the fragile, early stages of self-transformation. Like an artist who does not display her painting until it is completed, you *protect* your work in progress from premature criticism. Only when your masterpiece is complete, do you reveal it to the public, and by then it no longer "belongs" to you anyway. It is *art,* not a popularity contest, and it enters the world as it is. Your visionary heart-open life is your gift to the world. Not everyone will understand or appreciate it.

But some will.

How the Return Works

So how do you bring your gift back into the world? By simply living from your heart—by being more authentic in your words and actions every day and less fear based in your decisions—you will shift your relationships and expand your entire web of influence. "The world is a wasteland," says Joseph Campbell, describing the universal insight of world mythology. "You don't save the world by shifting it around and changing the rules. The thing is to bring the world to life by bringing yourself alive."[4]

We change the world by who we become, by the light and joy we radiate. You do not have to start a big new program or crusade. "The influence of a vital person vitalizes," says Campbell. Your heart knows the way. Follow it. Over time, this alone will transform your life.

At the beginning of this book, I stated that our greatest societal need at this time is not different technology, more information, or even more energy resources. Our greatest need is for different *people:* more heart-open, Earth-honoring individuals able to walk Earth with vision and power. The principles in this book will help create these different people and release them into the world.

MEDICINE FOR OUR CHILDREN THROUGH NATURE AND SHAMANIC JOURNEYING

To show what I mean by the claim that our greatest need is for different, more heart-open people, here are some of the specific ways I believe the Heart Path can be a powerful medicine for healing the woundedness in the world all around us, from our children to the planet itself.

Get Children Back into Nature

The Lakota name for children is *wakiaja* (or *wakan icagao*), which means "something sacred is growing." Yet we are raising the first generation of children that is completely isolated from nature. Children now spend 90 percent of their time indoors: twenty-eight hours per week watching television and five months of every year in front of glowing screens.[5] In his 2005 book *Last Child in the Woods,* journalist Richard Louv argues that this lack of outdoor time results in a wide range of behavioral problems he collectively calls nature deficit disorder or NDD.[6] Symptoms include attention deficit disorder, anxiety, depression, lower grades, obesity, and even myopia from lack of exposure to outdoor light levels. The causes of NDD include restricted access to natural areas, favoring regimented sports over imaginative play, the lure of the screen, and the exaggerated risk parents feel about "stranger danger" that is fed by sensationalist media.[7]

In South Bend, Indiana, the children in my inner-city neighborhood get outdoors but many rarely leave the neighborhood. When a friend of mine offered to take several teenagers down to the Saint Joseph River just five blocks away (a major waterway from which South Bend received its name), the teens were excited but admitted they did not know where the river was! Another colleague who runs wilderness adventure trips for inner-city teens in Chicago told me how anxious his streetwise kids became outside the urban environment. "The night darkness and the silence freaks them out," he said. One even refused to step into the pristine water of the Minnesota Boundary Waters Canoe Area. "There's crocodiles in the water," he said. "I saw it on TV."

Whole industries thrive on our fear of nature. I recently passed a billboard with a gigantic twelve-foot spider (blown up from its actual harmless size of one inch) that read, "What Lurks in Your Crawl Space? We Can Help! Call Ed's Exterminators Now!"

Parents who lack exposure to wilderness can also develop an exaggerated sense of risk in the outdoors. Many project their own shadow psyche and fears onto nature and acquire a perceptual hazmat suit of anxiety, which further separates them from the actual experience of nature. One client of mine, a young mother and tenured university professor, was surprised that I took my girls camping in national parks. "Oh, that's not safe," she said. "I've read the articles about violence in the parks." I was stunned. I knew her to be a careful scholar and devoted mother, yet her lack of exposure to outdoor adventure left a huge fear-based reality gap in her perception and parenting. The most dangerous creatures in the woods are not creepy men, marauding bears, poisonous snakes, or insects. It is ourselves and the foolish things we do that result in the most common injuries.

I was certified in Wilderness Advanced First Aid (WAFA) through the Wilderness Medical Institute in 2015. The most common wilderness injuries are burns from spilling hot water, sunburn from lack of proper clothing or sunscreen, frostbite from improper winter gear, blisters from ill-fitting footwear, twisted ankles, lacerations from one's own knife, and dehydration from not drinking enough water.

Exposure to outdoor settings naturally opens the heart. The most conducive settings for spiritual growth are not church buildings or religious retreat centers but the outdoors, where people are engaged with the living world around them. Nature has obvious calming and heart-opening effects, but the most helpful effect for people today may be its *disturbing* effect: the disturbing realization that human beings are rather small and vulnerable, dependent on the health of the natural world after all. Where television tells us that human beings are the most important thing in the world, nature tells us the opposite: that we are a part of something very large and beautiful, and we are not at the center of it.

Teach Children Shamanic Journeying

Shamanic practitioners are beginning to work with children at an early age to teach them to journey in short sessions of three to five minutes. Children are natural journeyers because their imagination is still open and they can easily picture going down a hole, talking with a secret animal friend, or becoming a tree or an animal. Their energy is wonderful in workshops, and they can dance and drum without the limiting self-consciousness of adults. Even soul extraction ("I'm going to take out the owie for you: I'll pull and you push") and soul retrieval ("You know how when something bad happens you go away to a safe place?") work well with children. Children who have nightmares can be helped by getting a power animal for protection, and instructing them how to make a little power bundle with favorite things to take to bed with them.

MEDICINE FOR AGING

Honoring Elder Wisdom

With our social emphasis on youth, high-speed communication, intellect, and sexuality, older adults come out looking like failed young people, worn-out versions of the attractive and agile generation. In this view it seems there is little for the aged to do but stay out of the way and quietly die off. But for our ancestors, the opposite was true. Age brought power derived from wisdom, leadership, and long vision for the big picture and all the stages of life. For this reason, rocks and mountains—the oldest created things—were considered the wisest beings.

The respect accorded elders in traditional societies was no polite door-holding for the elderly. After Lakota, Arapahoe, and Northern Cheyenne warriors had killed U.S. cavalry commander George A. Custer and all of his troops at the Battle of the Little Bighorn (1876), the young Lakota war chief Crazy Horse wanted to press on and attack the remainder of the treaty-violating U.S. Army stationed nearby. But according to Lakota elder Carol Iron Rope Herrera, the tribal grandmothers told Crazy Horse not to do so. "It would only result in our people becoming brutal and inhuman just like the white invaders," she said. "It would lead to no good." The grandmothers could easily see this but not Crazy Horse, who was only thirty-six years old at the time. And so the great war chief deferred to the grandmothers.

Lawrence Swalley, another Lakota elder, told a more humorous story of early U.S.-Indian relations. "White soldiers would come onto Lakota land and say, 'Take us to your leader.' So the soldiers would be taken to the tipi with the grandmothers in it. This made the soldiers angry, thinking we were insulting them. The grandmothers would wink and say, 'Okay, take the soldiers to go see the healer' or some older male in the tribe. The soldiers would talk with him and he would relay the conversation back to the grandmothers. It was all very amusing."*

Today, organizations are springing up that cultivate elder wisdom in all cultures and encourage the mentoring of youth and community. I have participated in a local chapter of Sage-ing International, an organization that helps elders reclaim their role as leaders and share their life wisdom for creating a better world for future generations.[8] This wisdom cannot come from our youth-obsessed, death-denying consumer culture. It can only come from elders who understand that dying is not a problem or punishment but the most ordinary thing in the world. My shamanic journey for guidance during the care of my dying mother (as discussed in chapter 12) brought me to our family ancestors who showed me what my anxious self could not admit: that my mother was going to be much happier reunited with her own ancestors, family, and friends who had died before her.

MEDICINE FOR THE MEDICAL PROFESSION

Care of the Soul

In modern health care the primary healer is the medical doctor—a scientist—playing a role that has completely replaced the varied roles of traditional healers in community. When we are physically sick or in pain, we naturally call the doctor. But when we cannot sleep, we also call the doctor. When we are anxious or depressed, we call the doctor. When our child is overactive and distracted in class, we call the doctor. When we

*From a conversation with Re-Member volunteers on Pine Ridge Indian Reservation, South Dakota, September 2014.

are obese, we call the doctor. When grandmother is confused, we call the doctor. When she won't eat, we call the doctor. And when she says she is tired and wants to die, we call the doctor. Who else would we call? In many cases a doctor's authorization is required to even access (be reimbursed for) other forms of healing. It's quite a racket. Medicine is the only game in town.

When we "medicalize" so many forms of human suffering, we cede responsibility for our conditions—including nonmedical issues like emotional trauma and spiritual crises—to doctors. As a result, we no longer know how our own bodies work. We have no idea what is causing a particular rash, or ankle pain, or our anxiety, or our depression. We do not know which of these conditions we might safely treat ourselves, or which would be better addressed by another form of healing. So we go to the doctor even though medical treatment is usually the most expensive of all options and unable to address spirit-based illnesses. There we are told what medication or other treatment to take whether we understand these or not, leaving the doctor's office no wiser about our illness, our bodies, or the relationship between body, mind, and spirit. Even our best doctors are reduced to the role of overworked technicians, and our sickest patients become passive recipients of yet more medications and technology.

Medical treatments cannot even heal all physical problems. While writing this book I had a bad bicycle crash. My chest struck the handlebars, and I drove myself to the emergency room with difficulty breathing and a stabbing pain in my chest. Thanks to X-ray technology, I learned I had a partially collapsed lung and possible rib fractures. I also learned there was nothing medicine could do for me. My body just had to heal itself (unless the lung completely deflated and then I would go to surgery for a chest tube). The total cost of my ER visit, X rays, and follow-up was over three thousand dollars. I received good diagnostic information from the medical health-care system but no healing. That was still up to my body and the passage of time.

We need to admit that physical and mental illness can have nonmedical causes. True healing is not the application of pills and scalpels but rather the art of evoking the will to live. The will to live is a spiritual matter, not a medical one, and the Heart Path is the most powerful medicine I know for activating the will to live in oneself or another person. Integrating shamanic approaches with modern healing would create a powerful partnership between medical science and the time-tested ways of our traditional healers.

Unlike patients today, our ancestors could turn to a whole range of curandero helpers when feeling unwell. These included the herbalist, the bonesetter, the midwife, the shaman, the ayahuascero, the priest, the storyteller, and the elders. Regardless of specialty, each healer understood that illness or unhappiness was often the result of losing balance with one's spiritual center and the natural world. Their different healing methods all had the same intent: to restore power and balance across the various realms of the body, mind, soul, and spirit worlds.

The issue is not about choosing between medical science or traditional healing—a false dualism. The issue is balance, wherein all available and effective healing approaches are considered and included.

At this time in our history, we don't primarily need more physicians and medical technology. That's just the limited perception of a healing model dominated by rationalistic assumptions about illness and a professionalized medical class. We need more healers with more effective whole-person healing practices, like shamanic practitioners who can address soul loss and teach the art of healing the heart.

MEDICINE FOR THE LEGAL PROFESSION

Rights for Earth, Too

Americans are protected by one of the most highly respected legal systems in the world, the roots of which reach back to the eleventh-century origins of English common law. Yet from the perspective of indigenous people and nonhuman creatures, American law is completely blind and not in the virtuous sense of fairness.

In law school I learned that a properly organized U.S. corporation is considered to have the same legal rights as an American citizen. The corporation is considered a "person" with protected rights to free ownership and use of property. Like people, corporations are entitled to own land and the animals and resources that come with it. Corporations can legally compete with actual human beings for the use of land and resources, and hire a busload of attorneys if needed to represent their corporate interests in court against individual people and the inherent interests of the creatures and resources on the land itself.

Animals do not get defense attorneys. The fish in rivers are not entitled to constitutional protection of life, liberty, or the pursuit of happiness. The mountains in which coal and minerals are buried are not protected from criminal breaking and entry, unlawful search or seizure. The air we breathe has no legal right to representation or medical care as a result of having been poisoned by industrial toxins. Only if a citizen or interest group (such as the Sierra Club, for example) brings a lawsuit on behalf of endangered land, species, or water quality does Earth occasionally get its day in court.

Surprisingly, recent legal movements in "less-developed" nations like Ecuador (2008) and Bolivia (2010) are granting constitutional rights—and protections—to nature itself. Reflecting the values of their indigenous population, these laws consider nature sacred, as the Earth Mother or Pachamama of South American indigenous cultures. Explicitly naming the devastating effect of climate change on their land and people, these laws essentially recognize a right to life for forests, animals, and rivers.

Critics—in industrial nations—have dismissed these efforts and their leaders (indigenous Bolivian president Evo Morales, for example) as being everything from naive to socialist to crackpot to anti-American. Morales has endured political scandals and economic turmoil, just as other South American leaders have, while attempting to balance economic realities with the Earth-honoring spirituality of his Aymara Indian people.

Meanwhile, the trees, rivers, and animals are not complaining.

MEDICINE FOR FAITH COMMUNITIES

Honoring the Earth

As I write this chapter I am visiting the San Francisco Bay area on Easter Day. Despite the city's size and its Christian saint's name, a relatively small percent (17.5 percent) of the population is attending church services. In Europe many of the great cathedrals are nearly empty on Sundays, serving more as museums now than active places of worship. Some clergy complain that anti-God forces in society are causing this dwindling membership and roll their eyes at the people who say, "I don't go to church; I find God in nature." It does not seem to occur to these church leaders that one problem might be that the church itself is losing its relevance in matters of vital importance, like the environment. A 2015 Baylor University study demonstrated the vital relationship between nature and spirituality. The study found that U.S. counties in regions such as the Pacific Northwest with more natural amenities—mountains, bodies of water, forests, warm weather—had lower percentages of people belonging to traditional religious institutions than counties in regions such as the Midwest with flatter landscapes and colder winters.[9]

While in seminary during the 1990s, I took a class called "The Church in the Modern World." Each student was required to give a presentation, and one woman gave a report entitled "Christians Do Not Care about the Environment." I had never heard this before and listened with interest as the student explained how the church's emphasis on ideology (human moral and sexual ethics, human salvation, and a heavenly afterlife) allowed some believers to view the natural world as unimportant, "fallen," or a God-given commodity for human exploitation. This perception runs deeply in the American psyche whether one is religious or not: Earth is not our mother, Earth is *real estate*.

In the late 1980s several prominent evangelical authors even coined the phrase *dominion theology* for a new political movement advocating the governing of nation and economic policy by Biblical law, including the Bible's well-known line from which the dominion phrase originated: "And God blessed (Adam and Eve) and God said unto them, 'Be fruitful, and multiply, and replenish the earth, and subdue it: and have dominion over the fish of the sea, and over the fowl of the air, and over every living thing that moveth upon the earth'" (Gen. 1:28, King James Version). Critics of the dominionist movement accused them of associating environmentalism with paganism, pantheism, and even terrorism, and that its followers seemed to accept the destruction of the Earth as a way to hasten Christ's coming. Although this is not a fair description of the entire dominionist movement one can understand the concern behind the student's paper.

Our world religions do not have to abandon their sacred scripture or traditions to be more engaged with the living Earth. Christian churches could easily link the ample scripture texts showing God's creative hand in the design and delight of nature with our urgent need to better honor our living Earth and its waters, air, and nonhuman kin all as expressions of our Creator God. The most obvious strength of religion would be its expertise with communal prayer, ceremony, and ritual, all practices for shifting consciousness and invoking the sacred that could be used to help connect the faithful with nature rather than dissociate from it.

For example, wilderness puberty rites and initiation ceremonies used to be the communal safeguards against grandiose egos and the abuse of human power. Young people would return from those initiations with a very clear sense that there was a higher power in the world, and they were not it. But we no longer have meaningful initiation rituals in social or religious life today, and without them we suffer the actions of men and women with great ambition but no spiritual depth. This is a dangerous imbalance, especially with young men. "If men are not led on journeys of powerlessness, they will *always* abuse power," says Father Richard Rohr, author and founder of Men's Rite of Passage. Traditional puberty rites could be so severe that some boys did not return from them. Yet how many more teens die today attempting to self-initiate through risk taking, gang membership, substance abuse, and violence? Rohr's five-day wilderness retreats for men are based on the pre-Christian initiation rites of our ancestors. Led by male elders, the retreats take men through an inner journey of powerlessness and support with drumming, ritual, silence, small groups, solo time, and teaching. The groups are open to any man regardless of religious or nonreligious belief and help men understand authentic power and its use in service of others and Earth.

We all need initiation rituals to help us slow down, become silent, connect with the energy of nature, and explore our connectedness to all things. True spiritual initiation helps us grasp the huge difference between emotion and conversion, between the temporary high of an ecstatic sermon, praise band, or service project and the ego-collapsing experience of a wilderness vision quest or a twelve-step recovery intervention by one's peers.

MEDICINE FOR THE WHITE PEOPLE

How to Slow Down and Be Present

In the summers of 2013 and 2014, I traveled to South Dakota to do volunteer work on the Pine Ridge Indian Reservation, known by its residents as the rez.* My experiences there with the Oglala Lakota people were a real lesson in mouth management and slowing down. From Lakota elders to children, I found that there was just no hurry with the people I met, who often seemed less interested in talking than in just being with me.

One day on Pine Ridge I was assigned to help with the construction of a small one-room home with Thomas, an Indian man who had moved to the rez from New York. His father was a Seneca Indian and

*You can read the full heart-opening (and heartbreaking) account of these visits on my website of short stories and commentary at www.Urban-Shamanism.org.

his mother, a Mohawk. As Thomas and I worked together, I soon found myself working faster than Thomas. I moved up and down the ladder more quickly, nailed and power sawed faster than him. I felt quite productive. When I told Thomas I needed another two-by-six board, he disappeared out to the lumber pile for a long time. When I finally went out to find him I discovered he was examining each board with slow hands, feeling the grain and sighting down the length of each one, looking for warps—in no hurry whatsoever.

I realized I was missing the entire point of the volunteer program: building relationships and not just houses. Thomas was present in the moment; I was not. My mind had been far ahead on the project and not there in the actual moment with Thomas or even the materials I was working with. Without a word, his slow deliberate actions taught me this: It's just a building. There is much to do here. Let's take our time, enjoy this day, and be grateful for the tree that gave up its wood to us. Once I slowed down and actually paid attention to the man, he opened up, and we had a wonderful afternoon together. And we still got plenty of work done.

During that same week we heard the Lakota creation story of Turtle Island, which explains the origins and temperaments of the white, black, red, and yellow people. "White people are the people of the element fire," said Lakota elder Larry Swalley. "White people talk fast, move fast, and desire to burn bright like Hollywood stars. They are good at making new technologies of fire like the light bulb, the gasoline engine, and the nuclear reactor." Then Swalley observed, "But when you play with fire, you can get burned by that fire too," even in spiritual practices. "When white guys build a sacred fire, they always build the fire too big," he complained. "This pushes people away from the fire and from each other. The purpose of the fire is to draw people in."

By contrast Swalley described Indian people as people of the earth element: red like the soil, grounded, heartfelt, and slow to move. "In conversation we can be slow to reply and are more likely to give a thoughtful response than a fast one. That's because it's more important for us to get it right with our hearts than to get some words out fast and have to correct ourselves later."

The initiated person understands that a bigger fire is not always a better fire and that real power and security comes not from dominating everything around you, but by becoming a valued and integrated part of the interconnected whole.

HEALING THE HEART OF NATIVE AMERICA

Although the days of colonial genocide may be over in the United States, the Indian nations of North America are still suffering from the loss of land, sacred animals like the buffalo, hunting traditions, language fluency, and social structures.* Trying to preserve Indian heritage while living in the modern world is a steep, isolated, and uphill battle for many native people today. Non-Indians may be ignorant of (or disinterested in) the full story of American history, and many Indians are tired of explaining that story and dealing with ongoing racism.

Further complicating the gap in non-Indian understanding is the fact that each of the 566 tribes recognized by the U.S. government today has a different story. The Oglala Lakota on the Pine Ridge Reservation in South Dakota live in the second-poorest county in the United States and suffer third-world levels of disease and decades of corruption in their tribal leadership. Yet the Pokagon Band of Potawatomi in northern Indiana and southern Michigan live in relative prosperity and contribute significant support and cash to

*The Belgian physicist, author, and shamanic healer Claude Poncelet, Ph.D., was invited to teach the Buryat people in Siberia how to do shamanic journeys, as their own traditions were completely lost during the decades of communist rule. See his book *The Shaman Within: A Physicist's Guide to the Deeper Dimensions of Your Life, the Universe, and Everything* (Louisville, Colo.: Sounds True, 2014).

non-Indian civic needs (like sponsoring South Bend's minor league baseball team and our local public radio station). The Lakota have no economic base on their arid prairie lands, few businesses, and 1930s-era conditions outside their reservation towns. The Potawatomi have steady income from businesses and a casino and better housing, schools, vehicles, and infrastructure.

The rise of the American Indian Movement (AIM) in the 1970s brought some recognition for the Indian cause but not a return of lost ways. One Lakota man named Marvin said to me, "The AIM people came to Pine Ridge and said, 'Hey man, be proud, you're Indian! Speak *Lakota*. Don't speak English, that's the white man's language.' But I didn't know how to speak Lakota. My grandparents only spoke it to each other, and I was sent to public schools off the rez." Marvin shook his head. "I wasn't a white man, but I didn't feel like an Indian either. I didn't know who I was."

How can Indians regain their power and relate to dominant non-Indian society at the same time? I believe the Heart Path can help because the entry point for healing is not insight-building about past trauma, mutual understanding, or even forgiveness. Rather, Indians and non-Indians all have journeys to walk, warriors' journeys, that involve asking a different kind of question than who did what to who in the past. That journey requires asking the same vital power-activating, forward-directed questions that are at the heart of this book: What is your spiritual center, the original and living heart of your people? What kind of life does the heart of your people really want to be living now and in the future?

In answering these questions, time would be spent developing a vision forward beyond the wounded trauma-based identity mired in past harm, injustice, and genocide. Not because the dominant society deserves to be absolved of responsibility but because it puts the identity of the Indian people back where it needs to be: in the heart of the Indian nations. Indians can use their own healing and shamanic practices to clear the heart of the deep wounding that blocks full power, participating in tribal-level healing ceremonies like soul extraction of intrusions, group soul retrieval, spirit depossession, and psychopomp work to assist the dead in fully crossing over.

One of the great benefits of using the Heart Path in relationship work is that couples (or old enemies) seeking healing do not need to *like* each other to begin walking the Heart Path and moving forward toward healing and power. The goal can be very self-focused: "healing my own wounds from this bad relationship." But in the process of engaging with our own wounds, we will also start to see our own illusions and fears. We see the hell we have been creating for ourselves and for others, and we begin to have compassion for others who are creating their own hell. This can melt the most hardened heart and open new possibilities between old enemies.

The Path of the Heart allows parties to come to the table as fellow spirit creatures rather than unequal strong and weak players or as perpetrators and victims. The Heart Path is not about race relations; it is about soul relations. I am reminded of a comment by the Dalai Lama when asked how he would approach peace negotiations in the Middle East. "First," he said, "I would invite everyone to dinner."

We need ambassadors of spirit in the world, to be the hosts at the banquet of kinship relations between people and cultures. Organizations like Re-Member on the Pine Ridge reservation have created a workable exchange program in which volunteers work on the reservation in exchange for opportunities to meet and learn from Lakota elders, teachers, and artists.[10] For example, at the beginning of the program, Re-Member volunteers hear about U.S.-Indian history from the mouths of Lakota elders. This is a painful class for non-Indian volunteers to sit through! But it begins the necessary ritual initiation process, the hero's journey of leaving the comfort of home and sleepy American dreams to descend into the heart of the Indian story.

Facing these dragons is difficult but not impossible. As in every odyssey, helping spirits, ancestors, and energy magically appear along the way. I have volunteered three times at the impoverished Pine Ridge Reservation, and each time I have driven home on an absolute high of energy, experiences, fractured illusions, and new friendships with real heart people.

MEDICINE FOR THE EARTH

This Is Paradise

In July 2013 I was lying under a great tree in the Peruvian Amazon having a direct interaction with the Queen Spirit of the Jungle. I was about ten kilometers downriver from Iquitos, participating in a traditional ayahuasca ceremony. An hour earlier I had swallowed a thick, bitter mixture of jungle plant medicines administered by an ayahuascero named Raul, part of a traditional healing ceremony to connect with the living spirits of the jungle.

Ayahuasca is not for the weak of heart: the first thing that happens after consuming the drink is a period of hard vomiting believed to be a therapeutic release of physical and psychospiritual toxins. This was followed by a direct and terrifying encounter with my psychological shadow, in which I was shown (and felt) the suffocating effects of my negative beliefs about myself and others. After enduring this initiation, the powerful spirit of ayahuasca (referred to as *la medicina*) slowly took over, and for several hours I had direct access to my soul, jungle spirits, and what I can only describe as a sort of metaintelligence: the throbbing web of all sentient life-forms around me. I was able to hear and communicate back and forth with the plants, trees, birds, and insects directly.

During this last of four ayahuasca ceremonies I participated in that week, I walked on unsteady legs from our jungle *maloca* (ancestral longhouse) out onto the muddy footpaths that crisscrossed the jungle. I was drawn to a particular stately tree and lay down in the bed of plants underneath it. A number of mosquitoes immediately appeared and explored my body head to toe. *This is going to be a long afternoon,* I thought to myself. Raul had discouraged us from using insect repellant because of the chemical (and relational) barrier that it puts up between self and natural world. I was wearing only hiking shorts and a tank top.

But then, without biting me, the mosquitoes abruptly disappeared.

As I lay listening to the sounds of the parrots and monkeys in the trees above me, I felt the approach of a great presence, silent but palpable. It was the queen herself, the spirit of the Amazon, and she had come in the form of a great translucent snake, the anaconda. I was so astonished that I forgot my original intent and questions, and after some time interacting with me, she "said" (telepathically) in her characteristically blunt way, "And you were planning to ask me about climate change?"

I had to laugh because she was exactly right. I had wanted to ask questions about the state of the planet and get answers on how we humans could help. But instead of answering, she seemed to disappear, without a word. *The ayahuasca must be wearing off,* I thought. I opened my eyes to the jungle canopy above me, now illuminated by the low evening sun.

I slowly stood up, not an easy task. Loud birdcalls and animal sounds drew my attention upward to the dark shapes of small monkeys leaping through tree canopy. Staggering over to a little clearing, I reached out to a small tree to steady myself, rested my chin in the natural fork of the tree, leaned against it and gazed at the luminous biosphere of color and life stretched out before me: emerald plants, cobalt sky, and the red-orange ball of the setting sun. Insects danced across the low shafts of yellow sunlight like diamond dust motes. My heart was wide open, and my mind was still.

Then suddenly the queen's voice was talking to me again as if she had been with me all along, just invisible. *See all this?* she said. *This is balance. This whole neighborhood of creatures. And you are one of them. You really want to know what to do? What to teach? Teach this. This is the formula. Paradise.*

Paradise. I understood! The queen was showing me a *vision* of what we have lost: the Garden of Eden. I felt like Adam, the first earth creature, who cast himself out of the paradise of balance with nature.* How

*The word *adam* in the original Hebrew of the Torah was not a man's name, Adam. It is a form of the word *adamah,* which means "ground" or "earth." In its biblical context, the word is a noun that can be translated as "earth creature."

could I best "help"? Not by railing against climate change, pollution, or coal-fired power plants, the queen seemed to be saying, but by helping to unleash the shamanic power of visions in other people, helping to create different people with a new dream for the planet. This new dream would incorporate balance and coexistence with all created things.

Paradise is not a faraway place, I realized. It is not a rarified concept of faith or theology or mythology. Paradise is right under our feet and is stretching out before us. We can touch it, talk to it, and learn from it.

I stood there motionless for a long time, as the sun set before me in the jungle. Eventually I realized that the queen had slipped away as quietly as she had appeared. She was finished with her teaching.

I am still gazing at paradise. Not in the Peruvian Amazon but in the inner city of my Midwest town of South Bend, Indiana. I wrote this book to share my vision and the Path of the Heart that I use to enact it in my life.

You do not have to travel to the Amazon jungle, some remote mountaintop, or an expensive spiritual retreat to find your power and life purpose. It can happen in your backyard, on a noisy street corner, or while holding the hand of an elderly person. Each of us has a vision, an angel mission awaiting release in our hearts, and the most important task we each have is to learn what that angel mission is and then bring it into the world. That involves uncovering the shamanic dream for your life and for the planet that sustains us like a mother.

What dream are you living? Is it a dream of hell filled with endless motion, working, shopping, traffic, anxiety, and the negative voices of people dead and alive murmuring in your head? Or is it a dream of paradise, a sacred dance in the cosmic ballroom of your life on this luminous blue planet with your most beautiful partner, your soul?

You can change your dream. And you can do it right now.

Aho.

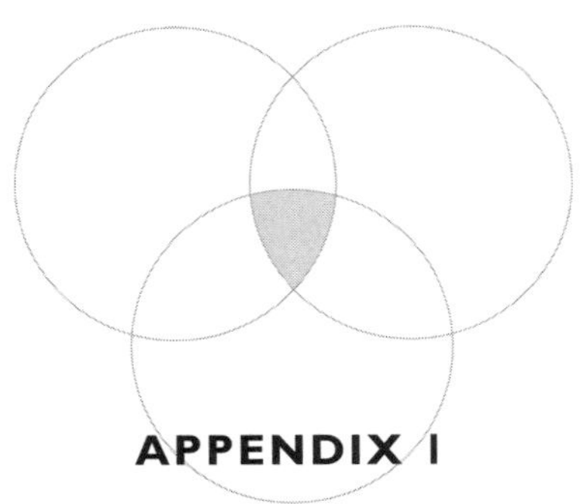

APPENDIX I

A Full Scan of Your Spiritual Heart

In this appendix I provide a powerful exercise to help you go deeper in exploring the full nature of your heart. I also include information on two additional exercises that are available for removing stuck emotional patterns and for experiencing the benefits of a wilderness vision quest without having to leave home.

Each of these exercises involves what I call process journaling, a way of writing in your journal that helps you to get to the heart of your life (or the traumatic root of a problem's pattern) and explore that from the position of your own healthy core. This is a form of inner work where you go through a set of steps to bring something to closure, or completion, or to make it finished and ready for use. As such, it is not the kind of passive journaling where you just ventilate feelings, report dreams, or write creatively in an open-ended manner. Process journaling helps you go somewhere, do something different, and get something done.

EXERCISE

☼ Thirty-Three Questions: Finding Your Heart of Aliveness

The following questions are an expanded version of the Ten Core Questions exercise in chapter 5, designed to help you get clear on your center, your heart, or core of aliveness. In this exercise you will look at three distinct areas in your daily life: experiences that bring delight and satisfaction, experiences that help the self grow and develop, and experiences that can be called spiritual.

The quality of your answers here is far more important than the quantity of words you produce. Do not rush to finish these exercises. You can do this work in your journal or with a partner. If you work with a partner, ask him or her to write down what you say, then underline key words so you will have a helpful written form to review.

I. Experiences That Bring Delight and Satisfaction

1. Recall a time, as recently as possible, when you did something that was *delightful*. This can be some small thing you really enjoyed doing or that brought a flash of joy. Write it down in your journal. Then get a bodily felt sense of that delight and ask yourself, what was the *crux* (the core or essence) of its delightfulness? Write that down. (You will do this two-part inquiry with each of the following questions.)
2. Recall a time when you did something or experienced something that made you feel *ecstatic*. Write that down. What was the felt-sense crux of this experience being ecstatic?
3. Recall a time when you were *passionately absorbed* in doing or experiencing something. What was the felt crux of its absorbingness?
4. Identify some natural thing or place you just *couldn't be without* because it so enriches your life, bringing you pleasure, calmness, or inspiration. What was the crux of that?
5. Identify some *everyday object you love*. It may be a simple item or trinket, or much larger in size, but you just love it. What is the crux of your loving it?

6. What do you feel instinctively is truly *ugly* in these three areas: in people, in places, and in things? Write down a specific example of each. Then, get a felt sense and identify the crux of the ugliness or undesirability of each.
7. What do you feel instinctually is truly *beautiful or attractive* in people, in places, and in things? Give an example of each, then the felt-sense crux of each.

II. Experiences of Personal Growth and Development

8. Recollect a specific time when you had to muster *courage* and take a risk to do something and as a result you were very glad you did. What is the crux of why you are glad you did it?
9. Recall a specific time in your life when you said something on the order of "to heck with what the neighbors think (or what my family thinks, or my spouse thinks, etc.), I am going to do it anyway, for me!" Why was it important to do this? State the crux of its importance to you.
10. What do you find *unnatural* to you, something that really goes against your natural grain? What is the crux of the unnaturalness?
11. List three specific things that automatically produce *boredom* for you. What is the crux of the boringness of each thing?
12. Think of three activities or things that can make you *miserable*. Name how they make you feel in your body. What is the crux of that misery?
13. If you could freely express your *wild self*, how exactly would you do so? What is the crux of this wildness in you?
14. Identify three specific things in your home and/or workspace that make you feel *physically uncomfortable*. What is the crux of why you feel uncomfortable?
15. What little change could you make in your house or apartment that would make it more *delightful* and *satisfying* for you? Name the crux of its delightful or satisfying quality.
16. What little change could you make in your home and/or your workspace that would make it more *comfortable* and *supportive* of you and/or your work? What is the crux of its comforting and supportive nature?
17. When you experience someone as truly loving you and supporting you,

what exactly do you feel in the middle of your body? Give it a little time for a felt sense to form here and describe it as concretely as you can. Metaphors and images are good to use here. What is the crux of that felt sense of love and support?

III. Spiritual or Self-Transcending Experiences

18. Bring to mind some good thing in your life that you are truly *thankful* for. What is the crux of your thankfulness for it?
19. Look around in your everyday life, in little and big things or experiences, and ask, "Where do I find holiness in my life?" Give three examples of this experience. Then name the crux of each.
20. Recall a time that wasn't pleasant, such as when someone you love was in crisis or suffering, but that afforded you an opportunity to *do something that was needed*. It may not have been pleasant, but it was deeply meaningful or satisfying to do: you did what the situation called for, even though there was no reward in it for you. What is the crux of its meaningfulness or of its deeply satisfying quality?
21. Recall a specific time when you did something that you knew in your heart *was wrong to do,* not because teacher, pastor, or parents told you so but because you just knew it in your bones. You felt it instantly and instinctually to be wrong. Describe where in your body you felt this wrongness. Identify the crux of this felt wrongness.
22. Recall a specific time when you instinctually knew something *was right to do* even though others disagreed. Identify where exactly in your body you felt this rightness and describe it in words as concretely as possible. What is the crux of this rightness?
23. List three *beautiful qualities* you want to leave your children and grandchildren (or others, like your friends and the community) as a legacy when you have passed on. What is the crux of each of these beautiful qualities?
24. Identify three experiences you would *like to have* before you die. What is the crux of each of these?
25. List three things you feel you must *accomplish before you die,* for your

life to be complete and to be satisfied that you did what you needed to do in this life. State why each is important to you. Describe the crux importance of each.

26. What is something that *pulls you out of your self-absorption* and opens you to the needs of others? What is the crux of its power to open you?

IV. Bringing It All Together

27. Go through your written answers above and find all your crux statements. Rewrite those on a separate page so you have a list of all your crux statements before you.
28. Go through this list and underline key words—words that have a significant feel or energy to them. After you have done that, take them all in, for a while, as a whole. When you are ready, write down anything surprising or useful that you notice, perhaps a pattern of some sort that is worth keeping in mind.
29. Now go through the rest of your replies to these twenty-six questions and underline any other words that seem key to giving you a sense of what brings your heart alive. List those on the separate page with the crux statements.
30. Now consider these two lists (the crux statements and the underlined key words) and circle those key words or phrases you feel are really important to remember. Write down why you want to remember *them* specifically.
31. Now get a felt sense of the whole of the two lists of key words. Hold them all in your heart and awareness. When you have that felt sense, being as precise as you can, use those words to write several fresh paragraphs or more about what you know in your heart to be you. You do not have to literally use each word but be sure to capture the heart and nuances of the whole collage of words and phrases.

This is your Core Self.

32. Now get a felt sense of all that—of your Core Self. What is the crux of your Core Self? Take some time to find a physical symbol or talisman of the crux of your Core Self.

Now, consider what it would mean to be living every day of your life from that core of aliveness. Take some time to imagine your life having in it the qualities you most deeply want, on a day-to-day basis, and let yourself get a felt sense of how *that* life feels.

33. Then ask: What stands between me and living that life? This is the same question we asked in short form after the mandala exercise in chapter 5, naming your dragons.

From here on, continue the work of the shamanic Heart Path: using the tools for opening the heart and the tools for removing the barriers that stand in the way of that.

GOING DEEPER THROUGH JOURNALING

I offer two additional process journaling exercises that can take you deeper in this work: Journaling from the Heart (JFH) and the Written Quest. Both are adapted from the brilliant work of the Jungian psychologist and shamanic practitioner C. Michael Smith. For more information or to order a copy of either exercise e-mail me at greatplainsguide@gmail.com. The cost of each exercise is $19.95.

Journaling from the Heart: To Ground Zero and Back

The JFH exercise is inspired by the practice known as "clearing of the heart" in Andean shamanism. In the high Andes there are stone temples that have a cave of the heart in them, which the Q'ero shamans use to this day. The caves are used for the clearing out of some wound-based emotional-spiritual pattern in the heart that keeps one from being fully alive and flowing with love into the world.

This JFH process was constructed and adapted to our modern cultural context to help us in clearing ourselves of some problem pattern, a COEX (*co*ndensed *ex*perience) system that keeps showing up in your life and prevents you from moving forward on the vision of your heart.* Examples include a persistent fear, an unusual reaction to situations, an anger pattern, an avoidance, or a procrastination habit. JFH helps address a disjuncture between how you want to be and how you are actually behaving.

The version of JFH that I offer is combined with a methodology for processing a wounding or trauma-based pattern. It is a powerful uncovering method, a way to dismantle COEX systems. You select a problem pattern you have noticed in your life and use the felt sense to search across time and memory for all instances of this pattern, finding your way back to its origins like following knots on a rope into a dark woods. When you arrive at that place of original wounding (ground zero), you stop and study the trauma details and its effects on your life and on others.

In the JFH process we are not reexperiencing the trauma itself but examining it with curiosity to see how a pattern of thinking and behaving was created that is not serving you today. We then find your unwounded, pretrauma self and draw on this healthy core of wholeness to re-vision and rewrite a new pattern to replace the old problematic pattern.

The Written Quest: Finding Your Core

The vision quest is a sacred ceremony of many Amerindian traditions traditionally done in a wilderness setting. It is a powerful practice of opening your heart to Mother Earth and the great life force to seek and clarify a strong sense of vision and purpose for your life when facing a key decision or life change, or just wanting to live with more focus and intention. This written version of the quest is an alternative way to get clarity on your purpose through an intensive journaling process, a good approach for those who cannot do a wilderness quest or who need to begin working immediately on clarifying what the big picture

*Czech psychiatrist Stanislav Grof, one of the founders of transpersonal psychology, devised the COEX concept to describe how the brain organizes experiences.

of their life is. In the written vision quest you open your heart to the great life force, to Mother Earth, and to the human community. You do this through a process of interiorizing while being firmly grounded in physical space and time.

The written quest will help you find your place in three arenas of life: your geographical place, your place in the life cycle, and your place in the human community. Your purpose arises in the context of these three arenas—from what is being called for—given your unique gifts, loves, and calling. The written quest is a powerful practice that will help you find your purpose and allow your life to transform.

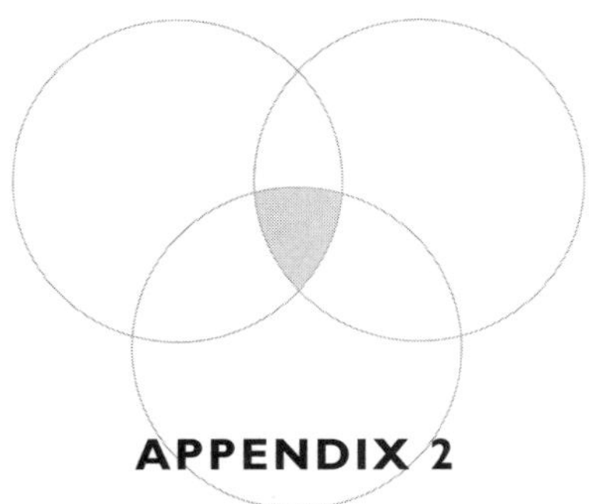

APPENDIX 2

Mindfulness in Daily Living

EXERCISE

☼ Tracking Your Daily Energy Tides

This exercise is designed to help you maximize your available energy for change by pinpointing the most vital and productive time(s) during the day for you. To get started, take out your journal and begin to reflect on the following questions:

- When during the day or evening are you most awake and alert, energized, and creative?
- When during the day or evening are you least awake and alert? Most sluggish or dull?
- At what point during the day do you seem to have the most physical energy?
- At what point during the day do you feel most solid, resilient, competent, and strong, your can-do time of day?
- When do you seem to be most fatigued, listless, lazy, or unmotivated?
- When do you seem to be most clear in the head and able to write, think, or speak coherently?
- When are you most sociable and talkative?
- When do you feel least sociable, needing solitude, quiet, or restoration?

- What time of day do you most enjoy reading? Least enjoy reading?
- When do you feel most positive, hopeful, and optimistic?
- When do you feel most down, anxious, overwhelmed, or irritable?
- When are you naturally drawn to go outside to enjoy nature and the outdoors?
- What part of the day do you feel most reflective, spiritual, or poetic?
- Is there a time of day when you are more likely to notice the mystical, the beautiful, the connectedness of life?
- What time of day do you feel most naturally yourself, without hindrance?
- Thinking back on situations when you tended to have helpful insights, solve problems, or dream new visions, what were you doing?
- Do you find times during the day when you are more likely to laugh, sing, act more silly or spontaneous?
- Are there times when you seem more open and forgiving of others, able to reach out or let minor offenses just slide off your back?

Now repeat these same kind of questions but focus on seasons of the year: What time of year do you feel most awake and alert, energized? And so forth. Then put all this together and sketch out your new understanding of your high and low energy tides each day, week, and season. The point is to make sure that you are synchronizing your key efforts along your Heart Path with the most conducive times of natural buoyancy, inner abundance, and power.

EXERCISE

❋ One Perfect Step

I call this exercise One Perfect Step (or Fox Walking) because it focuses very close attention on the physical sensations and movements involved in taking every step while walking. It is a form of mindfulness meditation that can be enjoyed indoors or out, but you will experience an additional level of benefit if you do this practice outdoors in bare feet.

Medical research shows that when we physically connect with Earth our body's electrical potential changes to match the negative electrical charge of

Earth. This phenomenon, called earthing or grounding, functions to "push back" the harmful positive electrical charges that surround us from power lines, cell phone towers, smartphones, computers, and our home's wiring and appliances. Grounding is believed to relieve pain, reduce inflammation, improve sleep, and enhance well-being. But shoes block us from this beneficial influx of electrons from Earth, as do the insulating qualities of asphalt, wood, rubber, plastic, and rugs. Conversely, stone, cement, grass, and soil allow for this grounding conductivity between Earth and our bodies. Thus I recommend doing this exercise barefoot and outdoors for maximum benefit. Read through this exercise to see all the steps before trying it the first time.

1. Begin standing next to a tree, wall, or chair that you can use to steady yourself during the following steps. Place your feet shoulder-width apart.
2. Taking three deep breaths, exhale each one slowly. Become aware of the ground supporting your entire body mass from below. It holds you up: you cannot "fall through Earth."
3. With superslow movements like a tall tree rocking ever so slightly in the wind, gently shift your weight from one foot to the other, back and forth. Keep your knees bent a little to help with balance. Draw your attention to the subtle firing of the many large and small muscles in your legs, feet, ankles, and hips as your brain and body help you stay erect and not fall over.
4. Now steady yourself with one hand on the tree or chair. Shift all your weight to your left foot (still keeping both feet on the ground), get solid there, and prepare to take a single, purposeful, superslow step forward with your right foot. (Note: We will not continue stepping and "walking" after this one single step yet. The point is to take one . . . single . . . step. That's it!)
5. You are now going to take the most *mindful step of your entire life*. Do this very, very slowly. You will breathe in as you slowly raise your right foot in the next step.
6. Now breathing in slowly, begin lifting your unweighted right leg ever so slowly with a completely loose ankle, your limp foot dangling from your lower leg until it is off the ground.

7. Lean slightly forward. Your right foot will instinctively want to step down to catch your fall. But instead of clomping your foot down in the usual manner, lower your relaxed right foot down to Earth in ultraslow motion as you exhale. Since your foot is limp, with toes hanging down, the ball of your foot will likely touch the ground first, instead of your heel. Allow this natural two-part landing of your foot: first the ball of your foot touching the Earth, and then your heel arriving down on the Earth after that, gently "kissing" Earth lightly as it settles. Breathe out as your foot fully settles onto the Earth.
8. Now slowly shift your body weight off the stationary left rear foot and allow your full weight to shift over to the right leg and foot. As you do so imagine you are pressing your right foot into soft clay, making a lasting impression of your foot on the Earth. Now *stop*. Don't move.

   Congratulations. You have taken one complete, mindful step! Perhaps the first ever in your life.
9. Now repeat this procedure in ultraslow fashion with the left foot. Keeping the right foot firmly planted, breath in as you slowly lift your left foot with a completely relaxed ankle, moving it slightly forward, then exhaling slowly and setting your left foot down on the Earth in slow motion ball-of-foot-first, followed by your heel coming down. Kiss Earth with your heel, and then impress the full print of your left foot into soft clay. Stop. Enjoy. Smile. No walking (yet).
10. Now that you understand the process, you can begin to move a tiny bit faster in more smooth and connected steps right . . . left . . . right. . . . Resist the impatient voice in your head that is bored, restless, telling you that you are not moving fast enough, getting anywhere, or accomplishing anything. That voice is killing us, every day. Instead, we are introducing a revolutionary, trance-breaking new practice designed to return your attention to the utter miracle of balance and movement in space, a slow ballet of breath, body, presence, and planet.

    And so repeat now, lifting the right foot again. Ever so slowly. Breathing in on the lifting of the foot, breathing out on the setting down of the foot. Pressing into soft clay. Kissing the Earth. Left foot. Right foot. Over and over. A little faster, a little more smoothly until you find a lovely sweet spot of slow movement, balance, and continual mindfulness. Breathing, lifting, moving, setting down, imprinting on Earth.

11. Now that you are slowly moving forward upon the Earth, imagine beautiful flowers blossoming from each of the footprints you are leaving behind. You are kissing the Earth, and it blooms with joy. She is your mother, supporting your every step of living.

As you slowly walk with this new mindfulness and joy, consider the following. It took you two years to learn how to walk as a toddler. You can move easily now! You tell your body to move, and it moves. You tell it to stop, and it stops. *This is where your power is. Here*, in the now, with each step. Nowhere else. Ever. Not in the last step, the last minute, or the last week. Not in the last boyfriend, the last marriage, your last home. Nor is your power in the next step that you haven't taken yet, in the next meal, relationship, promotion, paycheck, or job move. Just *this* breath. Only *this* step. Always *this* moment. Your body, mind, and spirit are lined up and working together right now.

To move mindfully like this is rare, and it is sacred. To *live* like this, moment by moment, will heal your life. But it will also help to heal Earth. Because you will feel, not just think intellectually, about your vital connection with Earth and about the interconnection between your life and the condition of the living planet. You will be awakening, and walking, as your ten-thousand-year-old indigenous self.

How to Use the Audio Tracks That Accompany This Book

This book includes four audio recordings designed to help you learn the core practice of shamanic journeying. You can download the tracks at:

audio.innertraditions.com/loarhe

1. Guided Skeletization Journey (16:03)
2. Guided Departure Station Journey (14:42)
3. Unguided Spirit Helper Journey (15:31)
4. Unguided Ancestral Spirit Journey (15:29)

These audio exercises are designed in sequence. Throughout the book I suggest that you listen to each track in conjunction with the sequential journeying exercise that it accompanies. Each one introduces an important aspect of the journeying process, so that by the end of all four tracks you will have the necessary elements to undertake basic shamanic journeys of your own design. The first two recordings are guided journeys that lead you step by step through the entire journey process. The last two recordings are unguided journeys that get you started with a clear journey intent, then set you loose to journey on your own accompanied by a solo drum.

You will hear a certain amount of repetition at the beginning of each of these audio journeys. This repetition is deliberate to help you maintain focus and carve out a familiar and predictable path into non-ordinary consciousness. Over time you will not need this repetition and will be able to shift consciousness easily into the unseen realms of the spirit world.

Notes

CHAPTER 1. SEARCHING FOR HEART IN A WORLD OF REASON

1. "Bolivia enshrines natural world's rights with equal status for Mother Earth," *The Guardian*, April 10, 2011, www.theguardian.com/environment/2011/apr/10/bolivia-enshrines-natural-worlds-rights.

CHAPTER 2. THE HEART PATH AS A HERO'S JOURNEY

1. Bill Plotkin, *Soulcraft: Crossing into the Mysteries of Nature and Psyche* (Novato, Calif.: New World Library, 2003), 51.
2. Maureen Murdock, *The Heroine's Journey: Woman's Quest for Wholeness* (Boulder, Colo.: Shambhala, 1990).

CHAPTER 3. THE SHAMAN AS GUIDE TO THE SPIRIT WORLD

1. Michael Harner, "Science, Spirits, and Core Shamanism," *Shamanism* 12, no. 1 (Spring/Summer 1999).

2. Joseph Campbell and Bill Moyers, "The First Storytellers," *Joseph Campbell and the Power of Myth,* episode 3, aired 1988, PBS documentary.
3. Fools Crow, *Wisdom and Power* (San Francisco: Council Oaks Books, 1991), 42.
4. See Claude Poncelet, Ph.D., *The Shaman Within: A Physicist's Guide to the Deeper Dimensions of Your Life, the Universe, and Everything* (Louisville, Colo.: Sounds True, 2014); Stanislav Grof, M.D., *The Holotropic Mind: The Three Levels of Human Consciousness and How They Shape Our Lives* (San Francisco: Harper SanFrancisco, 1990); and C. Michael Smith, *Jung and Shamanism in Dialogue: Retrieving the Soul/Retrieving the Sacred* (Bloomington, Ind.: Trafford, 2007).

CHAPTER 4. GATHERING AROUND THE SACRED FIRE

1. Peter Farb, *Man's Rise to Civilization as Shown by the Indians of North America from Primeval Times to the Coming of the Industrial State* (New York: E. P. Dutton, 1968), 28; Yehudi Cohen, *Man in Adaptation: The Cultural Present* (Livingston, N.J.: Aldine Transaction, 1974), 94–95.
2. Joseph Campbell and Bill Moyers, "The First Storytellers," *Joseph Campbell and the Power of Myth,* episode 3, aired 1988, PBS documentary.
3. EPA, *Inventory of U.S. Greenhouse Gas Emissions and Sinks: 1990–2013* (Washington, D.C.: U.S. Environmental Protection Agency, 2015).
4. Thomas Merton, "Things in Their Identity," chapter 5 in *New Seeds of Contemplation* (New York: New Directions, 1972), 29.
5. Bill Plotkin, *Soulcraft: Crossing into the Mysteries of Nature and Psyche* (Novato, Calif.: New World Library, 2003), 228.

CHAPTER 6. FACING YOUR DRAGONS

1. Joseph Campbell and Bill Moyers, "The Hero's Adventure," *Joseph Campbell and the Power of Myth*, episode 1, aired 1988, PBS documentary.

CHAPTER 7. A HARD LOOK AT YOUR OWN MIND

1. Don Miguel Ruiz, *The Four Agreements: A Practical Guide to Personal Freedom* (San Rafael, Calif.: Amber Allen Publishing, 2003).
2. Don Miguel Ruiz, *The Fifth Agreement* (San Rafael, Calif.: Toltec Wisdom/ Amber Allen, 2010).
3. Carlos Castaneda, *The Eagle's Gift* (New York: Simon & Schuster, 1981).

CHAPTER 8. POWER FROM THE BODY AND EARTH

1. "National Mosaic," National Weather Service, U.S. Views, Reflectivity: National Loop, http://radar.weather.gov/Conus/index_loop.php.
2. Wilson, Timothy D., David A. Reinhard, Erin C. Westgate, et al. "Just think: The challenges of the disengaged mind." *Science* 345, no. 6192 (2014): 75–77.
3. Richard Louv, *Last Child in the Woods: Saving Our Children from Nature-Deficit Disorder* (New York: Algonquin Books, 2008).
4. Dan Harris, *10% Happier: How I Tamed the Voice in My Head, Reduced Stress Without Losing My Edge, and Found Self-Help That Actually Works; A True Story* (New York: It Books, 2014).
5. Harris, *10% Happier.*
6. "Gatha-Poems," Plum Village: Mindfulness Practice Centre, http://plumvillage.org/mindfulness-practice/gatha-poems.
7. See also Thich Nhat Hanh, *Peace Is Every Step: The Path of Mindfulness in Everyday Life* (New York: Bantam, 1992).
8. Thich Nhat Hanh, *Peace Is Every Step*, 28–29.

CHAPTER 9. POWER FROM THE EAGLE MIND

1. *The Shamanic Times,* online edition, http://theshamanictimes.com/qeros-indigenous-prophecies-2012.html.
2. Serge Kahili King, *Urban Shaman: A Handbook for Personal and Planetary*

Transformation Based on the Hawaiian Way of the Adventurer (New York: Touchstone, 1990).

CHAPTER 10. POWER FROM THE CONDOR HEART

1. From a 1994 interview of Steve Jobs in *Steve Jobs: One Last Thing,* aired 2011, PBS documentary (Pioneer Productions).
2. Stanislov Grof, M.D., and Christina Grof, eds., *Spiritual Emergency: When Personal Transformation Becomes a Crisis* (New York: Tarcher/Putnam, 1989).
3. C. G. Jung, *The Red Book: Liber Novus,* ed. S. Shamdasani, trans. M. Kyburz, J. Peck, and S. Shamdasani (New York: W. W. Norton, 2009).
4. Jung, *The Red Book*, vii.

CHAPTER 11. THE GUIDED SHAMANIC JOURNEY

1. Sandra Ingerman, *Shamanic Journeying: A Beginner's Guide* (Louisville, Colo.: Sounds True, 2004), 77–81.
2. Alberto Villoldo, *Mending the Past and Healing the Future with Soul Retrieval* (New York: Hay House, 2005).
3. Ervin Laszlo, *Science and the Akashic Field: An Integral Theory of Everything* (Rochester, Vt.: Inner Traditions, 2004).
4. Ingerman, *Shamanic Journeying,* 42.

CHAPTER 12. THE UNGUIDED SHAMANIC JOURNEY

1. Ted Andrews, *Animal Speak: The Spiritual and Magical Powers of Creatures Great and Small* (St. Paul, Minn.: Llewellyn, 1993).
2. Archive for Research in Archetypal Symbolism, *The Book of Symbols: Reflections on Archetypal Images* (Cologne, Germany: Taschen Books, 2010).
3. Sandra Ingerman, *Shamanic Journeying: A Beginner's Guide* (Louisville, Colo.: Sounds True, 2004), 51.
4. 1 John 4:18, New Revised Standard Version.

CHAPTER 13. BRINGING YOUR SONG INTO THE WORLD

1. Dan O'Brien, *Buffalo for the Broken Heart: Restoring Life to a Black Hills Ranch* (New York: Random House, 2002).
2. Mark 6:4, New Revised Standard Version.
3. Bill Plotkin, *Soulcraft: Crossing into the Mysteries of Nature and Psyche* (Novato, Calif.: New World Library, 2003), 51–2.
4. Joseph Campbell and Bill Moyers, "The Hero's Adventure," *Joseph Campbell and the Power of Myth,* episode 1, aired 1988, PBS documentary.
5. *Play Again,* directed by Tonje Hessen Schei (Ground Productions, 2010), DVD.
6. Richard Louv, *Last Child in the Woods: Saving Our Children from Nature-Deficit Disorder* (New York: Algonquin Books, 2005).
7. Elizabeth Dickinson, "The Misdiagnosis: Rethinking 'Nature-deficit Disorder,'" *Environmental Communication: A Journal of Nature and Culture* 7, no. 3 (2013): 315–35.
8. Age-ing to Sage-ing International, www.sage-ing.org; see also Zalman Schachter-Shalomi, *From Age-ing to Sage-ing: A Revolutionary Approach to Growing Older* (New York: Grand Central Publishing, 1997).
9. Ferguson, Todd W., and Jeffrey A. Tamburello, "The Natural Environment as a Spiritual Resource: A Theory of Regional Variation in Religious Adherence," *Sociology of Religion* 76, no. 3 (2015): 295–314.
10. Re-Member, Pine Ridge Indian Reservation, www.re-member.org.

Index

Page numbers in *italics* indicate illustrations.

About the Author

Jeff Nixa, J.D., M.Div., CMT, is a shamanic practitioner and the owner and founder of Great Plains Guide Company (aka Great Plains Shamanic Programs), an array of shamanic healing programs including individual counseling, education programs, outdoor retreats, and wilderness trips. Jeff began walking the shamanic heart path in 2009 after experiencing a life-changing vision quest in northern Michigan.

A veteran spiritual guide, Jeff's work has spanned thirty years as a university campus minister, hospital chaplain, pastoral counselor, and massage therapist. Earlier in his career, Jeff earned his law degree from Lewis and Clark Law School in Portland, Oregon. He has been a professional associate with Crows Nest Center for Shamanic Studies USA and is a graduate of Sandra Ingerman's shamanic teacher training school. He has studied with the Harner Foundation for Shamanic Studies, shamanic healers in the Peruvian Amazon and the Andes mountains, Oglala Lakota elders on Pine Ridge Reservation in South Dakota, and Cree elders in Alberta, Canada.

Jeff lives in an inner-city neighborhood in South Bend, Indiana, with his wife, Regina, where he has created a beautiful backyard nature retreat for his fire-talk counseling sessions. He makes regular journeys into the Great Plains, the north woods of Minnesota, and the desert southwest, for teaching, reconnecting with nature, and writing. Jeff is an experienced wilderness backpacker, paddler, cyclist, and sea kayaker. He is writing a companion novel for this book, and posts his short story-commentaries on his blog at www.Urban-Shamanism.org. For more information on Jeff's programs or to contact him directly, please see his website at

www.GreatPlainsGuide.net.

BOOKS OF RELATED INTEREST

Speaking with Nature
Awakening to the Deep Wisdom of the Earth
by Sandra Ingerman and Llyn Roberts

The Accidental Shaman
Journeys with Plant Teachers and Other Spirit Allies
by Howard G. Charing
Foreword by Stephan V. Beyer

White Spirit Animals
Prophets of Change
by J. Zohara Meyerhoff Hieronimus, D.H.L.

The Book of Hoʻoponopono
The Hawaiian Practice of Forgiveness and Healing
by Luc Bodin, M.D., Nathalie Bodin Lamboy, and Jean Graciet

Shamanic Healing
Traditional Medicine for the Modern World
by Itzhak Beery
Foreword by Alberto Villoldo

The Gift of Shamanism
Visionary Power, Ayahuasca Dreams, and Journeys to Other Realms
by Itzhak Beery
Foreword by John Perkins

Soul Whispering
The Art of Awakening Shamanic Consciousness
by Linda Star Wolf, Ph.D., and Nita Gage, DSPS, MA
Foreword by Richard Rudd

Advanced Shamanism
The Practice of Conscious Transformation
by James Endredy

INNER TRADITIONS • BEAR & COMPANY
P.O. Box 388
Rochester, VT 05767
1-800-246-8648
www.InnerTraditions.com

Or contact your local bookseller